JEAN SIBELIUS AND OLIN DOWNES

Music Advisor to Northeastern University Press
GUNTHER SCHULLER

JEAN SIBELIUS
and OLIN DOWNES

Music, Friendship, Criticism

Glenda Dawn Goss

Northeastern University Press
BOSTON

Northeastern University Press

Library of Congress Cataloging-in-Publication Data

Goss, Glenda Dawn.
   Jean Sibelius and Olin Downes : music, friendship, criticism /
Glenda Dawn Goss.
     p. cm.
   Includes bibliographical references and index.
   ISBN 1-55553-200-4
    1. Sibelius, Jean, 1865–1957. 2. Composers—Finland—Biography.
  3. Downes, Olin, 1886–1955. 4. Music critics—United States—Biography.
  I. Title.
  ML385.G7   1994
  780′.92′24897—dc20
  [B]   94-22367

Designed by Diane Levy

Composed in Simoncini Garamond by Graphic Composition, Athens, Georgia.
Printed and bound by Thomson-Shore, Inc., Dexter, Michigan. The paper is Glatfelter
Supple Opaque Recycled, an acid-free sheet.

MANUFACTURED IN THE UNITED STATES OF AMERICA
98 97 96 95 94   5 4 3 2 1

For Beth and James,
who shared the adventure of Finland

ᏣᎸᏋ CONTENTS

Acknowledgments   ix

Introduction   1

ONE   *Jean Sibelius and Modern Finland Come of Age*   7

TWO   *Of Puritans, Preachers and Pioneers:*
The Childhood and Youth of Olin Downes   17

THREE   *Sibelius Discovers America*   39

FOUR   *Enter Igor Stravinsky*   75

FIVE   *The Thirties: Sibelius, Downes,*
and the American People   91

SIX   *Sibelius and the Sophisticates*   123

SEVEN   *Sibelius and Posterity*   139

Notes   151

Appendix A: Correspondence of Jean Sibelius
and Olin Downes   177

Appendix B: The Writings of Olin Downes
on Jean Sibelius   233

Bibliography   241

Index   257

ACKNOWLEDGMENTS

In a sense this book had its beginnings in the 1960s, when, as a student at the University of Georgia, I had the privilege of working with Jean Réti-Forbes on the Olin Downes papers. A personal friend of Downes, Jean was directly responsible for this extraordinary collection of twentieth-century documents coming to Athens. I will never forget the experience of going to the Hargrett Library to assist her in sorting subway ticket stubs and grocery lists from priceless letters written by such composers as Sibelius, Schoenberg, and Stravinsky. Jean did not live to realize her plan of writing a biography of Downes, but her understanding of the worth of his materials, together with her annotated inventory and her articles and typescripts, formed the starting point for my entry into Downes's world.

That world had included modern Finland, and my own trips to Finland, assisted by grants from the University of Georgia Research Foundation, have yielded many friends. All have contributed to my understanding of Sibelius and his critics. Laila Koukku devoted a disproportionate amount of her time to assisting me with the treasures of the Helsinki University Library; Professors Eero Tarasti and Erkki Salmenhaara have patiently responded to my numerous questions with information and assistance; Kari Kilpeläinen spent countless hours guiding me through the complexities of the Sibelius music manuscripts and, together with Leina Reijonen, nurtured my Finnish; Paul Sjöblom brightened many a dark Finnish night with his skills as raconteur and his memories of Downes and Sibelius; and Fabian Dahlström of the Sibelius Museum generously shared his apparently inexhaustible supply of knowledge, acquainted me with the beauty of the Finnish archipelago, and gallantly came to my rescue when my essential belongings (passport, return tickets, and money) vanished. To all and to the many able individuals who assisted me in the libraries of the Sibelius Academy, the Helsinki Philharmonic, the National Archives of Finland, and the Sibelius Museum in Turku, I extend my heartfelt thanks.

In writing a book like this it is particularly meaningful to have contact with the families of men like Jean Sibelius and Olin Downes, and in that regard I have been unusually fortunate. Several members of the Sibelius family received me with great courtesy and willingly reflected on their famous ancestor. I am grateful to them for their time and for granting me permission, through Erkki Virkkunen, to quote the materials included here. Because they are just a telephone call away, the Downes family has heard from me far more often. Rather than regarding me as an intrusion into their lives, they have instead been graciously accommodating and have granted permission to quote Olin Downes's letters. I am particularly indebted to Edward Downes, whose kindnesses over the last five years have made him a valued friend.

Many other friends and scholars have interested themselves in this project and through lively discussions and correspondence have greatly enriched the final result. I thank them all, even those who are not Sibelians, for they provided useful, often enlightening resistance. In particular I would like to acknowledge Richard Crawford, James Dowd, Egbert Ennulat, James Hepokoski, Lewis Nielson, Joe Scalise, Margareta Thompson, and Laura Youens for their readiness to read, translate, suggest, and argue. I would also like to express my gratitude to my publisher and editor, William Frohlich, for his steady encouragement, and to Tim Waters, who prepared the music examples.

The support of major research libraries was, of course, essential to this work. In addition to those in Finland already mentioned, I would like to acknowledge the British Museum, the Boston Public Library, the New York Public Library for the Performing Arts, the Rare Book and Manuscript Library at Columbia University, the Library of Congress, the Yale Music Library, the Robert Manning Strozier Library at Florida State University, and the University of Georgia Libraries, of which the Hargrett Rare Book and Manuscript Library is a part. In every case the assistance I received was exemplary, if not extraordinary, ranging from finding a rare document at my telephoned request (as Ken Crilley did for me at Yale) to supplying me with mattress and blankets (produced by Barbro Kvist of the Sibelius Museum). I would also like to acknowledge the *New York Times* for granting permission to quote from reviews and other articles printed in their pages.

My deepest appreciation is reserved for my parents, who, upon learning of my scheme to mortgage the house for Sibelius's sake and board a freighter bound for the far North, volunteered financial assistance, offered transportation to the port of embarkation, and answered my mail for an entire year. Such devotion and support go far beyond what any offspring has a right to expect.

Glenda Dawn Goss
Athens, Georgia, winter 1994

ᘒ INTRODUCTION

> . . . the ultimate significance of an art work is deter-
> mined not only by what its creator intended, or by
> that of which he was conscious when he produced
> it, but also by the meanings and the values discov-
> ered in it by many individuals and generations.
> —Olin Downes, 1937*

Few composers in the history of music have had so ardent a champion as
Jean Sibelius had in Olin Downes. Widely known through his position as
music critic for the *New York Times,* Downes acquired the nickname "Sibelius's Apostle." Many in America looked upon him as the resident Sibelius
expert. Sibelius mirrored that goodwill. He once professed "with much
beating of the breast over the heart" that Olin Downes was his very best
friend.[1] Through a mutual correspondence that lasted over twenty-five years
and through Downes's many professional activities in the composer's behalf,
we may chart the course of a friendship that illuminates important aspects
of Sibelius's life and work.

Although we may seldom pause to reflect upon them, the interconnec-
tions of people and events profoundly affect composers' lives, just as they
influence our own. In the case of Jean Sibelius, some little-known events in
the fortunes of three individuals—a Wall Street banker; his son, Olin
Downes; and a Midwestern composer-critic, Virgil Thomson—shaped his
fate in America. The far-reaching effect each man had on a composer half a
world away, as well as the impact of their actions on American musical life,
will become clear in the story that follows. Along the way we will learn a
great deal about the image of Jean Sibelius as an anachronism in the twentieth century.

The young Sibelius, who cut a bohemian figure with his slim physique and abundant hair, viewed himself as a modernist. Artistically, his works (up to and including the Fourth Symphony) moved steadily toward a modernism entirely his own. But in the decade after the Fourth Symphony that image drastically changed. In the twice-revised Fifth Symphony, audiences and critics heard a reassuring tonality. As if in confirmation of an artistic retreat, the composer's shaved head and increasingly portly stature appeared to symbolize a venerated conformist. What happened in the crucial years between the premiere of the Fourth Symphony in 1911 and the final version of the Fifth in 1919 has caused Sibelius ever since to be categorized, indeed stigmatized, as an also-ran, a Romantic composer fated to live in the wrong century.

Olin Downes played a key role in establishing that image. At the very time that British traditionalists and German romanticists were adopting Sibelius in Europe, Olin Downes was discovering the composer in America. As first Schoenberg and then Stravinsky began to explore the outer limits of music's language, Downes began to spread the gospel of Sibelius's music as salvation for the contemporary soul. He preached this message across America and around the world with an enthusiasm that did not abate until his death, two years before Sibelius's own.

Had Olin Downes been simply another newspaperman, his message would have made little difference. But Downes was an enormously intuitive, highly visible, and extremely influential critic. The generally conservative position of his newspaper, the *New York Times,* and Downes's intense personal dislike of certain moderns, especially Mahler and Stravinsky, reinforced the conservative appearance of those he championed. And Downes could be an opinionated, even overbearing personality. Although it can be argued that it is not possible to overpraise a great composer, the evangelical zeal with which he preached Sibelius to the American people had the effect of irritating and alienating key individuals. The critic's attitude, adulatory enough in the magniloquent prose of his newspaper columns, emerges from his correspondence with Sibelius as downright worshipful. There was also Downes's conviction that great music, including Sibelius's, belongs to Everyman. That philosophy, which cynics sneered had remunerative, commercial value for its promoters, and the critic's increasingly influential involvement with the American consumer industry helped to entrench Sibelius's music within the bastion of die-hard conservatism.

It was Virgil Thomson who was the most outspoken and articulate of

Sibelius's detractors in America. From the time he appeared on the New York music scene as critic for the *New York Herald Tribune,* attitudes toward Sibelius began to change dramatically in the intellectual circles in which Thomson moved, attitudes that persist even today. Thomson managed to impress upon his readers not only that Sibelius was unprogressive, but also that his music was superficial, "provincial" being Thomson's word. He decried its popular power, likening its effect to that of a Hollywood movie. And he incorporated into his newspaper columns the ideas of Theodor Adorno, the most vociferous Sibelius critic of all.

The resulting story is as sad as it is human: It shows how a composer, seized as an artistic cause and appropriated by a consumer culture, was given an image completely at variance with his image of himself, and one that arose without regard for the musical qualities of his compositions. It is a saga so fraught with the personal agendas of his promoters and detractors that it demonstrates with dramatic clarity how necessarily idiosyncratic is *Rezeptionsgeschichte,* or "reception history"[2]—an area of investigation increasingly modish in musicological circles. The Sibelius-Downes story cautions us about the dangers of studying how other people "received" a work of art as the basis for coming to our own understanding of it. The story does, however, provide the opportunity to question the assumptions of our predecessors—part of the reception historian's modus operandi—and to unmask Sibelius's critics and reveal their ideological and personal biases. Insofar as is possible at this point in history, we can thus make a serious attempt to wipe the slate clean of received opinions and make way for an uncluttered consideration of those truly extraordinary compositions, which deserve a valued place in the annals of twentieth-century music.

CENTRAL TO THE PRESENT STUDY has been a group of documents collectively labeled the Olin Downes Papers.[3] Acquired by the University of Georgia in Athens, Georgia, ten years after Downes's death, the collection contains over 50,000 letters, including correspondence between the critic and most of his leading contemporaries in the field of music. Among the hundreds of Correspondence Files is one marked "Sibelius, Jean." Here the composer's original letters to Olin Downes are preserved together with carbon and handwritten copies of the critic's side of the exchange. Downes initiated this correspondence in 1927 and continued it for nearly three decades—until his death in 1955. The full communication appears here for the first time. Even though the letters were written after the period of Sibeli-

3

us's greatest creativity, they provide a useful starting point for studying Downes's connection to Sibelius.

One may well be disappointed on first reading Sibelius's letters. While Olin Downes waxes lyrical, revealing much about himself and about music and musicians, Sibelius's writing is painfully brief and often stereotyped. In his later years the composer once told his secretary that his letters gave a wrong impression: "They are always attuned to what I think will best suit the person who gets them," he said.[4] Yet despite the composer's brevity and his studied politeness, his correspondence gains enormously in significance when studied in connection with other documents. And the Olin Downes Papers are replete with other documents: letters from listeners, composers, and critics; texts from lectures and radio programs; and reviews and occasional pieces concerning virtually every composer of any significance whatsoever in the first half of the twentieth century. Even though these sources are disconnected, they clarify many aspects of the relationship between composer and critic and provide solid ground for charting Sibelius's history in America.

Research on Sibelius has from time to time addressed his conservative image and even his relationship to Olin Downes. Although no one has set out to examine these topics in any systematic way, Erik Tawaststjerna's five-volume biography, *Jean Sibelius,*[5] makes various references to Downes and incorporates numerous European and American responses to the composer and his works. Where Sibelius is concerned, these copiously detailed volumes form the starting point for this study, as they do for that of every Sibelius scholar today.

In the matter of Jean Sibelius and his dealings with Americans, there is one earlier study. Forty years ago, Otto Andersson, Director of the Sibelius Museum in Turku, Finland, examined Sibelius's relationship to the United States. In *Jean Sibelius i Amerika,*[6] published in 1955, Andersson related the history of American performances of Sibelius's music and of the composer's visit to New England in 1914. He perceived "the Master" as widely beloved, and, glossing over any dissenting currents, gratefully and repeatedly acknowledged Olin Downes for championing Finland's favorite son.

A later study, which dealt with Sibelius and America only peripherally, offers a radically different perspective: Joseph Horowitz's *Understanding Toscanini.*[7] Although Horowitz's chief concern was obviously not Sibelius, he nevertheless discussed certain aspects of Sibelius's works in the context of American musical history and gave repeated consideration to Olin

Downes. In Horowitz's account, Downes figures largely as a culprit who manipulated Americans into preferring a "soft" diet of Toscanini warhorses and Sibelius symphonies.

The present study more narrowly focuses on the ties between composer and critic. Because it is largely biographical, those looking for a systematic analysis of Sibelius's musical language will not find it in these pages. Yet the music plays a crucial role, and one may turn to the several discussions of it here as a relief from the politically charged fray with which it had so little to do.

The time frame is that of the principal characters, both of whose lives ended in the 1950s. Their story has much to teach us about the way in which human connections affect the course of history. In the teaching of those lessons, the known dimensions of Sibelius's life are embellished with various details. Above all, the Sibelius-Downes story demonstrates how little the history of "musical reception" may actually have to do with music. It serves to remind us that each age and every individual must judge music afresh, for the reception that most deeply matters to each of us is our own.

~ ONE

Jean Sibelius and Modern Finland
Come of Age

Through Sibelius, who thinks in 3-2 time and speaks
with the voice of the early gods, a nation becomes
articulate.   —Olin Downes, 1909*

OF THE TWO PRINCIPALS in this narrative, only Jean Sibelius has received
extensive biographical treatment. Numerous biographies of varying
strengths exist,[1] but the best and most complete is Erik Tawaststjerna's
five-volume biography, *Jean Sibelius*. While later we will add various partic-
ulars to what is known of the composer's life, the present chapter summa-
rizes its main points.

Jean Sibelius was born in 1865. A second-born child, he hardly knew his
father, Christian Sibelius, a competent but extravagant doctor in the small
town of Tavastehus. Christian died in the summer of 1868, the victim of
typhus contracted from his patients. His son was then not yet three. Christian left his much younger widow in difficult financial straits. Seventy years
later, when Olin Downes referred to Christian as a surgeon in the territorial
battalion, Sibelius felt it important enough to draft a correction to his father's title: His father had been a regimental doctor, he wrote proudly, and
ylilääkäri, literally, "over-doctor," a title implying responsibilities and prestige beyond the average.[2] The right image of his family stock often concerned Sibelius, who liked to think of himself as cut from aristocratic cloth.

There was also the question of the family's Finnish roots, a matter far

7

more crucial to Sibelius's wider image than his imagined nobility. In America, Olin Downes repeatedly stressed Sibelius's Finnish ancestry: "In his own conviction Sibelius is wholly a Finn and is regarded by the people as their supreme spokesman in art."[3] This matter became widely discussed with the publication of Cecil Gray's biography of Sibelius in 1931, for Gray claimed that Sibelius was overwhelmingly Swedish, not Finnish. In Finland, citizens rose up in numbers to protest, and some Finns even wrote to the *New York Times* to set the record straight. Eras Suomalainen pointed out that Sibelius's antecedents, his traditions, his education, "everything, in fact, that may have contributed toward molding his herculean character, has been Finnish. He has stated so himself, time and again."[4] The same newspaper also printed a letter from Jean Sibelius, in which the composer communicated the twin points of his Finnish heritage and, if not aristocratic, then at least nonservile family background:

> My family has been traced back to the latter part of the seventeenth century, when my great-great-grandfather was the master of the Pekkala estate at Artjärvi. He was of old Finnish farming stock. . . . My mother's ancestors were Swedish. Together with this subject it should be mentioned that Finnish farmers from time immemorial have been free, as well as those of Sweden and Norway, and not "peasants" in the sense of servile subjection, as were those in France, Germany, Denmark, etc., not to speak of the serfs in Russia. Also, that many of the oldest and most powerful noble families of Sweden, such as the Kurcks, Carpelans, etc., have originated from Finnish farmer-folk. This, because the world at large seems to regard Swedish ancestry as being superior to Finnish. It is ridiculous, yet a momentous matter for us [Finns].[5]

Sibelius's identification with a specifically Finnish awareness was a gradual but essential part of his later personality. Fennomania, as Finnish nationalism was called, arose along with other Romantic nationalist movements of the nineteenth century. Goaded by centuries of Swedish rule and the prevalence of the Swedish language, as well as by the presence of their newer, Russian rulers, who occupied the country in 1808, Finns experienced a swelling national consciousness during the nineteenth century.

Three men in particular led the country's nationalist aspirations: Johan Vilhelm Snellman (1806–1881); Johan Ludwig Runeberg (1804–1877); and Elias Lönnrot (1802–1884). Their rallying cry, "Swedes we are no longer, Russians we cannot become; we must be Finns," took practical form in the demand for adoption of the Finnish language as the mother tongue. Yet it was a language that few of its advocates had mastered. Snellman published his political polemics in Swedish; Runeberg used Swedish for his fervently patriotic poetry. It was Lönnrot who took the crucial step of building a linguistic foundation. In 1835 he created a literary epic from poetry collected in Karelia, Finland's eastern region. He called his work the *Kalevala*.[6] When the longer, definitive version of the *Kalevala* was published in 1849, not only Finns but much of the outside world realized that Finland as a nation had not only a history but also a language and a literature. Before the *Kalevala,* the Finnish language had been widely disparaged. The *Kalevala* demonstrated that Finnish was a language capable of meaningful literary accomplishment. Furthermore, it portrayed Finns in heroic terms, as figures larger than life. While Jacob Grimm lectured admiringly on the *Kalevala* in Germany and Longfellow modeled his *Song of Hiawatha* on its poetic meter, Finns rallied to build a political consciousness on its cultural achievement.

Sibelius studied the *Kalevala* as a boy. He was placed in a school where Finnish was the language of instruction, a school newly founded in 1873 in his home town, now called Hämeenlinna rather than the Swedish Tavastehus. But in the Sibelius home the language spoken was Swedish, the traditional language of Finland's intellectuals and upper classes, many of whom, from the 1860s, had begun to resist the widespread change to Finnish. Swedish was also the language of Sibelius's earliest love letters to his fiancée, Aino, and to her father, General Järnefelt, even though both were ardent Fennomen. At Alexander University, where he went to study law, Sibelius preferred Swedish-speaking circles. And even in his later years Swedish remained the language of his thoughts, as his diary and most of his song texts suggest.

In 1885 Sibelius enrolled full-time at the Music Institute (later renamed the Sibelius Academy) in Helsinki. As a student, he had the reputation of a daredevil, a dreamer always "in his cups," dwelling in the land of fantasy, and with an eye for the ladies.[7] His principal teacher in Helsinki, Martin Wegelius (1846–1906), and the young Ferruccio Busoni (1866–1924), who joined the Music Institute in 1888, turned the budding composer's interests southward, toward Germany and Austria. Thus it was not until he left Finland that Sibelius began to awaken to his own country's musical potential. In Berlin in 1890 he heard Robert Kajanus's *Aino* Symphony, an experience that seems to have suggested to him the *Kalevala*'s musical possibilities. And while studying in Vienna the next year, he began to read the *Kalevala* anew and to plan a symphonic work based upon it.

On returning to Helsinki in 1891, Sibelius found that he already had something of a reputation for composing in the conventional German musical idiom. In 1889 his A-Major Suite for String Trio had caused Busoni to take notice and remember it as something more than a student work. A month later an A-minor string quartet distinguished him as the leading voice in Finnish music. Yet it was with a quartet in B-flat major that the Finnish image clearly began to take shape. Completed when he was studying with Karl Goldmark in Vienna, the Quartet found a prophetic advocate in Ilmari Krohn: "Let us hope to God that his inner struggle meets with victory; then the Finnish people will find their most sacred and inspired ideals enshrined in his noble harmonies. It is he who has given voice to the Finnish people's struggles."[8] Finns, widely experiencing the need to identify national heroes, such as those from the past represented in the *Kalevala,* began to see in Sibelius a living one.

The quest for heroes arose from the political climate, for it was just at this moment that Nicholas II moved to eliminate Finland's privileged autonomy as a grand duchy and to assimilate the country into Russia as a border state.[9] He first attempted to unify Finland's postal, customs, and exchange systems with Russia's. Soon he began to conscript Finns into the Imperial Army. By the end of the decade, Finland's Parliament had lost the right to pass legislation. The constant demands that Russian become Finland's administrative language, that Russian be taught in schools, and that Russians be appointed to public office galled the Finns at every step. In such circumstances, the *Kalevala,* the story of heroes, became a symbol for a nation that would not perish, Karelia became a kind of Finnish holy land, and Karelianism became the term for the fervent patriotism of the decade. The heightened political consciousness spurred a creative outpouring that became a real cultural Renaissance in Finland. The most creative liberals, a group that Sibelius was soon to join, included Robert Kajanus, composer and conductor; Sibelius's brothers-in-law-to-be, Arvid and Eero Järnefelt, one a musician, the other a painter; the writers Juhani Aho and Eino Leino; and, most important, the artist Akseli Gallen-Kallela.

Born the same year as Sibelius and bearing a Swedish name, Axel Gallén (1865–1931), like Sibelius, only began to realize the artistic value of his Finnish origins abroad. In Paris he painted the first version of his large-scale *Aino* (the tragic sister of Joukahainen in the *Kalevala*), just one year before Sibelius found inspiration in Kajanus's *Aino* Symphony in Berlin. Keenly aware of the avant-garde's turn away from materialistic civilization, Gallén saw in Karelian Finland that primitiveness so valued as modern in the international art world. In 1890 Gallén left Paris for Karelia to study the customs, utensils, architecture, and landscapes as inspiration for his art. Regularly moving between Karelia and the art capitals of Europe during the 1890s, Gallén, who by the end of the decade came to be regarded as Finland's most radical symbolist, established a vital connection between patriotism and modernism. Through Gallén's charismatic example, Finnish nationalism and the artistic avant-garde became one.

On his return to Finland in 1891, Sibelius, now the very picture of the unorthodox artist with his slender figure, wild hair, and fresh ideas, joined this circle of radical young intellectuals who opposed Russification and sought artistic inspiration and political protest in Karelianism. Organizing themselves under the name Young Finland (*Nuori Suomi*), some of the group founded a daily newspaper, *Päivälehti* (today *Helsingin Sanomat*), to give voice to their ideas. The program of Young Finland was "liberal, but highly Finnophile and nationalistic. They believed in the great future flowering of art, the 'Finnish Renaissance,'" as Gallén called the movement in his diary.[10] Partly directed by the writer Adolf Paul (Sibelius's friend and a friend also of August Strindberg and Edvard Munch), who joined the group from Berlin in 1893, the members began to question realism and philosophize about the unfathomable. One of them, the writer Eino Leino, described the prevailing mood:

> All old religious ideas are awakening and a time of new mysticism, new occult doctrines, invocations of the spirits and star-gazing wafts through the intellectual life of the end of the century. . . . The human spirit once again feels the need to fall on its knees before the great unknown spirit of the world.[11]

Gallén immortalized the group's ideas as well as his friendship with Sibelius in a remarkable painting, originally entitled *The Problem,* later called *The Symposium.*[12] There the artist depicts himself with Sibelius, Kajanus, and a face-down figure (usually identified as the composer and critic Oskar Merikanto) around a table, drinking and smoking, presumably in commemoration of their many infamous gatherings at such favorite haunts as the Hotel Kämp. Perhaps for this reason, that its young intellectuals should be portrayed amidst debauchery, the painting caused a terrible scandal, which drew attention away from the canvas's rich symbolism.

It was in this decade, the 1890s, that Sibelius first came to widespread public attention with his *Kullervo* Symphony, a work for orchestra, men's

Sibelius in the 1890s. Photograph courtesy of the Sibelius Museum.

chorus, and soloists based on an episode from the *Kalevala*. Certain qualities of the choral movements (the meter, the melodic construction, the extraordinary skill in setting the Finnish text) caused many to assume that Sibelius had borrowed directly from Finnish folk singers. And indeed, although it had been begun in Vienna, *Kullervo* was not completed until Sibelius, like Gallén before him, traveled to Karelia. Perhaps because the nationalistic tag later became a stigma, the composer denied this experience to his biographers, from Rosa Newmarch to Karl Ekman to Olin Downes. Yet Tawaststjerna has documented that in the fall of 1891 Sibelius visited the legendary Larin Paraske, the illiterate artist who had the extraordinary ability to sing literally hundreds of the *Kalevala's* runic chants.[13] Only afterwards did the composer unveil his new symphony.

Based on the story of the tragic Kullervo, the hero in the *Kalevala* who is too strong to live among ordinary mortals and who unknowingly seduces his sister, *Kullervo* is thoroughly imbued with nationalistic spirit, from the setting of selected *Kalevala* verses for chorus and orchestra in the third and fifth movements to the programmatic nature of themes and keys and their treatment in the purely instrumental movements. The most powerful expression of the composer's Karelianism may well be the symphony's center, where Sibelius created an unforgettable chantlike men's chorus with a distinctive 5/4 meter. For all his misgivings about Finnish, the composer skillfully wedded the *Kalevala* text to the unison melody in a way that preserves the language's nearly unvarying first-syllable emphasis. While the orchestra maintains its five-beat ostinato, the choral recitation accentuates sometimes the first, sometimes the third, sometimes the fourth, and sometimes the fifth beat, shifting according to the stress in the spoken language. Carefully chosen rhythmic values and prescribed metrical accents provide the means of superimposing the correct rhythmic declamation of the vocal line over the orchestral groupings.[14] (See Ex. 1.)

This chorus is eventually followed by a moving recitation in which Kullervo and his sister both reveal their identities. Kullervo initially sings in the key of A-flat major; his true musical relationship to his sister, the dominant of her C-sharp minor, is thus "hidden" enharmonically, just as it is hidden dramatically. A heartrending lament from the hero catapults the movement to its end. Partly because it spoke to Finns in their own tongue and undoubtedly because the music has extraordinary vitality, *Kullervo* was an enormous success.

In the wake of this triumph, Sibelius not only won the hand of Aino

Ex. 1.

Järnefelt in marriage, but also, recognized suddenly as a national figure, received a decade-long government stipend that eventually became a lifetime grant.[15] In light of the long fallow period at the end of Sibelius's life (referred to as the "silence of Järvenpää," after the small village where the composer lived in later years), it has sometimes been mistakenly concluded that this stipend made Sibelius so comfortable that he ceased composing, rather like the professor who abandons serious research upon receiving tenure. Nothing could be further from the truth. At the time the stipend was awarded, 1897, the most famous works, *Finlandia* and *Valse triste,* had not yet been composed. Nor had a single one of the seven symphonies seen the light of day. For an explanation of Sibelius's "great tragedy," as one daughter referred to the unproductive last years, one must look for another explanation.

By 1900, Sibelius's music began to be heard abroad. Conductors in England and in America frequently programmed his works. Sibelius himself traveled widely. Between 1900 and 1923 he journeyed not once but many times to Paris, Prague, London, Berlin, and various cities in Italy. He even came to the New World: In 1914, he arrived in the United States as the guest of Carl and Ellen Battell Stoeckel. It was then that Sibelius's life began to intertwine with that of Olin Downes. Conducting a program of his works at the Norfolk Music Festival on June 4, 1914, Sibelius impressed the eager young Downes as one of the two most effective conductors the critic had ever witnessed. "He cast a spell that no other conductor has ever bestowed upon the works he then interpreted," Downes remembered.[16] Afterwards, a brief conversation with the composer provided an opening with which the critic would later begin his correspondence.

Sibelius left America intending to return, but the outbreak of World War I thwarted those and many other plans. After the war, his travels gradually ceased altogether. And after 1926, having completed his Seventh Symphony and the great tone poem *Tapiola,* his composing ceased as well. What was effectively a retirement did not, however, prevent foreigners like Downes from coming to Ainola, the composer's rustic, lakeside home in the little village of Järvenpää, some thirty kilometers from Helsinki. The composer died in splendid old age, nearly ninety-two, loved and honored in his homeland and during his lifetime as few composers have been. Yet everyone, supporters as well as detractors, puzzled over the mystery of a much-rumored Eighth Symphony and the meaning of the "silence of Järvenpää."

Sibelius's genius had first impressed itself upon Olin Downes in Boston. It was there, in 1907, that Karl Muck's interpretation of the First Symphony had won many Americans to Sibelius's music. Olin Downes, then a fledgling music critic for the *Boston Post,* spoke out like a voice in the wilderness heralding the messiah. Since the reasons Downes came to revere Sibelius almost as a god have a significant bearing on the role the critic would play in the composer's life, it will be useful to pause here to consider the background of Sibelius's Apostle.

TWO

Of Puritans, Preachers, and Pioneers: The Childhood and Youth of Olin Downes

> . . . to find a prototype for Olin Downes, you must
> go back to the early days of America, for he is in
> character one of those men who laid the plans for
> our country today.   —"Meet Olin Downes"*

OLIN DOWNES SHOULD HAVE HAD an easy childhood. Born on Mozart's birthday, January 27, he came into a family of excellent means in the year 1886. His father, Edwin Quigley, was the son of a Methodist minister. He was also a successful Wall Street banker. Quigley provided splendidly for his growing family. Residing at Orange, New Jersey, rather than New York City where "Neddie" worked, the Quigleys owned an estate that boasted thoroughbreds, carriages, coachmen, gardeners, and other trappings of the wealthy. The young boy's mother, Louise Corson Downes, cared for her only son (a second child like Sibelius) and two sisters, Frances and Dorothy. Downes seems to have aspired from his earliest years to become a pianist and began music lessons when he was eight.

But in January 1895, the comfortable world of the Quigleys collapsed. Edwin was arrested for dealing in fraudulent bonds and placed in a cell on Murderers' Row. As the details of his actions came to light, they were reported daily in front-page articles in the *New York Times*.[1] Quigley had created huge losses, not only in New York's Mercantile National Bank but also

Olin Downes the aspiring young pianist, about age seven. Photograph by Brady, Orange, New Jersey. Olin Downes Collection, Hargrett Rare Book and Manuscript Library. Reproduced by permission.

in banks in Ohio, Pennsylvania, and Iowa. Still other institutions, reported the *New York Times,* were preparing to absorb their damages quietly.

On January 26, 1895, only one week after the scandal broke, Quigley pleaded guilty to forgeries amounting to $320,000. He was sentenced to fifteen years and six months in Sing-Sing Prison. His son Olin, just nine, found life changed irrevocably. The stable of thoroughbreds and the carriages were sold at auction. By March, Quigley was declared insolvent. To combat such an unthinkable crime, Quigley's wife, Louise, took the strongest possible measures: she not only divorced Edwin, she also eradicated the name of Quigley from her own life and that of her children forever.

Louise Corson Downes was no ordinary individual. She proudly traced her ancestors back to three van Corson brothers who had come to America from Amsterdam in the eighteenth century.[3] In the family genealogy, her great-grandfather, Enoch Addis, had crossed the Delaware with George Washington that cold Christmas Day in 1776. Enoch eventually acquired large estates and considerable wealth, at one time owning nearly all of Addisville, Pennsylvania. Another forebear had accompanied Sherman on his march to Atlanta; still another had signed the Declaration of Independence. But of all the ancestors, Sarah Jane Corson, Louise's mother, may have been the most remarkable.

Born in 1822, Sarah Jane Corson was graduated at the age of seventeen as valedictorian of the first class at Pennington Female Institute, the first Methodist institute for educating women. Sarah Jane's homely appearance did not dampen her tenacity, her integrity, or her Christianity. After an early spell as a schoolteacher, Sarah Jane married Charles S. Downs (spelled without the *e*), a traveling Methodist Episcopal minister. Sarah Jane reared the minister's two sons as well as their own daughter, Louise. After the Reverend Downs died in 1870, Sarah Jane supported her family, in part through literary contributions to the *New Jersey Courier* (in later years, she determined to study journalism). When it became clear that she could afford to send only one child to college, Sarah Jane unhesitatingly chose her daughter. Olin's mother, Louise, who was graduated in 1876 from Pennington Seminary, thus spent a year at Bordentown College.

It was during Louise's teenage years that Sarah Jane became involved in the Women's Christian Temperance Union. In 1881, at the age of fifty-nine, Olin Downes's grandmother became the WCTU's New Jersey president. For ten years she led the forces of temperance. In that decade, New Jersey's temperance unions increased in number from 26 to 208 and the membership to some 8,000. Her contemporaries credited the spectacular success of the unions to her fearless leadership and nicknamed her the "Andrew Jackson" of their National Executive Committee.

As did many prohibitionists, Sarah Jane also campaigned ardently for women's suffrage, "the surest method of overthrowing the liquor traffic and all other sins against our home." Significantly, her high-minded attitudes embraced music, which to her provided a striking resemblance to the influence of women. Both music and women, she believed, were "ennobling and elevating." She wrote, "The society of true women will lift humanity to a higher plane. So a soul filled with music will have aspirations for the good and lovely."[3] In 1886 Sarah Jane delivered a thundering address to the Temperance Union, the theme of which was Down with the Saloon! "It is a Woman's Crusade against a mighty wrong! A bloody battlefield is before us, upon which lie a hundred thousand slain! A still unconquered enemy, still strong and mighty! 'Woman to the rescue!' is inscribed on many a streaming banner!"[4]

In 1886 Sarah Jane's grandson was born. The baby boy was named Edwin Olin. The family recalls today that "Olin" was the last name of a prominent and admired American—quite possibly the Methodist Episcopal minister Stephen Olin (1797–1851). If the psychology of a name has any relevance to a child's development, then "Olin" was a momentous choice: Stephen Olin was a preacher, an author, and an educator, and his surname is both Anglo-Saxon and Swedish.[5]

Five years after the birth of Edwin Olin, Sarah Jane died in full feminist stride at the home of her beloved daughter. Young Olin, his elder sister, and his father and mother were at her side. At the deathbed, Louise knelt: "Mother, while life lasts, you will be my ideal of womanhood, of motherhood, of all that is purest and best."[6] Sarah Jane's last words rang with conviction: "Liquor traffic *will* be outlawed. Blessed is he who helps."[7]

Louise Corson Downes, upright and formidable even as an old woman, carried out the promise she had made her dying mother. She opposed the demon drink all her life long, executing Carry Nation–like hatchet maneuvers against Satan's saloons. She also battled for women's rights. In *The New Democracy,* published in Boston in 1910, Louise (who now spelled Downes with an *e*) sounds forth on the rise of women as the harbinger of a new, truly democratic era.[8] Louise liberally sprinkled her often obtuse and bizarre prose with quotes from two treasured sources, the Bible ("Set bounds about the mount, and sanctify it," Exodus 19, v. 23) and Walt Whitman ("And I announce as the glory of these states, that they respectfully listen to proposition, reforms, fresh views and doctrines"),[9] and occasionally Goethe.

Yet for all her feminist rhetoric, it was her son, rather than her daughters, on whom she fixed her hopes. ("My son is a genius!") Her opinions only hardened with the years, and she created a tense and jealous triangle with Olin and his first wife, Marion.[10] Yet Downes was devoted to her. In 1931 he dedicated his book *Symphonic Broadcasts* "to my mother who made possible my experiences of music, apropos of many concerts we have enjoyed together."[11] When Louise died in 1940 at the age of eighty-three, Serge Koussevitzky paid her tribute: "In death as in life Louise Downes remains a living symbol of American womanhood with the soul of a poet, the mind of a thinker, the vision of a prophet, the heart of a mother."[12] His mother's death caused Downes anguished turmoil, and he wrote Sibelius several distracted letters of unusually great length in which he described his mother's "Christ-like body" and her "heroic struggle."

It has seemed important to dwell at some length on Olin Downes's "ministerial forebears," as he once called them, because it was the family legacy of evangelical, high-minded zeal that gave Olin Downes his name, formed his personality, and characterized his championship of Sibelius. As is often the case with zealots, the overbearing enthusiasm they bring to a cause can galvanize as many into opposition as into support. Although Downes adopted a liberal position in his political views, the fundamentalism evident in his musical tastes would eventually create bitter enemies for Sibelius.

AFTER THE LOSS of the family's New Jersey estate, Louise moved her family to Boston. In Boston the young Downes would learn to be a music critic. It was also a city that would prove particularly sympathetic to Sibelius. In later years Downes would use his Boston connections to benefit the composer, even after the critic had relocated to New York. On another front, the indignities the young critic suffered in Boston and the lessons he learned about how composers' reputations may be assisted perhaps explain why he took some of the actions toward Sibelius that he did. It is thus useful to consider the city's cultural climate and some of its leading personalities in the world of music.

Boston in 1900 smelled as much of the Old World as of the sea. Home of the Handel and Haydn Society since 1815 and of the Boston Symphony Orchestra since 1881, Boston's cultural life had been molded by the Puritans and fashioned after England. When the colonists founded the New

Louise Corson Downes. Olin Downes Collection, Hargrett Rare Book and Manuscript Library. Reproduced by permission.

World's first institution of higher learning, they named it after the Puritan minister John Harvard, whose estate and books provided its beginnings. From the outset, the history of Boston and that of Harvard were intertwined.

For all its English and Puritan ties, however, Boston was culturally in awe of Germany. "A musical suburb of Munich" was one description of the city around 1900.[13] The reverence for Germany went beyond music. In Henry James's *The Bostonians,* which appeared in book form in the year of Olin Downes's birth, the Southerner Basil Ransom inspects his Boston cousin's books and discovers "that his cousin read German; and his impression of the importance of this (as a symptom of superiority) was not diminished by the fact that he himself had mastered the tongue. . . ."[14]

In music, German ideals clearly held sway. Among the composers who have been called the "Boston Classicists," John Knowles Paine (1839–1906) had studied in Berlin, George W. Chadwick (1854–1931) in Leipzig, and Horatio Parker (1864–1919) in Munich. All three held stern reverence for the past, specifically the German past, and their attitudes came to characterize their academic institutions. At Harvard, where Paine restricted musical offerings to the intellectual pursuit of *musica speculativa,* America's first music professor at its first university passed on German ideals to such pupils as Arthur Foote, Frederick Converse, Daniel Gregory Mason, and John Alden Carpenter. Chadwick in turn occupied an influential academic position as director of the New England Conservatory, a post he filled from 1897 to 1930. And at Yale, where Horatio Parker taught the music history classes, German composers received overwhelming emphasis.

The very narrowness of the academic tradition eventually engendered a reaction. One Boston transplant, Arthur Farwell (1872–1952), urged a corrective to the vision. We must "cease to see everything through German spectacles!" he cried in 1903.[15] A few years before, Charles Ives (class of '98), begrudging the rigidity of his Yale professor Parker, who failed to see the imagination in his student's work because it did not conform to what Parker had learned in Germany, found stimulation and fresh ideas in his native New England.

But while Ives and Farwell turned to America for inspiration, the academics simply transferred their affections from one European country to another. For despite the seemingly entrenched tradition, Boston's reverence for German culture had begun to weaken just at the time Olin Downes located there. German unification in 1871 and Germany's subsequent rapid economic growth worried Americans, a worry exacerbated by the jingoistic posturings of the Kaiser and the patriotic rhetoric of Theodore Roosevelt.[16] As Americans in general came to view France as the more successful model of European democracy and a source of commercial and military cooperation, Boston's musical community became visibly more Francophile. William Foster Apthorp (1848–1913), critic for the *Boston Transcript,* edited a collection of essays and lectures by Hector Berlioz and tried to emulate the "French style of personal criticism"—enlightened but never dogmatic.[17] In Charles Martin Loeffler (1861–1935), the city gained a composer for whom French music held a special allure. Born in Alsace, Loeffler immigrated to Boston in 1882, where he lived for more than two decades. His *Poème païen,* based on the eighth eclogue of Virgil, combined the piano with orchestra in a wash of arpeggiated and whole-tone parallelisms worthy of any French impressionist. To be in the vanguard, Olin Downes recalled later, "was to quote with familiarity from the text and music of *Pelléas.* And there was *La mer.* . . . Snobism [*sic*] was particularly rampant at the time. . . . If you knew anything, your gods were Fauré, Chabrier, Debussy, D'Indy, Charpentier— providing you were such an unashamed vulgarian as to relish his opera written about Parisian working people and cabbage soup."[18]

Above all, Boston music critic Philip Hale (1854–1934) enjoyed a love affair with France.[19] He began to promote Debussy when that composer was virtually unknown in America. Hale could discourse upon what Louis XIV ate for dinner and on the remarkable *Commentaires sur les épistres d'Ovide* by Claude Gaspar Bachet, Sieur de Meziriac. And he crusaded for French composers: the "colossal originality" of Berlioz, the "flawless beauty" of Debussy, the "cunningly and gorgeously orchestrated" Ravel. Of all the Francophiles, it was Philip Hale who most deeply influenced the young Downes. Hale sported a *Yale* degree, although eventually Harvard forgave him and conferred a degree of its own. Hale was known for his integrity, for not hiding behind the editorial *we,* and for speaking out against the Germanic cultism that idolized Johannes Brahms and Johann Sebastian Bach. "There is, it is true, a gospel of Johannes Brahms," he wrote in 1896, "but Brahms, to use an old New England phrase, is often a painful preacher of the word—Brahms is a safe play in Boston. Let me not be unthankful; let me be duly appreciative of my educational opportunities in this town."[20]

In countering the German cult, Hale wrote conversationally, with tongue in cheek, not as the bearer of Truth. When he wrote about "great" composers, in tones far from solemn, he ridiculed the snobbish element in the public. And he did not hesitate to tweak the nose of the establishment, which included Boston's highly respected father of music criticism, John Sullivan Dwight. "Bach," he noted, "is one of the great fetishes in music. . . . No matter how formal, how dull a page of music looked or sounded, Mr. Dwight was in ecstasy the moment he was told the page was signed with Bach's name."[21]

After practicing law from 1880 to 1882, Hale had pursued the traditional path to higher musical knowledge that led through Germany. In his study of keyboard and composition, he seemed to be following in the footsteps of the Boston Classicists, Paine, Chadwick, and Parker. Although he continued to perform, in 1889 he came to Boston to write, first for the *Boston Post* and eventually for the *Boston Home Journal*. When in 1903 Hale moved to the *Boston Herald,* he began thirty years of a reign that some referred to as that of "Philip the Great," others, as "Philip the Terrible" (Charles Ives had his own epithet for him: "Auntie Hale"). Two years before, Hale had taken over from Apthorp the writing of the Boston Symphony's program notes, a task he transformed into a literary art.

Olin Downes learned a great deal from Philip Hale. Eagerly reading the *Herald* after each Symphony performance, he absorbed Hale's sympathy for French music, Hale's skepticism of the establishment, and even his turns of phrase: Downes audaciously compared Dan Emmett with Bach—with Emmett coming out the better. ("There are people who think that the dullest fugue Bach ever wrote—and let me assure you, he wrote a number of dull ones—is superior to Dan Emmett's *Dixie,* one of the most remarkable tunes ever composed."[22]) In January 1907 Hale responded to Sibelius's First Symphony by writing: "If there be a moment of gayety [*sic*], it is rough rollicking and knives are quickly drawn."[23] Downes reprocessed that description in a later review that used the phrase "knives are quickly drawn." Hale approved of Sibelius's music for its "little thought of woman or of love" and referred to its "Berserker rage"; Downes echoed the same sentiments, using identical vocabulary, even years later, when writing about Sibelius.[24] No doubt Hale won his sympathy when from time to time he treated academics with contempt and when he quoted Walt Whitman (a favorite poet of Downes's mother).[25]

Although Hale sometimes mocked the institutions of higher learning, the New England academic scene had also begun to experience a change in attitude toward French music. Even at Harvard, that venerated institution whose history was so enmeshed with Boston's own and whose German-trained professors had steadfastly emphasized the Germanic tradition, certain individuals began to legitimize French musical culture. Edward Burlingame Hill (1872–1960), the grandson of a Harvard president, had gone to Paris and studied with Charles-Marie Widor; he later published a book entitled *Modern French Music.*[26] On becoming a Harvard professor himself, Hill began to spice up the formerly all-German curriculum, first with a course that included the works of Tchaikovsky and Franck, and then with one entitled "D'Indy, Fauré, and Debussy." He also dwelled lovingly on Chabrier, Charpentier, Dukas, and Ravel.[27] Through his teaching, Hill influenced a new generation of composers to be open-minded, even enthusiastic, about things French. One of these students would later excoriate Sibelius skillfully and repeatedly. His name was Virgil Thomson.

BUT OLIN DOWNES'S RESPONSE to Boston's new Francophile fashion took a very different turn.

One of the guiding lights during Downes's formative years as a young critic was a Frenchman, Romain Rolland. Downes considered Rolland "the nearest personification of the ideal music critic that we know," an opinion he made clear in his earliest years at the *Post* and which he affirmed toward the end of his life. Rolland (1866–1944) was a true Renaissance figure: a writer, a historian, a critic, a novelist, a man of civil action, and more. In his criticism he stressed the importance of intuition over reason; in his view of history, he championed the idea of a noble, superior soul triumphing over adversity. His Nobel prize–winning novel cycle, *Jean-Christophe,* portrays a composer as hero, and Downes returned often to its precepts. He reviewed the work in a column in the *Boston Post* on May 12, 1912, and referred to it again on January 5, 1913, April 20, 1913, and June 22, 1913. Soon after Rolland's death in 1944, Downes devoted an entire article in the *New York Times* to him, toward the end of which he quoted the Frenchman's words from the preface to the seventh volume of *Jean-Christophe:* "I needed a hero with a pure heart and unclouded vision, whose soul should be stainless enough for him to have the right to speak: one whose voice would be loud enough for him to gain a hearing."[28]

Rolland's words also voiced Olin Downes's needs, for the critic's search for a musical hero was a major factor in his response to Jean Sibelius. Downes repeatedly described the composer and his music in heroic terms. The music of Sibelius, he said, is "music of intense masculinity, from which the erotic element which influences almost all the music of the nineteenth and early twentieth century is entirely absent. This is a man, a hero of the North, and I have called him at times the last of the heroes in music."[29] The composer himself contributed to that image when he affixed the words "the hero can never lose heart" to his tone poem *Pohjola's Daughter.*

One does not have to look far to discover why the young Downes so desperately needed a hero. In his own home, his father, a boy's first hero, had failed him in the most bitter of ways and at the most critical of times. During the wounding experiences of childhood and adolescence, Downes must have often yearned for a man to guide him through the rites of human passage. And then there was also the example of his mother. In the face of the tragic turn her life had taken with Edwin Quigley, Louise's "immense and fanatical heroism" fed Downes's own, and made the heroism of Sibelius's music so important to him.

Downes's heroes were invariably manly. "There is no more virile music written today," he often proclaimed of Sibelius's music. "The man who can write with such force, such sheer strength and fertility of invention, who can, so to speak, throw manners to the winds and bring back the gods, is quite beyond price in an overcultivated age."[30] Sibelius, he said, was a "new, clean, great man," the word *clean* seeming to refer to moral rectitude; not all composers bore comparison. Debussy, for one, came from surroundings slightly precious and far too perfumed. *La mer* had prompted Downes to ask:

> . . . Is it a great, vital art? Is it elemental enough to appeal to succeeding generations and differing epochs of thought and expression? Is it not rather a new taste, a rarity, calculated to appeal to the refined sensuousness of a hyper-refined age? To us this music lacks the vast elemental note, and with its prismatic opalescent hues seems rather the sea conceived by a dreamer lying on his couch in a sumptuously upholstered apartment and puffing blue rings of smoke into the air.[31]

Downes would presumably have agreed with Ives's famous observation that Claude Debussy needed to hoe some corn.

Like Boston-born, Harvard-educated Ralph Waldo Emerson, whose correspondence shows that on a trip to Europe he was seeking a master, or "the man,"[32] Olin Downes would go abroad for the same reason and his journey would produce one. On one occasion, after a long visit with the composer, he addressed Sibelius as "dear Master, whom I love and adore." Over the years, Downes, like Emerson, seems to have convinced himself that to be self-reliant, nonconformist, and do battle for the Right and the Noble was as heroic a feat as swinging a battle-axe. Although Downes often coupled Sibelius with the name of Walt Whitman, the last words he wrote about the composer mention Emerson: "Emerson says somewhere that when we are little children we take for granted the presence of the gods about us; that in later life the din and confusion may cause us to lose sight of them; but that with the clarification of the years our sight is restored, and we see again that the gods are there, and that they never left us. Sibelius never forgot them, or relinquished their guidance to the truth."[33] Seeing his own aspirations toward truth, clarity, and manhood reflected in Sibelius's music, Olin Downes portrayed this composer as a virile, living hero to men and women all over America.

ON THE SURFACE of Boston's cultural life the question of German versus French allegiance seemed the most in evidence. However, there simultaneously flowed through the city a deep undercurrent of high-minded, even puritanical, regard for the past. The past was visualized as a distant realm of perfection and treated with a veneration that extended back to antiquity. This attitude was symbolized visually by the Greek and Roman statutes placed reverently around Symphony Hall. It was embodied in Horatio Parker's most famous composition, the oratorio *Hora novissima,* a setting of 210 lines from the twelfth-century Latin poem *De Contemptu Mundi.* And it surfaced in the idolization of Vikings and other Nordic figures. In 1881 George Chadwick composed *The Viking's Last Voyage,* featuring baritone solo and a men's chorus with orchestra. Horatio Parker, it will soon be seen, cultivated contacts with his own live "Viking," Sibelius. Rupert Hughes, writing about American composers in Boston in 1900, exclaimed, "What would part-song writers do if the Vikings had never been invented? Where would they get their wild choruses for men, with a prize to the singer that makes the most noise?"[34]

Admiration for Nordic people developed swiftly in the United States in the early years of the twentieth century, fueled considerably by fears of growing immigration from southern and eastern Europe.[35] During the 1890s, most immigrants had been British, German, or Scandinavian, and the press now indulged in speculations about racial superiority. It was commonly believed that anthropologists favored the Nordic people, whose energy and capable natures were surely bred by natural selection in the fierceness of Northern winters. A "Ku Klux Klan school of anthropology" identified old-stock America with the Nordic race, which, it was claimed, embodied morality, energy, and cleanliness. There was widespread agreement that from central and southern Europe came whiffs of decay, especially from Vienna, the home of a nervous sickness where a psychic frailty rotted away a society covered by a veneer of culture. Quick to applaud physical prowess, many Americans found confirmation of Nordic and specifically Finnish racial superiority in the Finnish runner Kolehmainen, who, in 1913, broke the existing five-mile indoor track record by an astonishing 11²⁄₅ seconds.[36]

To this conservative, high-minded, and elitist city came Olin Downes, an idealistic, hopeful, and aggrieved youth. He longed to be part of the Harvard circle, the one that would soon so readily welcome Virgil Thomson. But it remained stubbornly closed to Downes. His mother's financial situation was such that, after the eighth grade, Downes had to leave school forever. This inability to afford a Harvard education in the midst of a culture of Boston Brahmins left Olin Downes with both a permanent abhorrence of elitism and a passionate desire to fill the gaps in his education. That yearning for acceptance and education stayed with him always. Lucien Price recalled that, one summer in the 1930s, Downes arrived in Saratoga with the Koussevitzkys, lugging Jakob Burkhardt's *Civilization of the Renaissance* for light summer reading.[37] But it was the exclusion from the Harvard sanctum that cost untold quantities in emotional pain. Even his obituary, over fifty years later, referred to it.[38]

The experiences of his teenage years solidified his populist outlook. Downes not only had to relinquish the dream of becoming a pianist, but he also began to shoulder his family's financial burdens. He took various jobs, farming in the summer, accompanying vocal students in the winter, laying sewer pipes in the broiling heat, playing piano for a men's exercise class in the evening. He gave piano lessons, and he ran an elevator—at the *Boston Post*. There in 1906 he became the music critic for a readership decidedly plebeian in its tastes, as the young Downes discovered when he used the three-syllable word *increment* in a column. The *Post*'s publisher, Edwin A. Grozier, called the new critic in to demand his intention in using such a word. Downes carefully explained that *increment* was not to be confused with another, somewhat similar-sounding noun. Grozier was still aghast. "Increment, excrement!" he snapped. "It's all the same to readers of the *Boston Post!*"[39]

The formative experiences at the *Post* together with the un-Harvard–like lessons of his youth proved a potent mixture. Working with Italian laborers over the sewer pipes, Downes had heard the men sing as they worked; he heard farm hands whistle as they plowed, and he watched the exercise class practice to his piano version of *Bedelia*. Downes came to believe with every fiber of his soul that music belonged to the people. Music correlated with life.[40] Had not his mother's favorite poet, Walt Whitman, heard America singing?

> . . . the varied carols I hear,
> Those of mechanics, each one singing his as it should be blithe and strong,
> The carpenter singing his as he measures his plank or beam,
> The mason singing his as he makes ready for work, or leaves off work,
> The boatman singing what belongs to him in his boat, the deckhand singing
>   on the steamboat deck,
> The shoemaker singing as he sits on his bench, the hatter singing as he
>   stands,
> The wood-cutter's song, the ploughboy's on his way in the morning, or at
>   noon intermission, or at sundown,
> The delicious singing of the mother, or of the young wife at work, or of the
>   girl sewing or washing,
> Each singing what belongs to him or her and to none else,
> The day what belongs to the day—At night the party of young fellows,
>   robust, friendly,
> Singing with open mouths their strong melodious songs.[41]

It should not be thought, however, that Olin Downes was without musical education. He somehow managed piano lessons with Carl Baermann, who had been a pupil of Liszt.[42] At various times he took theory instruction from Homer Norris, John P. Marshall, and Clifford Heilman, three Boston educators who taught composition.[43] There was a period of four months during which he immersed himself in scores at the Library of Congress. Downes later said, however, that he had learned the most from the "remarkable Dr. Louis Kelterborn in Boston, who started his career as a student of jurisprudence under Nietzsche at Basel and became a remarkably broad-minded musician."[44] Over four years, "the two played music for four hands, explored together entire periods of the literature of opera, oratorio, chamber music, and argued, often violently, about them. Sometimes the views of the pupil were of an alarmingly youthful and radical nature."[45]

Kelterborn may well have contributed to Downes's belief in musical heroes as well as to his knowledge of Nietzsche, who showed up frequently in the young critic's *Post* columns. (Downes once called for a twenty-minute intermission between *Ein Heldenleben* and the *Tristan* Prelude and *Liebestod* because, he groaned, "Only an Over-man may survive the *Heldenleben* with an appetite for more."[46]) Perhaps it did not escape Downes that Nietzsche's philosophy had much in common with Whitman's. "Beware of the scholars!" Nietzsche says in *Zarathustra*. "They hate you for they are sterile."[47] Whitman, too, saw the archenemy of life's joyous affirmation in the "dry-as-dust scholars and preachers." Like Nietzsche, Whitman foresaw a future of great men, of heroes. Paralleling Nietzsche's *Übermensch,* Whitman's heroes were self-reliant, individualistic, and defiant of convention. In *So Long!* he writes:

> I announce the great individual, fluid as Nature, chaste, affectionate,
>   compassionate, fully arm'd . . .
> I announce myriads of youths, beautiful, gigantic, sweet-blooded,
> I announce a race of splendid and savage old men . . .[48]

Somehow, Whitman and Nietzsche, idealists both, maintained an abiding faith in humanity. Whitman embraced the masses, in whom he heard the Song of Himself. Zarathustra, coming down from the mountain, is asked why he is not content to remain alone in the forest. His answer: I love mankind. Whitman's individual and Nietzsche's *Übermensch* both sought salvation for the human race. C. N. Stavrou, who examines this parallel between Whitman and Nietzsche, asks a penetrating and insightful question that seems to have particular significance here:

> Is the Messiah complex universal—latent in all? Or does it manifest itself with pronounced strength in certain temperaments? Are those who labor under severe handicaps, or encounter rejection, failure, insult, mistreatment, abuse, injustice early in life, more inclined to transmogrify their misfortune, whether real or imaginary, into a universal agony of Promethean proportions, and, with a grandiloquent gesture, shoulder the world's ills, and pen a gospel of salvation?[49]

Stavrou's question seems answered in the affirmative by Olin Downes. Rejected by his contemporaries, humiliated by his father's financial and moral failure, Downes, experiencing his own personal agony, gradually took on the world's aesthetic ills, for which his flourishing pen preached the gospel of music by the heroic Jean Sibelius.

For music lovers, Boston's most wondrous offering was its incomparable symphony orchestra. Downes found ways to save his pennies for a seat at the orchestra, and he was usually first in line for student tickets. He found the experience extraordinary, unsurpassed. At the symphony, one was "plunged deep beneath the surface of a sea of tone and the swirling, clamouring waters had met overhead. This was intoxication, confusion, joy past the telling. Coral caves, gleaming pearls, mermaids, and monsters, would not have been so enchanting!"[50] Symphonic music would always retain a powerful allure for Olin Downes. Once more, it suggested to him his mother's favorite poet. "All music is what awakes from you when you are reminded by the instruments . . ." Whitman had caroled in *A Song of Occupations.*

In 1904, the Boston Symphony under the direction of Wilhelm Gericke presented Sibelius's Second Symphony. Downes, eighteen at the time, later recalled a ponderous, unimpressive performance of a work far ahead of its time.[51] But three years later a different conductor performing a different work brought about a revelation: It was Karl Muck conducting the Bostonians in Sibelius's First Symphony. Downes arrived at the concert with a tepid review half-formed in his mind. He had already examined the Boston Public Library's score of the symphony, in whose jacket were pasted earlier reviews.[52] One German critic, he discovered, had granted the work's *Stimmung,* but, perhaps unable to appreciate Sibelius's thematic ellipses or his fluid interplay between two tonic keys, had concluded that the work lacked form. Downes thought he knew what to expect. Then the music began. A haunting clarinet lamentation unfolded over a timpani roll.

Ex. 2.

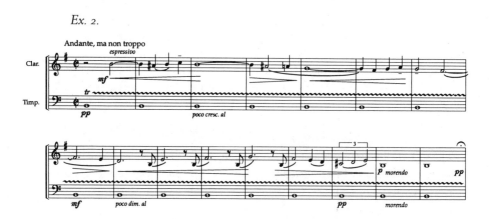

32

Gradually, the review Downes had planned to write was eroded—by the lyrical second movement, whose *Andante (ma non troppo lento)* unexpectedly becomes aggressive and then turns majestic when its slow and fast themes precipitately combine.

Ex. 3.

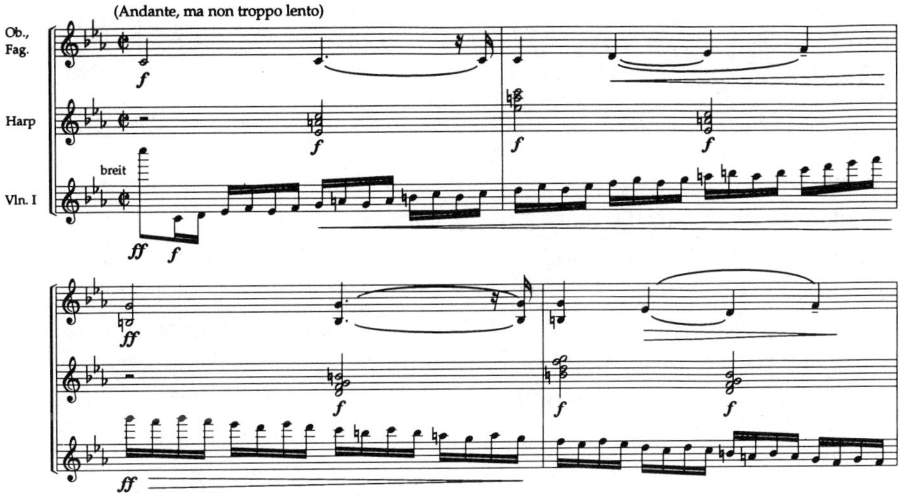

The two themes resolve into a ringing dissonance in the brass—perhaps what Sibelius meant when he spoke of trying to forge the *silverklang.*

Ex. 4.

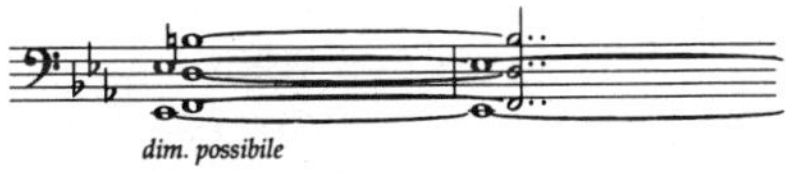

Then came the Scherzo, whose percussive string writing and elemental theme convey a savage primitivism.

Ex. 5.

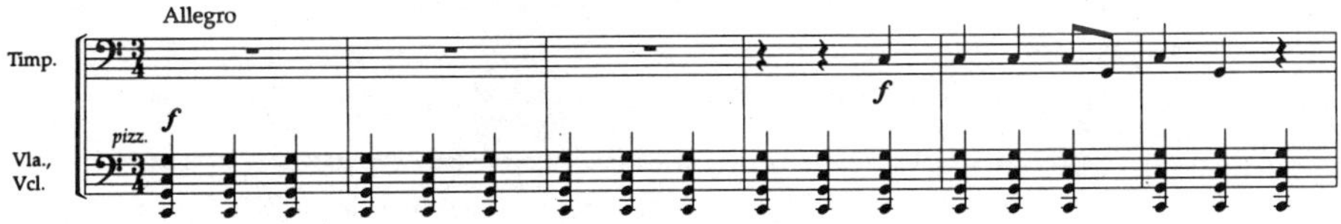

And then the Finale, "somewhat fantasy-like," Sibelius wrote. Its beautiful second theme, presented over an immense, thirty-three-measure pedal tone, seemed to Downes to embody the spirit of Finnish folksong.[53]

Ex. 6.

Olin Downes had found a home. "Here, oh God, was again grandeur, honor, nobility: Again the dignity of the human soul and the cry of the human spirit which nothing can kill, and which therefore never dies. . . . A hero was in the world and had spoken. I felt then that somewhere in the world there was a home."[54] To this he added: "The only comparable emotion that I have known, from art that can properly be called in its quality 'contemporaneous,' was when I first read lines of our incomparable American poet, Walt Whitman."

In Sibelius, Downes found a pure, living hero, a resonance with his own soul. Evoking images of a primeval past, of a giant advancing in seven-league boots, Downes began to champion Jean Sibelius. Slowly at first, then with increasing momentum, he found his critical stride. Here was a voice from Valhalla! Here was music "disconcertingly" vital! Here was a hero, but an undiscovered one—neither German nor French, but a Norseman who made articulate an entire nation, whose music expressed the "very bottom consciousness of a people—more, of humanity."

Although Olin Downes, like other Americans, had been slow to appreciate the Second Symphony, it was this work that finally confirmed him as Sibelius's apologist. In the Boston of 1904, no one, including Olin Downes, seems to have had a favorable opinion of the Second; even six years later, the *Boston Globe* reporter described it as the least interesting modern work of the season, in places "grewsome" and even "neurotic." The eerie bassoon theme in the slow movement, which Sibelius marks "lugubrious" and which he sets in duple meter against a pizzicato walking bass in 12/8, probably prompted these reactions. (See Ex. 7.) As late as 1916, Louis Elson in the *Boston Advertiser* was complaining that, despite the work's "attractive weirdness," its composer indulged in too much meaningless repetition, a

Ex. 7.

charge that the most sympathetic have leveled at the symphony's Finale because of the incessant replay of its circular theme and its driving ostinatos.

Ex. 8.

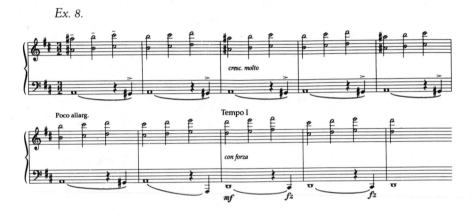

Surprisingly, even the first movement failed to impress Americans. Yet its treatment of the traditional sonata exposition showed considerable innovation, both in the character of the main theme and in the manner in which it is presented. The ingredients displayed in the first three measures—an eleven-note iteration and a stepwise ascent in compound meter

Ex. 9.

are gradually revealed to be essential to virtually all the remaining themes. They form the accompaniment to the ensuing woodwind melody, which employs the stepwise idea in retrograde.

Ex. 10.

The stepwise ascent is heard again in the horn call, this time in augmented values that unexpectedly slow the progress of the exposition.

Ex. 11.

And when the new key area of F-sharp minor arrives, at which point a new theme would be expected, there is instead the first theme again, only with an added counterpoint and reorchestrated to allow the winds to participate.

Ex. 12.

Not until the 1930s would the opening of this symphony lead Cecil Gray to claim that Sibelius had created a new symphonic principle, assembling thematic fragments in the exposition, merging them into an "organic whole" in the development, and dispersing them again in the recapitulation. (Sibelius, however, took exception to this view, which misled a whole generation of musical analysts. "I do not," he said in later years—one imagines with

36

some annoyance—"build my themes out of small fragments").[55] In early twentieth-century America, however, the Second Symphony was widely regarded by critics and audiences as simply morose. In Boston it consistently depressed Philip Hale.

But when Max Fiedler conducted the Second in 1909, Olin Downes sang a different song. Of course the Second Symphony was gloomy. It was dangerous, too: "It should not appear on too many programs. It might do incalculable harm to art, for it is sufficient to beat down the guard of the cleverest philosophy of esthetics ever formulated by dilettanti!"[56] Here was a symphony "gloriously rude," Downes chortled, about as welcome in Back Bay parlors as an unwashed Norseman in skins smelling of cod-liver oil. His delight with the coarseness he saw in Sibelius, indicated by such adjectives as "rude" and "unwashed," suggests that he had found in the composer an artistic symbol with which to combat Boston snobbishness. He also found in Sibelius a heroic father figure to replace his own disappointing one and a cause for which he could crusade in the service of art.

Downes's enthusiasm quickly became known. Just after the birth of Edward Downes in 1911, Philip Hale greeted the new father with a jovial, "Well, Olin, congratulations. Is it Sibelius or Sibelia?" From the printed page, Downes was sermonizing passionately. He did not advocate, he championed. He did not negotiate, he battled.

In Olin Downes's own words, "Young men should be formidable!" and formidable he was. In 1931 he was described as "a big fellow, with sizable neck, massive shoulders, thick chest, wrists of sapling girth, legs that tread with heavy impact," and a temperament of heroic cast. One startled observer recorded Downes in the act of writing a review, "arch[ing] his shoulders over a long piece of yellow, blue-lined paper and swing[ing] at it with a thick-leaded pencil as if driving a gouge cross grain on a block of oak."[57] Descendant of crusaders for other causes, Downes transformed that crusading spirit into preaching Sibelius with passionate obsession. "Was there ever a more imperative need of new force, at any stage in the history of the musical art?" he thundered.[58] Here was a "rebuke of cynicism, self-consciousness, decadent exaltation of style at the expense of substance." Jean Sibelius was "one born to go down in battle." Olin Downes seemed determined to accompany him.

THREE

Sibelius Discovers America

I have seen and experienced more in six weeks than
I normally do in many years.*   —Jean Sibelius

OLIN DOWNES AND JEAN SIBELIUS met for the first time in June of 1914. The occasion was Sibelius's first and only trip to the United States. Although it might naturally be assumed that Downes had arranged the visit, older, more established Americans, all of them intimately connected to New England, were in fact responsible.

In the summer of 1913, Horatio Parker, the distinguished Yale professor and composer, one of the Boston Classicists, invited Sibelius to write some songs for American children. Sibelius responded with *Three Songs for American Schools:* "Autumn Song," on a poem by Richard Watson Dixon; "The Sun upon the Lake Is Low," to a verse by Sir Walter Scott; and "A Cavalry Catch," on a poem by Fiona Macleod (a pseudonym for William Sharp). Parker included the songs in his Progressive Music Series, a graded instructional course published in Boston in 1916. Parker's admiration for the Finn had apparently preceded his invitation, for Sibelius believed that the Yale professor's prize-winning opera *Mona* had been modeled after his own music.[1]

It was also through Parker that another, more important invitation arrived: to be the guest of honor at a music festival in Norfolk, Connecticut. This annual event (which survives today as the Norfolk Chamber Music Festival) had been created by Carl and Ellen Battell Stoeckel, wealthy music lovers with important connections to Yale. Carl Stoeckel's father had been chapel organist and a music instructor at Yale and was eventually named Battell Professor of Music; Ellen was the daughter of Robbins Battell, a Yale graduate of 1839 who was an affluent amateur composer.[2] A letter from Carl Stoeckel to Horatio Parker shows that it was Parker who suggested to the couple that Sibelius be invited. Writing on August 18, 1913, Stoeckel thanks Parker for the list of prospective festival guests and adds that he would like to begin with Sibelius. In correspondence, Sibelius communicated his travel plans and the names of the works he intended to conduct to Parker.[3]

Only later did Carl Stoeckel write to Olin Downes about Sibelius's prospective visit.[4] Stoeckel explained that a friend who knew Sibelius had suggested that the composer be approached for a contribution to the Norfolk Festival. The contribution could be a work already in manuscript or something newly composed. Stoeckel made it clear that no conditions were being attached to the type of composition, only that Sibelius furnish something in one of the "lighter forms," as the concert was a summertime festival. The composition, which arrived in the spring of 1914, was entitled *Rondo der Wellen* (eventually to be called *Aallottaret,* or, in English, *The Oceanides*). Stoeckel immediately suggested that the composer conduct the work himself, together with other compositions of his own. To this Sibelius agreed.

In view of the enthusiasm for Sibelius in the Boston area, it does not seem surprising that the first and, as it happened, the only public appearance the composer ever made on an American podium was in New England. He arrived in the New World in the late spring of 1914, and over the next three weeks the Stoeckels introduced him to such influential Americans as Walter Damrosch, George Chadwick, Horatio Parker, Henry Hadley, Alma Gluck, and even former president William Howard Taft. On the evening of June 4 they featured the composer conducting a program of his own works before an invited audience that included Henry Krehbiel, Walter Damrosch, Maud Powell, and Olin Downes. The centerpiece of the program was the newly commissioned work, which the composer had dedicated to his hosts.

The Oceanides had twice been revised: three movements had been reduced to one, and then further alterations were made during the transatlantic crossing. Sibelius had written for an orchestra of grand proportions, perhaps in keeping with the expected grand scale of things in the New World. (Stoeckel's letter mentioned to Downes that the composer's own description of the new work was "Composition for grand orchestra.") He called not only for flutes, but also for piccolo; not just oboes, but English horn. He further enriched the woodwind section with bass clarinet and contrabassoon. He specified a large brass section—four horns, three trumpets, and three trombones (but no tuba, an instrument he did not like—*schwerfällig,* as he described it—and, after the Second Symphony, an instrument he generally did without). For percussion he asked for timpani, bells, and triangle; to the string choir he added two harps. With these instruments Sibelius treated his New World audience to some of his most memorable orchestral effects, such as the combination of harp, glockenspiel, and clarinet over a shimmering backdrop of string tremolos.

Ex. 13.

"If you don't create an artificial pedal for your orchestration," he once said, "there will be holes in it, and some passages will sound ragged." [6]

Although premiered as *The Oceanides,* the work's earlier name, in English, *Rondo of the Waves,* would seem to imply rondolike elements in the design. Through a combination of tone color and melody, the composer defined two contrasting blocks of material (flutes playing in thirds in one; oboes and clarinets over swirling harp glissandos in the other) that do in fact alternate in slow motion. In neither block is there a sense of regular meter or of a stable harmonic center. With Sibelius conducting the premiere, their accumulating power built in climax after climax, creating at the end of the work a final shock that left the audience stunned, then brought them to their feet shouting with enthusiasm.

In the reviews, critics made comparisons to Debussy, probably beguiled by the work's harmonic and metrical ambiguities and by Sibelius's choice of the "confectionery" instruments: harp, glockenspiel, and triangle. "He has become . . . an arch-impressionist," wrote Olin Downes.[7] It is indeed conceivable that the composer filled his commission with New Englanders' Francophile preferences in mind; he may well have learned of American musical tastes through Horatio Parker.

From this first contact, Downes left a vivid description of the composer at this moment in his life:

He is not an unusually tall man, but one of considerable girth, a really immense build, with what would be in a less highly organized individual the heaviness of Northern physique. Quite the contrary! Few men have I seen with a face that is such a sensitive record of impulses and impressions, despite the massive jaw and the somewhat large features. His manner is impulsive, and his speech very quick so that the experience of an interviewer peddling considerable French to a man that threw out jerky sentences and abrupt, energetic phrases in that language, and usually bit them off before they were concluded, had better be imagined than described.[8]

Downes's view of the occasion was widely disseminated in the essay he published the following week in *Musical America,* an essay boldly entitled "Creative Genius in Music Honored at Norfolk."[9] In it he reviewed the works Sibelius had conducted that evening: *Pohjola's Daughter,* music from the *King Christian Suite* (which he referred to as *King Stephen*), *Swan of Tuonela, Valse triste,* and *Finlandia.*

Toward the end of Sibelius's stay, the Stoeckels escorted their guest to Yale University. There on June 17, to the strains of *Finlandia, Valse triste,* and *Spring Song (Vårsång),* the faculty conferred upon him an honorary doctorate—once more the work of Horatio Parker. In April, Parker had requested this honor in behalf of Sibelius from the Committee on Honorary Degrees. In his petition, Parker had commended the composer's dedication to "impersonal" symphonic works, rather than to dramatic music more assured of immediate success.[10] His words were persuasive, and the degree was bestowed in recognition of the composer's vibrant nationalism and spreading reputation:

> By his music intensely national in inspiration and yet [in] sympathy with the mood of the West, Dr. Sibelius long since captured Finland, Germany, and England, and on coming to America to conduct a Symphonic Poem, found that his fame had already preceded him here also. Still in the prime of life, he has become, by the power and originality of his work, one of the most distinguished of living composers. What Wagner did with Teutonic legend, Dr. Sibelius has done in his own impressive way with the legends of Finland as embodied in her national epic. He has translated the Kalevala into the universal language of music, remarkable for its breadth, large simplicity, and the infusion of a deeply poetic personality.[11]

For Sibelius, America was a revelation. He was moved by the aristocratic hospitality and generosity of the Stoeckels (he later called them a mixture of Harun al-Rashid and Sinbad);[12] he was delighted with New York's sky-

Sibelius in his Yale robes. Painting by Sigurd Wettenhovi-Aspa, 1921; photograph by Gustaf Welin. Reproduced by permission of the National Museum of Finland.

scrapers and his private bathroom (his first night in America he arose three times to shower); and he was astonished by the excellence of the music found in America, which he had assumed would be mostly of the popular variety ("The orchestra is wonderful!! Surpasses anything we have in Europe").[13] Perhaps the most heartwarming of all was the stature accorded him as a composer and the enthusiastic response to his newest symphony, the Fourth. To understand the impact of these discoveries upon a composer who, to gauge by the adulation lavished upon him in America, would seem to have no cause for self-doubt, we must look at Sibelius's life in the years before his journey to Norfolk.

IN THE DECADE prior to his visit to America Sibelius had experienced various difficulties. One concerned his standing as a composer. In 1904 his own teacher and mentor, Martin Wegelius, had published a Finnish edition of the *History of Western Music*. Brushing aside all Finnish composers with the sentence "We must first have a music before its history can be written," Wegelius, an ardent Wagnerian, had singled out the Germanic composers, Mahler and Strauss, as the twentieth century's giants.[14] Such a dismissal from his own teacher must have cut deeply. Yet Sibelius could have consoled himself with the considerable success he was at that moment enjoying in Germany. And Germany seems to have been the forum he viewed as requisite for achieving lasting significance. There, in the summer of 1902 at the Heidelberg festival of the Allgemeiner Deutscher Musikverein, Sibelius had established himself as one "round which the greatest hopes of the music of the future would center."[15] The glow of that moment had hardly dimmed, even thirty years later, when Sibelius related to his biographer, Karl Ekman, the pleasure it had given him. His memories included conversations with the Festival's principal conductor, Richard Strauss.

But success had brought its difficulties. In its wake Sibelius sensed that Arthur Nikisch, conductor of the Berlin Philharmonic, had cooled toward him, and the composer suspected the plotting of rivals. His suspicions were confirmed when a friend tried to comfort him: "Now you are thoroughly recognized . . . the intrigues are beginning."[16] In Berlin, three years later, when Sibelius conducted his Second Symphony at a concert series sponsored by his friend and promoter Ferruccio Busoni, the composer found himself ". . . at the centre of battle. Fired at or praised. Mostly the latter."[17] While the praise was gratifying, the reservations proved significant. A review of one of his works in the *Neue Zeitschrift für Musik* was symptomatic

Sibelius at his desk at Ainola. A portrait of the composer's parents hangs on the wall. Photograph courtesy of the Sibelius Museum.

of a chauvinism that would ultimately relegate Sibelius to the periphery of German musical life. While praising the composer's orchestration and motivic handling, the critic nevertheless concluded loftily that "it is not a symphony destined and worthy to be ranked among the great symphonies of our masters from Haydn to Bruckner."[18]

Against this background came the Third Symphony, composed in 1907. The critics recognized immediately that Sibelius had veered sharply from the Romantic grandeur and extravagance of the Second. This symphony employed a smaller orchestra than did its predecessor—no tuba and one less trumpet—and chamberlike textures that lent a tautness to the language rare since Mozart. At the same time the symphony reinterpreted the conventional four-movement plan, fusing the scherzo and finale into a single structure. In contrast to works gigantic in scope and grandiose in instrumental resources being composed by Mahler and Strauss, the Third Symphony was of such lean proportions that it now seems a startling augury of post-war neoclassicism. Sibelius had eschewed the kind of writing he criticized in his contemporaries, music of huge dimensions and with showy instrumenta-

45

tion. Writers of such music, he said, could be likened to a dragon: "fire in your mouth and scare the children."[20]

In the Third Symphony, Sibelius had begun to concentrate and refine the inner musical relationships demonstrated in the first movement of the Second Symphony: the "profound logic," in his famous and oft-cited description, that creates an inner connection between all the motifs. These connections could be heard both thematically and harmonically in the new work's first movement. The two principal themes are the opening in C major,

Ex. 14.

and the contrasting theme in the surprising and seemingly incompatible key of B minor.

Ex. 15.

The first theme seems inspired by eighteenth-century Vienna;[20] the second by Finnish folksong. But Sibelius transforms one into the other in a passage in which the sixteenth-note first theme gathers energy and then takes flight.

Ex. 16.

46

And in the course of the development section, he emphasized the underlying unity of his two themes by converting the second into

Ex. 17.

The apotheosis, which reveals unmistakably that the two radically different themes spring from the same source, also ushers in the recapitulation, accomplished harmonically when the temporary tonic B is transformed into the leading-tone, which, accompanied by a huge orchestral crescendo, resolves dramatically upward.

Ex. 18.

The recapitulation thus seems to have been preordained, achieved by means of that musical logic of which Sibelius had spoken to Mahler that very year. With increasing confidence Sibelius was now permitting his ideas to

shape his music, even to the extent of generating new musical structures. The most radical manifestation of this in the Third Symphony is in the final movement, in which the composer synthesized scherzo and finale into one grand whole. The movement begins with nimble themes in 6/8 time, their flight through the orchestra recalling Sibelius's description of "thoughts crystallizing out of chaos." Eventually, these thoughts coalesce into a hymn of certain determination and grandeur in a march-like tempo.

Ex. 19.

This must surely have been the passage Olin Downes had in mind when he declared the Third Symphony to contain "hints of the large utterance of the early gods." Rather than being treated in a conventional way, the hymn theme revolves in circular fashion, its reiterations driving the symphony to a close in a triumphal C major. This hymn first is heard in its full form where normally a trio would follow the scherzo; only in retrospect does the listener discover that the "trio" has actually been functioning as the finale.

The Third Symphony had puzzled listeners in Finland. Abroad it was widely rejected. Even for a devotee like Downes, who for years knew the work only from score, the symphony "fell short in its development and at last miscarries." Downes particularly rued its abrupt ending, "with an effect of incompleteness and the need of a capstone for the tonal edifice." [21] Sibelius himself once indicated that he was not entirely satisfied with the Third Symphony, "my most unfortunate child," as he told Downes. [22] As a mature symphonist, Sibelius may have been unhappy with the development section in the first movement. Possibly he was dissatisfied with the finale; his use of reiteration was perhaps too similar to the bombastic repetitions of the Second Symphony's finale. In any event, his Anglo-Saxon critics were heartless.

Henry Krehbiel groaned that Sibelius would go down in history as the composer of a single significant work, the First Symphony; staunch British supporter Rosa Newmarch found the Third Symphony weak. Opinions had hardly changed by midcentury. In 1952 Harold Rogers remarked, "It was interesting to hear [Sibelius's Third Symphony] last night, if only to note once again how badly a composer can write." [23] At least Olin Downes had

48

the humility to admit, in the last year of his life, that perhaps he did not understand the Third Symphony.[24] No one seemed able to appreciate the composer's attempt to distill the essence of a single key, an idea that would achieve its ultimate expression in *Tapiola*.

Thus at the time of the premiere of the Third Symphony, Sibelius's professional position appeared somewhat equivocal. At that very moment a new problem arose: He was diagnosed with a throat tumor and sent to a Berlin specialist for treatment.[25] The tumor proved to be benign, but its threatening presence forced Sibelius to confront his own mortality. It even coerced him, at least for a time, into a drinkless and cigarless existence. Something of the depth of his reaction to these events may be gauged from the diary he began in 1909, in which he could vent his frustrations and discouragements in private.

This diary clearly reveals the crisis in the composer's creative life.[26] At the time he began work on his Fourth Symphony, Sibelius seems to have felt a pressing need to secure his international reputation once and for all. "Now or never," he frequently exhorts himself. "Am I nothing more than a 'nationalistic' curiosity, who must rank second to any 'international' mediocrity?"[27] Another diary entry makes plain that he realized he had moved steadily away from his nationalistic beginnings and into uncharted realms. "Looked at the *Kalevala* and it struck me—how I have grown away from this naive poetry."[28] These and other entries leave little doubt that Sibelius hoped the new work would establish his place, not as "just another representative composer from this corner of the world," but as a leader in the vanguard of modernism. The composer's expectations had never been higher. Nor had the time ever been more critical. Having reached middle age and in what seemed to be questionable health, Sibelius had to seize the chance to become a great composer.

Significantly, it was the Fourth Symphony upon which Sibelius pinned his hopes. Begun as early as 1909, it cost him enormous effort—down to the moment of its premiere in the spring of 1911. Even then, Sibelius revised the score once more before sending it to his Leipzig publishers, Breitkopf & Härtel. He himself provided the work's quintessential description: "[My Symphony] stands as a protest against present-day music. It has nothing, absolutely nothing of the circus about it."[29] Not surprisingly, subsequent commentary has stressed the work's compression and economy, qualities evident in a first-movement sonata exposition of merely fifty-three measures and a scherzo without a repeat. More so than in any previous work, Sibelius

49

created in this symphony a work whose themes and harmonies are thoroughly integrated and explained by a single unifying musical idea, in this case the tritone. No extraneous material can be found. "Never write a superfluous note," he once told a student. "Every note must be experienced." [30] One senses that the composer of the Fourth Symphony experienced these notes in a totally new way.

The significance of the recurring tritone has often been remarked. Its bleak outlines begin the symphony.

Ex. 20.

Sibelius instructed that this passage sound "as harsh as fate." From the moment it is articulated, the tritone establishes the melodic and tonal foundation of the work, the "compelling vein that runs through the whole." In the second subject, for example, it is the same tritone, but now transposed—and distorted with octave displacement—to the highly contrasting key of F-sharp major, a tonality which is already determined by the opening motif.

Ex. 21.

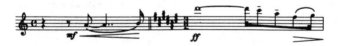

Sibelius proceeds with unassailable logic, allowing the tritone to generate the formal design as it simultaneously defines melodic and harmonic motion. There is no better illustration of this than the second movement. The sunny and *tranquillo* mood of this scherzo, which begins in the key of F major, is repeatedly disrupted by tritonal intrusions. Such abrasive contrasts were doubtless what prompted Walter Damrosch to remark that the Fourth was "the strangest thing in symphonic form he had ever encountered." [31]

Gradually, the scherzo is overtaken by an entire section derived from these disruptions, a section that serves as the trio (*Doppio più lento*) and, at the same time, makes a stunning contribution to symphonic thought. Whereas the traditional trio was a contrast within a minuet or a scherzo, this trio is an inevitable outgrowth of the disruptive forces within the scherzo itself, here redeemed and placed in the service of a higher structural function. Marked by violence (Sibelius instructed it be performed "brutally"), the section plays such havoc with symphonic proprieties that it rules out the normal practice of the scherzo's repeat. As a result, the movement halts abruptly, with only a whisper of the opening scherzo theme—an ironic distortion of the term *scherzo,* which originally meant "a joke." One can only think of Schumann's response to musical humor turned awry: "How must gravity be clothed if jest goes about wrapped in dark veils?"[32]

The third movement gives the impression of being the symphony's spiritual center. The music is contemplative in nature and must have occupied a special place in Sibelius's mind, because he asked that it be played at his funeral.[33] There are also distinct musical connections in mood, key, and theme between this movement and Sibelius's one mature string quartet, the quartet entitled *Voces intimae* (Intimate Voices). With its beautiful hymn, which rises from the depths of the orchestra, the symphony's slow movement was described by Sibelius as "compassion personified."

Ex. 22.

The conflict created by the tritone, transmuted into compassion in the third movement, is played out in the finale. The interval dominates the thematic material, especially the opening,

Ex. 23.

and provides the harmonic substance, most notably when the strings rush forward in A major while the woodwinds proclaim E-flat major. (See mm. 78ff.) This movement has a certain buoyancy that seems curiously inconsistent with what has come before. The key (a jubilant A major), the saucy ascent of the opening theme, and the sudden appearance of rejoicing bells seem to be at odds with the despondency of the rest of the symphony. Such friction, however, can be laden with meaning. Consider the instrument Sibelius now introduces—a percussion instrument whose exact character has given rise to lively discussion among commentators and inconsistencies in performance. The confusion concerns whether large bells are meant, as suggested by the word *Glocken* in the printed score, or whether that word is an abbreviation for *glockenspiel* and thus implies the small bells. The parts used at the premiere, which might provide clarification, can no longer be located. The composer's fair copy is marked *Stahlstäbe,* generally taken to mean large tubular bells, but Olin Downes was convinced that Sibelius had intended the "heroic" large bells. He enthusiastically praised Stokowski's decision to use large bells in his performance of the Fourth. The music itself, however, suggests that if Sibelius had heroism in mind it may well have been a heroism inspired by Mozart.

Admiration for Mozart ran like a leitmotif through Sibelius's writings and conversations. "Do you know whom I consider the two greatest geniuses of the orchestra?" he demanded of his student de Törne. "You will be surprised to hear it: Mozart and Mendelssohn."[34] Mozart, of course, had used the small bells in his opera *The Magic Flute,* a work whose Masonic symbolism reveals its composer's spiritual awareness. The significance in that opera of the number three, which is found in the number of characters in certain scenes, the number of repetitions of certain chords, and in the number of sharps or flats in certain key signatures, seems to be echoed in the Fourth Symphony. Sibelius's bells, which make their appearance in the key of three sharps, sound three different tones. And significantly, in light of the grinding hopelessness of the preceding movements, they cheerfully turn the tritone into a stable tonal unit.

Ex. 24.

The first appearance of the bells is preceded by a viola theme

Ex. 25.

that is strangely reminiscent of the piccolo motif in Papageno's aria "Ein Vogelfänger bin ich ja"

Ex. 26.

and which engenders a response from the flutes. Throughout the finale the bells appear consistently in keys of three sharps or three flats with one important exception: the movement's center. There they sound in augmentation in the "triumphal" key of C major (see mm. 230–37), the key that also accompanies the victorious Pamina and Tamino in *The Magic Flute*. And in the chaotic last moments as the symphony heads toward its close, when the disruptive forces seem to have scattered themes and a sense of tonal center to the winds, it is the bells that insist upon tonality and help swing the remaining instruments toward a consensus of key. (See mm. 436–44.) A work that stood at the brink of atonality and one whose materials were the sonic world's equivalent of despair, the Fourth Symphony demonstrated both the continuing vitality of the symphony as a musical genre and its power to express the most profound human feelings. At the very time the Fourth Symphony was being composed Sibelius noted in his diary, "A symphony is not just a composition in the ordinary sense of the word; it is more of an inner confession at a given stage of one's life."[35]

Sibelius himself conducted the premiere of the Fourth Symphony in Helsinki on April 3, 1911. Silence met the final bars. Then in the following days a critical furor erupted in reviews that ranged from attempts to fathom the symphony's "program" to charges that Sibelius now spoke in a language no one could understand. When the symphony was played in Sweden some months later, the audience hissed; in Copenhagen, they did nothing; in London, they expressed bewilderment. One Londoner ventured that the symphony might represent a stuffy garret with a view of chimney stacks on a foggy night.[36]

Perhaps these dismal critical failures would have been redeemed had the German community regarded the symphony as a leap into modernism. But the Germans seemed able to view Sibelius only through the spectacles of Romantic nationalism. In a review of the Fourth Symphony's score, Ernst Rychnovsky, while praising the composer's evident maturity, could only conclude that Sibelius "here again creates out of the inexhaustible springs of national experience."[37] *Die Musik,* the Berlin periodical that carried Rychnovsky's review in 1912, published a lengthy article the following year by Walter Niemann entitled "Jean Sibelius und die Finnische Musik."[38] Emphatically, Niemann, whose voice seemed louder than any other in Germany, insisted that Sibelius be understood in terms of his roots in northern melancholy, in unyielding nature, and in the soul of the Finnish folk—features, Niemann stressed, that helped to redeem the composer's formal and organizational weaknesses as a symphonist. As to Sibelius's being in the vanguard of modernists, there was not a word. Here and elsewhere, including his little book *Jean Sibelius* published in 1917, the voluble Niemann, himself a composer in the late Romantic style and a writer on musical topics from Johannes de Garlandia to Johannes Brahms, promulgated an image of Jean Sibelius that with each passing year appeared as outmoded as it was uncomprehending of the scores.

In 1912 when Walter Damrosch performed the work in New York the critics were thrown into disarray. Of their confusion, Philip Hale observed that it was hardly a good thing for brethren to dwell together in unity. Damrosch confessed that he had in duty offered the work to the American public, and that its first performance could well be its last. Critic Krehbiel huffed that the composer had now joined the futurists; Louis Elson observed primly that Sibelius had no business "in the pasture of Schoenberg"; and Philip Hale conceded that the work was a stumbling block, later remarking that the composer "does not trim his sails to catch the breeze of popular favor."[39]

Olin Downes had announced the news of Sibelius's Third and Fourth symphonies at the same time, in a *Boston Post* article in 1912. Whereas the Third was "neither fish, flesh, fowl nor good red herring," the Fourth was another matter. "Here is a composer who imitates no one, unless it be the contour and the harmonic color of the beautiful folk music of his own land," Downes proclaimed after studying the score:

> ... the art of Sibelius is one of the most vital needs of the musical art of today. It is, in some splendid particulars a return to the past. To sit in Symphony Hall and hearken to the roar of the winds, to see Red Eric whirling his sword, to hear the shouts of the heroes feasting in Walhalla—this can hardly be felt or communicated to such a degree by any other art. This is not a small thing, and the man who can sit down and sheerly pen such music is not a small man. The natural epic manner is his; there is the greatness and the sweetness, or the

rugged strength and fantasy of nature; there is also the note of the super-natural . . . but of love, as men know it, nothing. . . . We do not miss this, while we are thrilled by the eternal and unconquerable heroism of the music, its natural might, its Berserker rage.[40]

But Downes was describing the Sibelius he knew from the First and Second symphonies, from *En saga*. When at last he actually heard the Fourth Symphony, he must have been stunned. Publicly, he remarked that Sibelius had "developed the gentle art of making enemies to a point hitherto unsuspected by even his most enthusiastic admirers."[41] Only years later did he admit that his first response to the new score had been, "Where were the instrumental colors? Where was the grand gesture, the heroic challenge of the preceding works?"[42] After the 1913 performance he withheld judgment, perhaps not wishing to appear confused or to have written too hastily the previous August.

The discouraging reception of the new symphony precipitated a searching introspection by the composer. Self-doubts, always his demons, now pursued him more than ever. When the Swedish daily news, *Dagens Nyheter*, reviewed the Finnish Male Choir and praised Toivo Kuula and Selim Palmgren but mentioned nothing of Jean Sibelius, his distress became evident in his diary. His mood hardly improved when, through a chance remark, he learned that his music was gaining little hearing in Russia and that in Germany his Op. 61 songs had been heartlessly attacked.[43] He even showed a petty jealousy toward his friend and promoter Robert Kajanus, fretting that Kajanus had connived to displace him as the father of Finnish music. Increasingly, his diary from the period reveals indecision about his artistic direction and dismay that his creative ability might be on the wane. As the composer struggled inwardly, his friends began to notice outward changes: Already by 1908 his wild look had begun to soften. His proud, slim figure began to veer toward the rotund, and the Christmas after the Fourth Symphony's premiere, a contemporary referred to him in print as "fat and juicy."

Sibelius became eager to hear new music. In Paris and Berlin he followed the latest developments in European circles. He began to feel more positively disposed toward Claude Debussy, in whom he thought he recognized something of a kindred spirit, and Arnold Schoenberg, a composer of the avant-garde whom he found fascinating in spite of himself. In Berlin in early 1914 Sibelius was moved by a song of Schoenberg's (his diary does not specify which) and intrigued by "something important" in the *Kammersymphonie* (although he also complained it gave him an earache). The Second Quartet (with its prophetic soprano voice entering on the words "I feel the air of another planet") captivated him.[44]

It was in the throes of this compositional crisis and the disappointing responses to the Fourth Symphony, so devastating to a person of Sibelius's hypersensitivity, that the composer made his visit to the United States. How gratifying it must have been to Sibelius to be acclaimed a composer of strength and originality; how reassuring to find well-placed Americans, such as Carl Stoeckel, Horatio Parker, and Olin Downes, promoting his work; and how splendid, at last, that the Fourth Symphony was beginning to be appreciated. For in the summer of 1914, Sibelius discovered American critical opinion favorably disposed toward the new symphony. The composer wrote home joyfully, "America's best critics have written warmly about my Fourth Symphony."[45] Indeed, despite his ambivalence on first hearing the Fourth, Olin Downes praised Sibelius's "absolute mastery of his medium," the "uncompromising, powerful, and imaginative" qualities of the music, and, above all, the harmonic idioms which "place him in the very vanguard of the leading innovators of today."[46] Six months after meeting Sibelius at Norfolk, Downes would find in the Fourth Symphony the antithesis of French affectation: "No 'precious,' ultra-modern Frenchman ever steered more completely clear of the obvious or expected," he wrote, "and yet this symphony is as direct, as uncompromising, as inevitable as any one of the representative works of a man whose creations have always been remarkable for their simplicity and primeval power."[47]

Nor was Olin Downes alone in his acclaim. At the second performance of the Fourth Symphony in Boston in October 1913, listeners observed that the work improved with hearing and that it contained melodies of "sharp-set beauty and . . . concentrated power."[48] Best of all, in an article for *Musical America* entitled "Sibelius: A Musical Redeemer," Arthur Farwell uttered the words Sibelius must have most wanted to hear: "Why is it that [the critics] have much to say about Sibelius being a product of the wild and sombre north, and nothing to say of the manner in which he grapples, in his works, with the great musical questions of the day?"[49] Sibelius felt rejuvenated. "It is as if I find more and more of myself," he exulted from Norfolk.[50] On his return to Finland, he expressed his profound gratitude to Stoeckel for the efforts to advance his reputation; he had begun to experience joy, he said, in his work.[51] Norfolk's "wonderful peace," he wrote, had been of the greatest importance for his art. And indeed, within a month of the composer's return from America he began to plan first one new symphony and soon thereafter another. A sketchbook that dates from the period immediately following the Norfolk visit contains ideas for both the Fifth and Sixth symphonies, and also for the Seventh Symphony and *Tapiola.*[52] Although more than a decade would be needed to refine and give full expression to these ideas, the visit to the New World was a central event in nurturing the seeds of the composer's last four, and arguably his greatest, works.

If the Norfolk visit had given Sibelius welcome encouragement, it energized his promoters in America as well. The personal encounter with Sibelius seems to have spurred Olin Downes to new heights of enthusiasm. The summer before the visit, Downes had printed portions of Ernest Newman's article "After Wagner—What?" prefaced with his own call for a fruitful change in music.[53] In the wake of Sibelius's appearance in New England, Downes seemed to have found the answer to Newman's question. "Out of the North has come a new prophet," he thundered, "Jean Sibelius." In a three-part article spread over the summer issues of the *New Music Review and Church Music Review,* Olin Downes preached the gospel of Sibelius as salvation for the twentieth-century soul. This was music "of singular originality and power, heroic, primeval music, a vitalizing force of exceptional value to the modern art of composition."[54] Such music is "even more important to men," Downes proclaimed, "than to art." Downes's announcement would prove deeply prophetic in a way he did not intend; increasingly, men managed to overlook Sibelius's art as his music was drafted to serve interests of their own.

The December after Sibelius's visit there was heard in Boston a work that only solidified Downes's high-minded position vis-à-vis Sibelius: Arnold Schoenberg's *Five Pieces for Orchestra.* This was music "very terrible, physically hurtful—and this is but sober statement of fact," Downes fumed. His own puritanism and prejudices showed clearly in his review: "For us this music, however original and masterly in workmanship, is exceedingly unhealthy and disagreeable, having neither the grandeur of cleansing tragedy nor the uplift of a great composition that makes all men akin."[55]

Although Downes had praised *Verklärte Nacht,* perhaps because it reminded him of Wagner, whose music he loved, he took a dim view of what was now coming out of decaying Vienna. Not only was such music unwholesome, it was positively un-American. He said as much in a review of *Die glückliche Hand:* "The composition of Schoenberg's . . . is highly decadent in a very interesting meaning of that word, and in an extreme of pessimism, looking, in fact, toward death. In this it seems to us the antithesis of anything 'American.' At least, we hope so."[56] The music was fetid. "The impression one gets of this dying art," Downes grumbled, "is akin to the thought of

some struggling creature left by a receding tide, perishing on strange sands."
For Olin Downes, as for many Americans, Schoenberg's putrescent music
contaminated the concert hall with an effete radicalism, while Sibelius, that
"new clean great man," strode forth the virile hero.

And it was as conquering hero that Sibelius had arrived in Finland after
the New England visit. He was full of plans to return to America for a conducting tour, for which Breitkopf & Härtel's New York office had promised
full publicity. In the interim, conductors in the United States, from Damrosch to Stransky, Muck to Altschuler, filled their programs with his works.
The increased opportunities to hear his music seemed to bode well for initiating the reluctant into the mysteries of such "advanced" works as the
Fourth Symphony.

But war came, and with it came irrevocable changes. Germany, the musical Mecca Sibelius still hoped to conquer, now turned into the enemy. Finland's position as a Russian duchy automatically placed her at war with the
Germans. And in the war's aftermath, Sibelius, marginalized as a nationalist
in the best of times, had little chance of holding his own as a modernist in
such fiercely nationalistic centers as Berlin and Munich. Moreover, the German defeat brought down with it the prosperity of Sibelius's publishers,
Breitkopf & Härtel and Robert Lienau; Sibelius transferred his publishing
contracts to Wilhelm Hansen in Denmark. And Sibelius's troubles in Germany were further compounded by the suddenly diminished status of Busoni, his strongest champion, who, as a result of the war, suddenly found
himself shunned by Germans and Italians alike. Settling for a time in Switzerland, Busoni eventually returned to Berlin, but by then he was ill. When
he died in 1924, there was no one to take his place as an advocate of Sibelius.

Ernest Newman also blamed the war for this setback. In Great Britain,
the war made it impossible to arrange repeat performances of the Fourth
Symphony, a work unusually demanding on its listeners.[57] Although Breitkopf & Härtel's London office, being Swiss-managed, was allowed to continue releasing Sibelius's music for performance during the war, it was primarily Valse triste and Finlandia that were played. In the view of Sir Arnold
Bax, these and other "trifles" gave Sibelius the reputation of a popular, light-
weight composer rather than an advanced modernist.[58] When Sibelius again
appeared in England, in 1921, it was with a new work, the more accessible
Fifth Symphony, and a new image, a shaved head and a portly figure.

The war also affected Sibelius in America. It scuttled his immediate plans
to return. It distracted Olin Downes, who had intended to acquire all Sibeli-

us's scores, the better to advocate his cause. And most injuriously, the war's nationalistic tensions led to the imprisonment of Karl Muck, the conductor most enthusiastic about Sibelius's music in America. Muck's ignorance of a demand by American journalists to begin each concert with the national anthem was twisted by them into a cavalier and traitorous refusal that landed him in a Georgia prison for the duration of the war.[59] Muck's replacements in Boston, Henri Rabaud and then Pierre Monteux, were indifferent to the Finn, and performances of Sibelius's works fell off significantly. The Sibelius "cult" that had flourished for a time in New England withered. Significantly, Olin Downes, Carl and Ellen Stoeckel, Horatio Parker, and others remained enthusiastic toward Sibelius, but the one person empowered to assist the composer in a substantial way appeared to be Muck—the conductor, not the critic, the patron, or the professor. And the composer's ultimate proving ground would be the concert hall. This lesson would not be lost on Olin Downes.

SIBELIUS'S DISCOVERY of the New World, around the time of the Great War, marked a crucial moment in the composer's self perception and in the development of his work. Increasingly pigeonholed by chauvinistic Germans as a mere "nationalist," even in the face of his newest, most advanced symphony, Sibelius appreciated that he was being enthusiastically adopted by Anglo-Saxon critics, who saw in him a savior heroically bearing traditional aesthetic principles into the twentieth century. From this time forward he exhibited concern and an interest in his American reputation, which can be documented in his correspondence and in his diary, with its numerous references to important figures in American musical life including Parker, Downes, Muck, Chadwick, and the New York music publisher Carl Fischer. Sometimes the reference is no more than a postal address, yet the accumulated evidence demonstrates an acute sensitivity to his status in the United States. On January 3, 1921, for instance, the composer entered a London address for Olin Downes. In this same entry Sibelius noted that he had cabled the message "Yes!" to Rochester, New York. He was referring to an invitation he had received to accept a professorship at the Eastman School of Music. The affirmative reply prompted the *New York Times* to announce the appointment publicly.[60] But Sibelius, with his penchant for vacillation, soon changed his mind.

He did not, however, change his decision to continue along the path of symphonic exploration in the face of the radical departures of Schoenberg and Stravinsky, the second of whom, it will soon be seen, particularly incensed Olin Downes. The choice of going "his own way," as he referred to it, seems to have been bolstered by the American visit. Its most dramatic outward manifestation was the shaved head, extraordinary for the time and for someone as fastidious as Sibelius in matters of style and dress. Although a much more conservative haircut than that of the 1890s bohemian was evident when Sibelius visited Norfolk, the decision taken toward the end of the war to shave his head in its entirety appeared to be a powerful metaphor for stripping away all nonessentials, a decision that seemed to announce visibly the composer's unyielding pursuit of his own course.[61] That course lay with the symphony, and therein lay the rub. Already by the end of the nineteenth century the symphony, by virtue of its history and its conventions, had come to symbolize musical orthodoxy. While such turn-of-the-century composers as Mahler and Scriabin stretched the genre beyond its previous limits in size and tonal daring, younger composers such as Stravinsky and Schoenberg, at the forefront of musical modernism, preferred to write for the ballet, opera, and chamber ensemble. The avant-garde generally avoided the symphony unless their purpose was to outrage or parody. Ironically, they were called neoclassicists; those who worked within the symphonic tradition were beyond the pale.

Like many wild young men of the late nineteenth century, the youthful Sibelius had been fired by Wagner's example and had attempted to compose opera. But opera, although it would tempt him repeatedly, was not his medium. One such projected early work, based on the *Kalevala* and called *The Building of the Boat,* had been abandoned, although its overture seems to survive in *The Swan of Tuonela*. Sibelius's lack of success with opera, the classical aspects of his musical experiences in Finland and especially in Vienna, the seat of conservative symphonic tradition, and his own inclinations seem to have led him inexorably to symphonic expression.

For many among the intelligentsia of the twentieth century, Sibelius's devotion to the symphony rather than, for example, to "progressive" quartets in the manner of Bartók and Schoenberg was enough to warrant dismissing him as regressive.[62] It was a devotion that signified little in the European centers where he most wanted to compete, especially inasmuch as his promoters harped on the traditional and nationalistic aspects of his scores. Olin Downes's insistence on the "heroic" qualities in his symphonies intensified the suspicion that Sibelius was simply unable to make the leap into the modern world, and the widespread popularity of such "easy" pieces as *Finlandia* bolstered his image as an orthodox conservative who catered to popular tastes. However much at odds it was with the composer's complex and original thought, the image of a Romantic nationalist clung like a wet shirt. By the end of World War I, that perception seemed both widespread and firmly planted. In 1918 Paul Rosenfeld began an article on Sibelius in the *New Republic* with Romantic Northern images:

> Others have brought the North into houses, and there transmuted it to music. And their art is dependent on the shelter, and removed from it, dwindles. But Sibelius has written music innocent of roof and inclosure, music proper indeed to the vasty open, the Finnish heaven under which it grew. And could we but carry it out into the northern day, we would find it undiminished, vivid with all its life. For it is blood-brother to the wind and the silence, to the lowering cliffs and the spray, to the harsh crying of sea-birds and the breath of the fog, and, set amid them, would wax, and take new strength from the strengths of its kin.[63]

Like Walter Niemann, who the previous year had emphasized Sibelius's Finnish qualities above all else, Rosenfeld viewed Sibelius as the Norseman, an artist who preserved intact the "racial" inheritance of Finnish peasants.

Olin Downes tended to embellish the Nordic image with references to Sibelius's heroic qualities and with puritanical praise for his virility and disdain for sensuousness. When Pierre Monteux finally conducted the composer's Third Symphony in a Boston season that offered little by Sibelius, Downes wrote:

> Looking back, he [Sibelius] was the only man whose music, before 1914, rumbled and reverberated war-red war [*sic*]. This note, so stern, so terrible, in the music of perhaps the one man we know whose expression is supremely touching and yet utterly devoid of the note of sex, appears in retrospect so prophetic that one wonders, after all, if any composers, simple or sophisticated, know what they are writing about. One wonders if the spirit of the old heroic north did not elevate itself to some height from which it could view the acts, the thoughts, and the soul of the whole world, and then, descending again to earth, send out its message in the person of this Sibelius, whose name, anyhow, is a symphony of sweet sounds.[64]

Downes wrote that among his contemporaries, including Strauss and Debussy, Sibelius was the most "incredible," a product of his Northern origins:

Let us not be misunderstood. We don't mean that Sibelius is necessarily the greatest of these three composers. He is most incredible. He is incredible because of the manner in which he emerges from the north, a giant of a far gone, heroic, antique past. No one living in America can possibly understand how such a composer can exist today. His music is a saga. It is a tale of great deeds of yore, of things supernatural which confronted the fathers of men, of a pagan past which—thank the Christian God—still smoulders under northern snows.[65]

When only one year later the composer's Fifth Symphony was heard in the United States, conducted by Monteux in April of 1922, American critics heard confirmation of the Sibelius they had in mind: certain tonality, orchestral grandeur, and an affirmative, even heroic tone. Olin Downes breathed a sigh of relief: "It was with apprehension and relief that this music was heard by the writer. It had, of course, met with wide approval. But there had been signs of a possible decadence in the Fourth Symphony, and a man of Sibelius' power, a composer with his unique possession of the spirit of heroic tragedy, could ill be spared."[66]

The opening of the first movement of the Fifth Symphony is devoid of the warmth of strings,

Ex. 27.

and when the strings do at last enter, they provide an eerie sound screen against which the woodwinds play their themes.

Ex. 28.

Downes was hard-pressed to explain how this melancholy first movement could develop without a break into the equivalent of a second movement that was bright, joyous, and reminiscent of Haydn.

Ex. 29.

Rather than dwell on the analytical complexities of how Sibelius achieved that fusion of first and second movements, Downes concentrated instead on the work's nationalistic and heroic qualities, a trait that probably endeared him to Sibelius, who once remarked, "Let it be understood that one does not come at the true inwardness of music through analysis, and that in what the analyst writes he speaks not for the composer but for himself." [67] Downes wrote of the echoes of bleak moors and "the tragic outcry of the human confronted with fate" and of a finale in which "the composer returns to his native heath and to the mood which those who understand him know and love." [68] The mood to which Downes refers is almost certainly that of the finale. Its soaring theme is presented in three metrical layers, an example of Sibelius's well-developed ability to realize contrasting possibilities simultaneously within musical time.

Ex. 30.

For Downes, this passage was Sibelius's "native heath," for Tovey, "Thor's Hammer Theme"; more recently, it has been called Sibelius's "Swan

Theme." The desire by listeners to give this musical moment a name surely springs from the recognition that Sibelius is expressing something powerful about human experience, something that must go beyond a mere technical description of themes treated rather like the rhythmic layers of a medieval motet. Sibelius himself would later say that the Fifth, Sixth, and Seventh symphonies were "more in the nature of professions of faith" than the earlier works. It was this spiritual quality, which after the American visit Sibelius would explore and refine, that would prove to be the most important to Olin Downes.

In his later years Sibelius would complain about music in the contemporary world: "How endless a lot of well-composed music is—but nothing else than note-scribbling. The inner life is absent. They've built a huge shipyard—but where is the ship?"[69] The depth of his own inner life was suggested partly by the public persona he cultivated with his monklike isolation and tonsured pate, but mostly by his music. At the very time he was grappling with the Fifth Symphony, the composer was also working on music for a play by Hugo von Hofmannsthal, *Jedermann* (*Everyman*). Sibelius wrote a good deal of incidental music throughout his life, although little of it is heard outside Scandinavia. This particular work is interesting for the programmatic meaning the setting suggests.

A medieval English morality play, *Everyman,* symbolizes all humanity. The play recounts the mission of Death to summon every individual before God to account for the time each has spent on earth. Everyman, deserted by his fair-weather friends, despairs of finding anyone to accompany him on this last journey. But he repents of his sins, and, redeemed by his belatedly declared Faith and his few Good Works, sets forth on his pilgrimage into Eternity. The play drives home the moral that it is easier for a camel to pass through the eye of a needle than for a rich man to enter the kingdom of heaven.

Hugo von Hofmannsthal had found in *Everyman* an ideal vehicle with which to protest the materialism of modern society. His *Jedermann* deals with the love of material things far more than did the original medieval play, and his satirical condemnation of worldliness extends almost to the point of expressionism. Written in 1911, Hofmannsthal's play is susceptible to multiple interpretations: On the one hand he confronted social and religious problems of his day; on the other he seemed conscious that certain dimensions of his story might be truly understood only by later generations.[70] To this end, he wrote simply enough to be understood by the peasant, yet subtly enough to appeal to the sophisticate. Speaking to the average man, Hof-mannsthal's Everyman is "a rich man who is not exactly bad." Everyman is spiritually supported by a mother who speaks with the voice of Christian morality and who steadfastly tries to guide her son to the path of right-eousness.

Sibelius's music, composed in 1916, consists of individual movements that are wedded to the play; there is little opportunity for symphonic logic. Some numbers are treated as melodrama (*Werke* and *Glaube*) and others have choral or solo parts, yet the dramatic and musical associations are re-vealing. The work opens with a threefold fanfare, sounding a cluster of whole tones.

Ex. 31.

The prologue that follows, which also features whole-tone relationships, is marked *Jumala,* meaning God. In contrast with Jumala's prevailing diaton-icism, the Devil makes his appearance to the sound of the tritone, in his ultimate attempt to capture Everyman's soul. The Devil's scene is memora-ble for its intensely chromatic lines, which, though often seeming rootless, finally come to rest in D minor. Sibelius thus demonstrates his own historical sense—through the tritone's age-old association with the Devil, the Dorian mode's association with faith, and the organ's fauxbourdon-like passages as accompaniment to Faith and Good Works as they assure Everyman of God's grace. At the play's close, as Everyman makes his way into the grave accompanied by the voices of angels, Good and Evil stand harmonically opposed: piano and horns sound out F-sharp, but cellos, basses, and bas-soons stubbornly prolong C. The organ, however, with its near constant perfect fifth, seems to urge the recalcitrant instruments upward into D ma-jor and finally succeeds in dramatically lifting them—as though heaven-ward—through a whole-tone relationship. (See Ex. 32.)

In these final measures of *Everyman,* there may well be a world of mean-ing for understanding Sibelius. Drawing as he often did on the rich possibili-ties offered by the tritone, Sibelius seems to confirm in this drama that

Ex. 32.

within conflict itself there is resolution, that, just as light and dark, good and evil, are found in Everyman, so whole tone and tritone, harmonic control and harmonic freedom, may likewise occupy the same musical space. One has meaning only in the context of the other.

Of Hofmannsthal and his literary compatriots, such as Thomas Mann, it has been said that they remained true to the laws of their own development rather than join the Expressionist movement, that they concerned themselves with the rejuvenation of man in an age which had become extremely problematic, and that they brought to their work a rich historical inheritance with which they associated the process of renewal.[71] That assessment applies with clarifying accuracy to Jean Sibelius. Staying on the periphery of the musical fashions of his day, he followed his own musical laws to maturity, yet he did not shrink from the challenges of his complex age. Just as Hofmannsthal had sought to rejuvenate mankind, so Sibelius endeavored to rejuvenate the symphony by bringing to it a wide-ranging and profound historical inheritance. Through the ancient association of the devil with the tritone and the chromatic, God with the modal and diatonic, Sibelius, like Hofmannsthal, spoke in terms simple enough to be understood by the majority, as he had in *Finlandia* and in *Valse triste*. The deeper significance of his music has not yet been as widely understood.

SIBELIUS FINISHED HIS LAST two symphonies before Olin Downes undertook the first of his five journeys to Finland. Downes, who would become a personal friend of Sibelius's, especially treasured the Sixth because Sibelius presented him with an autographed score. The ideas for the symphony date back to the latter part of 1914, although the work was not premiered until February 19, 1923. The symphony made clearer than any of its predecessors how the genre had become for Sibelius a profession of faith. Downes likened it to Joan of Arc harkening to her voices. Other critics thought the work was inspired by Beethoven, whose own Sixth Symphony seemed recaptured in its pastoral spirit. Still others were reminded of Palestrina because of the prominence of the Dorian mode, the exquisite string polyphony, and the pure diatonicism—an unfamiliar sound in the dissonant, experimental twenties.

Ex. 33.

Sibelius had once noted in his diary that "many present-day composers, in their endeavours to preserve their place in the public eye, through constantly having to produce something novel and sensational had lost the power of composing anything based on the old ecclesiastical scales." [72] This, he concluded, was "reserved for me and others who could live in greater peace." The Sixth Symphony is a testament to that peace, nurtured by pastoral living at the composer's country home at Lake's End. That his peace was not without its occasional disruptions is heard in the tonal intrusion on the modal purity. (See Ex. 34.) One disruption that must have particularly disturbed Sibelius and deeply taxed his inner resources during the completion of the Sixth Symphony was the unexpected death of his brother Christian in the summer of 1922. The youngest and sunniest of the Sibelius siblings, Christian, a physician like their father, had been a bulwark for the composer during his tempestuous youth and had provided a safe haven for

Ex. 34.

Sibelius and his family during the time of civil war. Perhaps it was significant that Sibelius set the symphony in the Dorian mode, which in his setting of *Everyman* he associated with heavenly matters and faith. And his decision to use C major as the unusual second key area takes on significance as well, juxtaposing as it does a "lower," hence earthly, key next to the D Dorian. One thinks of the key symbolism in Haydn's *Creation,* in which the key depicting the earthly status of Adam and Eve is a whole step lower than the key portraying the divine act of creation. That Sibelius held a deep faith in the beauty and reality of the heavenly Dorian world seems to be expressed by the outcome of the first movement—as well as by the outcome of the symphony as a whole. Freely exploring the possible relationships between the two key centers in the first movement with no clear indication of his end in view, Sibelius alternates resourcefully between the two worlds of D and C until the movement's final measures. There a D-flat scale rises to C major, a key center prolonged by the whole orchestra as if in conclusion. But after a fermata, strings and woodwinds, *poco tranquillo,* lift the final measures upward—into D Dorian.

Ex. 35.

The superb fluidity with which Sibelius alternates between keys is one of the Sixth Symphony's most distinguishing features. A splendid example is the prominent theme of the last movement, a rising Dorian scale that unexpectedly finishes with an "out of key" C minor chord (to be immediately repeated in sequence a step lower).

Ex. 36.

This theme has been regarded as embodying the impulse that generates the entire symphony; versions of it occur in every movement. That a variant of it was originally sketched for use in the Fifth Symphony would seem to add to its value in Sibelius's mind. In the final measures of the Sixth Symphony it is transformed into a deeply expressive hymn, one that reaches out of its Dorian context for such startling realms as D-flat, E, and C-flat major. Yet the serene conclusion in Dorian attests to the composer's "inner," as Sibelius referred to his innermost self. Although by no means religious in the conventional sense of that word, Sibelius once noted that "it is impossible to define a religion—least of all in words. But perhaps music is a mirror."[73] Music such as we hear in the Sixth Symphony serves as just such a mirror, reflecting (to use Sibelius's own words about Bruckner) a strangely profound spirit in a world of pathos.

In his last symphony and the tone poem *Tapiola,* Sibelius completed the realization of musical ideas that had begun to germinate in the afterglow of his American trip. Although it is not surprising that these two works, completed in the mid-1920s, share certain features, what they do share is perhaps unexpected. There are not only the slow tempo and the expressive timpani roll with which each begins, there is also the one-movement form. Essential in a tone poem, the one-movement design was virtually unheard of in a symphony. Yet in hindsight this symphonic plan appears inevitable from a composer who had linked the third and fourth movements of his Second Symphony (with the direction *attacca*), fused movements in his Third and Fifth symphonies, and intimately linked all the movements of his Fourth Symphony (by ending each with a unison note that pivots effortlessly into the following key). In his last two great works, Sibelius closely linked the two genres, the symphony and the tone poem, virtually erasing the largely artificial distinction between "absolute" and "program" music.

At one time Sibelius had called his Seventh Symphony "Fantasia sinfonica." As a work-in-progress, he described it in 1918 as "joy of life and vitality, with appassionato passages."[74] The music begins as if to introduce one of the beautiful daydreams that sometimes provided his inspiration, but this one turns somber.

Ex. 37.

The Seventh Symphony could well be used to demonstrate the truth of Schoenberg's admonition to his students that "there is still a lot of good music to be written in C major."[75] That key is embodied in the work's most famous theme. What enhances the theme's significance further is that its broad rhythmic values are given to the trombone, an instrument whose historical associations with the religious create a sense of mysterious otherworldliness at each of its three appearances.

Ex. 38.

Sibelius's own description of his working methods in regard to these last works is revealing. "As usual," he said, "I am a slave to my themes and submit to their demands."[76] This submission probably accounts for the decision to cast the symphony in one movement, rather than the three originally projected, and for the delivery of the central trombone theme to woodwinds and strings.

Ex. 39.

This transformation into a buoyant *Allegro moderato* enables it to function as one of the "movements" within the overall plan. This section is sometimes referred to as the "Hellenic rondo," the composer's original name for what he thought would be the symphony's last movement. Yet no one recognized better than Sibelius that "the final form of one's work is . . . dependent on powers that are stronger than oneself. Later on one can substantiate this or that, but on the whole one is merely a tool. This wonderful logic—let us call it God—that governs a work of art is the forcing power."[77] It was undoubtedly such power that led to the symphony's ineffable closing moments, when the strings soar into the ether and Sibelius expresses in unforgettable sound his "joy of life and vitality."

Ex. 40.

No artifice this, no mere mechanical elaboration. Sibelius once lamented that too many present-day composers "made one think of court councillors composing," and, the ultimate damnation, "their works made one think of doctors' dissertations."[78] In an age of contrivance and "the kind of species labelled 'intellectual,'" Sibelius through his music insisted that "we human beings need much more than the kind of reality that is accessible to the five senses. He who does not understand that fact is unfortunate."[79]

It seems fitting that in this complex of late works whose creation was given forward momentum by Sibelius's visit to the New World, the last should be specifically composed for America. Walter Damrosch, who had met Sibelius during the trip to New England, commissioned the composer to write a work for the New York Symphony Society. Sibelius responded with *Tapiola*. He dedicated the music to Damrosch, who gave the world premiere in New York on December 26, 1926. What caught everyone's ear then and since was the construction of a nearly twenty-minute work from a single, short, unremarkable thematic idea that is stated in the first three measures. "Avowedly slight," said Downes, who complained of too little contrast and a pervading formlessness.[80]

Ex. 41.

While on the surface one hears the "perpetual variation" of the initial thematic idea, at a deeper level the composer creates an extraordinary sense of stasis. A slow-moving ostinato dramatizes an inertia that is both tonal and rhythmic.

Ex. 42.

Ernest Newman heard in *Tapiola's* monothematic plan an attempt to portray the infinite variety of life in the forest, all of which springs from a common source. Asked by his publishers to explain the title, Sibelius referred to the realm of Tapio, the forest god in Finnish mythology. He then inscribed his own verse at the head of the work: "Wide-spread they stand, the Northland's dusky forests,/Ancient, mysterious, brooding savage dreams;/And within them dwells the Forest's mighty God,/And wood-sprites in the gloom weave magic secrets."

No work demonstrates more vividly Sibelius's keen perceptions of the natural world. Here was a composer who was moved to musical expression by the call of the nightingale at Ainola; by the majesty of swans in flight; by the smell of flax drying in the sun, an experience that once sent him rushing home from a walk to capture the pungent fragrance in music. *Tapiola* betrays a spirit acutely attuned to nature's moods, in this instance those of savage dreams and dusky forests. Perhaps the Northland's gloom seemed most terrifying in the still of night, the time when Sibelius did most of his composing. "A fearful thing, this eternal stillness," Sibelius recorded in his diary. He proceeded to cast this stillness in *Tapiola*—in harmonic immobility and even in silence. (See Ex. 43.)

Ex. 43.

Appropriately, Sibelius called *Tapiola* a symphonic poem rather than a tone poem. As with *The Oceanides,* the New World's resources perhaps suggested the orchestration, amplified in comparison with the contemporaneous Seventh Symphony by an additional flute alternating with a piccolo, a bass clarinet, and a contrabassoon. The sounds the composer derives from this ensemble contribute to *Tapiola*'s most chilling moments.

Ex. 44.

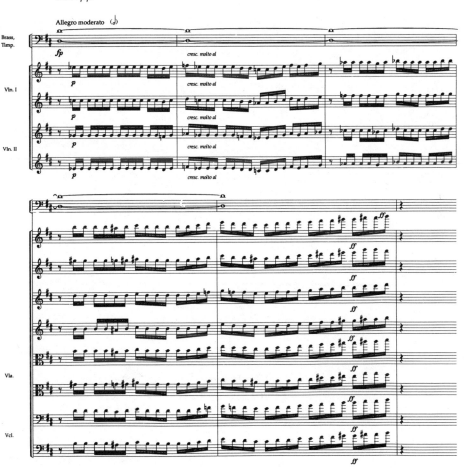

Moreover, they are thoroughly idiomatic to the orchestra, being virtually impossible to reproduce on piano in any satisfactory way. For all his admiration of Beethoven, Sibelius once observed that Beethoven's orchestral technique betrayed a pianist at work, a criticism that could not be leveled at Sibelius.

Tapiola, we now know, would be the end of Sibelius's odyssey. From our present perspective we can also see that the journey from *Kullervo* to *Tapiola* via the incomparable seven symphonies covered a remarkable distance; later observers would wonder whether further travel was even imaginable. Indeed, one explanation advanced for Sibelius's creative impasse is that subsequent works from such a composer would have been pointless, or at least thematically, tonally, and formally inconceivable.[81] In 1926, however, no such thought clouded the horizon. Instead, Sibelius's Eighth Symphony was awaited with eagerness and with certainty.

FOUR

Enter Igor Stravinsky

From *Oiseau de feu* to *Sacre du printemps* . . . his way
seems perfectly clear, after which this humble commentator cannot follow the singular and unpredict-
able divagations of Stravinsky's muse.*
—Olin Downes, 1924

CORRESPONDENCE BETWEEN SIBELIUS and Olin Downes began in the
1920s, at the end of the composer's period of most profound creativity. Initiating this correspondence, Downes drew on his by now well-established
Boston connections. He proposed an American tour be arranged for Sibelius by the Boston Symphony's manager, William Brennan. Reminding the
composer of their meeting in Norfolk (although he erred on the date),
Downes first asked to be sent as many of Sibelius's scores as possible. Then
he urged the composer to consider seriously the idea of conducting his own
instrumental and choral works across the United States.[1] Downes added
that he planned a trip to Finland and hoped to visit Sibelius in person.

The reasons Olin Downes decided to write Sibelius at this particular time,
reasons not immediately evident from his letter, are clarified considerably
by the circumstances of the critic's life in 1927. Three years before, on January 1, 1924, Olin Downes had become music critic for the *New York Times.*
After seventeen years it might have seemed that Olin Downes was a permanent fixture at the *Boston Post.* But the opportunity arose to interview for
Richard Aldrich's position at the *Times,* and the critic found himself in-
stantly captivated by New York's musical vitality. The night before his interview, he heard Leopold Stokowski conduct new music by Stravinsky and

other composers. The audience jeered, and Downes was exhilarated. "It was just the right introduction," Downes remembered, "that first evening in New York. Here was the freedom of ideas, here was merciless competition, here was quarter neither asked nor received, here was living. I never lost that sensation. I am one of the abandoned persons who think that New York is the finest city in the world and the most formidable challenge offered to men of ideas in all America."[2]

One of the first things Olin Downes encountered on moving to New York was a veritable Stravinsky cult. In 1922 Lawrence Gilman, critic for the *New York Herald Tribune,* had pitted Stravinsky against Sibelius. "The most radiantly distinguished of contemporary music-makers is Igor Stravinsky— King of the ultra-moderns, secure upon his throne," Gilman had written; Sibelius, on the other hand, "forbidding," conspicuous for works "sombre, drastic, infinitely remote from sensuous pleasings . . . steeped in the harshness and sternness of the North," is not a king but a "tragic poet," of whom it may ultimately be said, "He never spoke out!"[3]

Downes reacted strongly to Stravinsky's growing popularity. In Boston he had found *Firebird* "a well nigh perfect masterpiece of its kind" and *Petrouchka* "a marvel of genius." In New York the first performance of *Le sacre du printemps,* heard on the same program as Sibelius's Violin Concerto early in 1924, prompted Downes to devote the whole review—glowingly— to Stravinsky, with Sibelius mentioned only in passing.[4] But by 1924 Stravinsky had moved well beyond *Le sacre.* The previous year Stokowski had performed Stravinsky's *Symphonies of Wind Instruments;* the following June, Downes, in Paris, heard the composer play his Piano Concerto with Koussevitzky conducting. The critic was skeptical. "The concerto bears out the supposition that Stravinsky has become more and more capricious in his musical output," he complained.[5]

New Yorkers welcomed Stravinsky's music with increasing enthusiasm. Among other works, the *Song of the Haulers on the Volga,* the Concertino for String Quartet, *Le chant du rossignol, Pulcinella, Octuor Ragtime,* the Piano Concerto, and *L'histoire du soldat* were all performed in the city during Downes's first fourteen months there.[6] Then Stravinsky visited New York in person. Downes titled his Sunday article in January 1925 "Stravinsky Visits America at Forty-three." The prophet of the early ballets, Downes found, "had succumbed utterly to the aimlessness, the superficialities, and the pretenses" of the age; Stravinsky's bizarre experiments now seemed "empty of the impulse of beauty and feeling. . . . The same kind of deterioration has been noted with other moderns, particularly with Richard Strauss and Debussy. They suddenly failed at the height of their powers. But they had produced much more than Stravinsky when this took place, and each of them had passed his fortieth year."[7] A few days later when the composer played his Piano Concerto, Downes praised his "magnificent virtuosity" but worried, "Is there really any such thing as music which has no echo of the passions of the human heart? Perhaps. If so, then Stravinsky may really be on the track of a new music. . . ."[8]

Stravinsky's growing abstraction, his insistence on intellect over emotion, his widening distance from his "racial" roots, all increasingly alienated Olin Downes. Moreover, it could not have escaped him, and must have rankled, that the most outspoken Stravinskyites were an elitist group of Harvard men.[9] For the occasion of Sibelius's birthday in 1925, Downes penned another lengthy article, "The Sixtieth Year of Jean Sibelius; His Contribution to Modern Music." He described Sibelius's position as one of unaccountable neglect. "His lot up to the present time has been the rather common one of the original and heroic spirit that does not easily meet or court the crowd." In lofty prose, Downes declared that Sibelius "has been passed over in a period which exalts technic above expression, style and artificiality over feeling, for a hundred lesser men who have not, as artists, the right to latch his shoes."[10]

The critic painted a pathetic picture of the composer "in straitened circumstances," implying that the terrible war in which Sibelius and his brave countrymen had defied the tyrant Russia had left the composer destitute. (Elsewhere, he called Stravinsky the "Russian bear.") Actually, Sibelius was probably as well off in 1925 as he had ever been. On that birthday, his sixtieth, the Finnish government had increased his pension; his Danish publisher, Hansen, sent a substantial sum; and a nationwide drive launched to pay him tribute brought in 150,000 Finnish marks. It was only his popularity vis-à-vis Stravinsky that sagged.

The critic seems not to have been content to leave Sibelius's fate to circumstance. He noted approvingly that Stokowski and the Philadelphians had garnered audience enthusiasm with an exceptional performance of Sibelius's Fifth Symphony. And he must have remembered that Muck's outstanding interpretations of the composer's scores in Boston had once assured Sibelius of a following there. What was needed was a conductor devoted to Sibelius's cause. What better conductor than the composer himself? If Stravinsky's presence could win converts, so too could Sibelius's.

Downes's first letter to Sibelius was designed to implement such an idea. The idea seems to have tempted the composer who, characteristically, vacillated. Through the summer Sibelius deliberated, and only in August did he finally cable Downes a refusal: "Closely engaged with new works regret being unable at present moment decide for tourne stop for kind letter best thanks wishing you welcome to Finland. Sibelius"[11]

To this brief message Downes responded with such an outpouring of requests and self-revelation that Sibelius must have been taken aback.[12] Running on for more than three single-spaced, typed pages, Downes's letter fixed the date of his visit and then proceeded to ask for the presence of a translator; as many of Sibelius's scores as possible—without charge; arrangements to have the scores shipped to him in the United States, as he would by no means have room in his luggage; as many four-hand piano arrangements of the works as were available; a guide to take him fishing in the Finnish woods so that he might realize his dream of catching a salmon, though a sturgeon would do; and advice on buying property in the Finnish countryside. Sibelius's response: "Very welcome to Finland. Sibelius."

Although delayed, Downes finally arrived in Finland on September 10, 1927. (A report of the visit was later published by a fellow staff member at the *New York Times*.)[13] Downes, it seems, was met at the border by a written greeting from Sibelius, whom he discovered anticipating his visit in the lobby of the critic's hotel. There ensued a long and remarkable evening during which Downes had his first encounter with Scandinavia's notorious *akvavit,* as well as with Sibelius's legendary ability to consume it. Talk flowed as freely as liquor as the composer introduced Downes to a café with a bottle of Haig & Haig at each place. When the bottles had been emptied in the early hours of the morning, Downes foggily groped his way back to his hotel, while Sibelius strode solidly out of the establishment as "steady as Plymouth Rock."

Other details of the first meeting in Finland between Sibelius and Downes can be gleaned from the correspondence. In a letter composed aboard the SS *De Grasse* as Downes sailed back to America, the critic wrote:

> I do retain as a priceless memory the strength, the spirit, and the *reality*—the marvelous *reality*—which your music, and now yourself, have for me. Neither the man nor the music is a mirage! Both are true, and both have held out to me friendship and courage. After all, it is the grasp of a man's hand that we need most of all. The things you said to me I shall always remember, and they shall always mean to me strength in my life, new hope and faith for the future.

The young critic embarks for Europe. Olin Downes Collection, Hargrett Rare Book and Manuscript Library. Reproduced by permission.

You see, I was *not* mistaken, either in Sibelius or Finland. These are not fantasies or dreams or illusions. They exist, and they are my friends. It is quite enough. I expect to return to Finland again, and to shake your hand, either there or when you come over here. But whether we ever meet again or not, I shall know that you are always near, and for that life will be less lonely. Olin Downes[14]

Sibelius left his impressions in the diary. "Olin Downes from New York here with me," he wrote. "Extraordinary critic." [15] In later years he told a mutual friend, "Downes appeared on the scene like a revelation." [16]

From this time forward many of the critic's communications to the composer read in part like love letters, so romantic are they in tone. One began "Dear Friend and Great Master, whom I love and adore" and ended: "Salute! You have made me proud to live, as I shall be proud to die. Of all the things God has given me, there is nothing more precious, more *happy,* than *Sibelius.*" [17]

The visit to Finland had given Downes's admiration for Sibelius a deep, personal dimension. And now, as chief music critic for the *New York Times,* Downes was more than ever in a position to publicize his views. To his heroic image of Sibelius, Downes began to add a sanctifying essence: Sibelius was an antidote to the poison of Stravinsky's emotionlessness. Sibelius was god, Stravinsky was devil, the role Igor wished to play in his own *L'histoire du soldat.* Like an apostle, Downes began to advance his mission with strategic good works.

STRICKEN WITH PNEUMONIA on his return from Finland, Downes forgot to mail the letter written on shipboard until some months later. When he discovered the sealed-but-not-stamped envelope, he enclosed with it another missive to which he attached the following postscript: "I have read with the greatest interest the score of your Sixth Symphony, and of course your inscription in it makes it the most valuable musical volume that I have in my library. I have also told two conductors about this work and I think it likely that it will have a performance here next winter." [18] The score of this symphony, personally inscribed to Downes, provided an ideal vehicle for the apostle to effect a good work. If Sibelius could not be enlisted to combat the Stravinsky cult in America personally, Downes would find the next best thing: the most outstanding conductors and orchestras America had to offer. His correspondence with Sibelius often mentions conductors. In 1928 he wrote to recommend Henry Hadley, the composer-conductor whom Sibelius had met at Norfolk. Later Downes sent his son Edward, who aspired to conduct, to Ainola, as well as Antonia Brico, the first notable woman conductor in America.[19] Now, in the late twenties, Downes approached Serge Koussevitzky, the new conductor of the Boston Symphony, with the Sixth Symphony. He wrote Sibelius in June 1930: "I have not told you, I think, how much Koussevitzky admires your music—now. I think I told you that when he came to America he did not like it. Now he is very enthusiastic, and introduced the Sixth symphony—which I think one of your greatest works—with remarkable effect here this winter."[20] Significantly, Downes brings up Stravinsky: "We were having an argument when he was in this city one day, and I told him how much I disliked the late works of Stravinsky. He said, 'Perhaps you do not understand them. You should hear them often before you decide. Remember how at first I didn't like Sibelius!' That is a real conversion, and a useful one too."[21] Downes's choice of the word *conversion* was a meaningful one. In later years Koussevitzky would tell a journalist, "Sibelius is my god!" Olin Downes was the evangelist who brought him to the altar.

The new convert proved a particularly energetic disciple. In the 1932–33 season, Koussevitzky made history when he performed the first cycle of all seven Sibelius symphonies. Downes, who had visited Sibelius for a second time at Ainola in 1929, preceded a third visit with a letter in which he crowed: "Do you know that Koussevitzky is going to play *all* your symphonies next season. He has greatly changed his opinion about these works since he first came to America. That was in 1924. At that time I asked him how he liked the music of Sibelius, and he said, 'But it is so dark!' Now he is one of your warmest admirers...."[22] Once again Downes brings up the satanical Stravinsky: "When he [Koussevitzky] tried, a year ago—and in vain—unsuccessfully—to make me admire one of the later works of Stravinsky, he said to me, 'Remember how I changed about Sibelius. You must now try to be also open-minded about Stravinsky.' To which I replied, 'There is no comparison. Stravinsky *was* a great composer. Sibelius *is* a great composer.'"[23]

In November 1932, as Koussevitzky was conducting Sibelius's first Symphony, *Tapiola,* and *Swanwhite* in Carnegie Hall, Downes declared that no conductor in America had done as much for Sibelius's music as Serge Koussevitzky.[24] The Boston conductor's fervor proved enduring. Between 1925 and 1948 Koussevitzky programmed works by Sibelius at least seventy-four times.

It was not just the opportunity to hear the music that made Koussevitzky so important. It was also the publicity, sometimes of a sensational nature, that he created. One example can stand for many. In December 1937 Koussevitzky was preparing a joint program with the Helsinki University Chorus that was to include Sibelius's *Tulen synty* (*Origin of Fire*). En route to Boston from Germany, the complete score and the string parts simply vanished from the ship.[25] Under the conductor's skillful management, the loss was turned into a *cause célèbre*. In Leipzig, Breitkopf & Härtel agreed to transmit the music by wire facsimile to Berlin (probably the first music ever transmitted by fax). From Berlin, radio flashed the pages to New York. In New York, the music was photographically enlarged and delivered by special courier to Boston. And in Boston, Koussevitzky had the parts transcribed by hand for the orchestra only hours before rehearsals began. Those in the New York receiving station marveled that music, for the first time ever, had been transmitted transoceanically by radio. The world followed the historic proceedings in the pages of the *New York Times*. Finns especially were astounded and delighted that Americans would go to such lengths to have their Sibelius.

Finland recognized Koussevitzky's extraordinary services in Sibelius's behalf. On the composer's seventieth birthday, in 1935, Koussevitzky received an invitation to conduct the opening concert of the Sibelius Festival. The government decorated the conductor for his service to Sibelius by naming him Commander of the Order of the White Rose.[26] With his father-in-law living in Finland, Koussevitzky's ties to the composer grew increasingly personal, and his appreciation for Finnish art in general grew as well. It was a Finnish architect, Eliel Saarinen, whom Koussevitzky selected in 1937 to design the pavilion at his beloved Tanglewood.

As late converts sometimes are, Koussevitzky was particularly zealous. He very nearly missed salvation, for he was already well into his fifties and enamored of Stravinsky when he arrived in America and saw the light. Koussevitzky had started out as a double-bass player—by default, there being scholarships at the Moscow Conservatory only for horn, trombone, and double bass.[27] Eventually, Koussevitzky established a position of widespread recognition and distinction as a conductor of the St. Petersburg Imperial Orchestra. He took his orchestra up and down the 2,300-mile Volga River, not once but three times, playing in towns along its banks with guest artists such as Alexander Scriabin. His reputation as a champion of new music—and Stravinsky—began before World War I: when Debussy conducted and

Busoni performed with Koussevitzky's Petersburg Orchestra, and Koussevitzky himself gave the first concert performance of *Le sacre du printemps.*

After the Bolsheviks came to power, Koussevitzky and his wife, Natalia Uškov, moved west, first to Berlin and eventually to Paris. There Olin Downes interviewed him shortly before his sensational arrival in Boston and found Koussevitzky to be "the conductor of the hour . . . a storm center of friends and enemies, of intrigues and rivalries."[28] *Les concerts Koussevitzky* had achieved renown for their brilliance and ultramodern repertoire, but public opinion divided sharply over Koussevitzky's intrinsic musicianship.

Koussevitzky took the helm of the Boston Symphony in the fall of 1924, the year Downes left for New York. There the conductor continued to divide opinion. The orchestra found his rehearsals a nightmare, his temperament tyrannical, his iron will implacable. One of the orchestra members, violinist Harry Ellis Dickson, recalled that he could "argue with composers over their own music and, with rare exceptions, prevail," and proceeded to illustrate the point with a story about Aaron Copland that preserves Koussevitzky's colorful English: "'Aaron,' he [Koussevitzky] would say to Copland in the balcony while we were rehearsing a new work, 'vy do you write mezzo-forte? You know mezzo-forte is di most baddest nuance *qui existe.*' It must be pianissimo.' And Copland would nod in agreement."[29] During the Koussevitzky regime, Dickson counted one hundred and five players in the orchestra and "one hundred and six ulcers. One man had two."[30] Particularly ulcerating was the ordeal of trying to begin together:

> He would begin a piece [Dickson remembered], holding his arms rather high in the air, then bring them down ever so slowly, as though daring anyone to begin. I remember my first rehearsal and how frightened and confused I was. During the intermission I went to Alfred Krips, who was then assistant concertmaster, and asked, "How do you start? What's the secret?" He answered, "I'm not quite sure. All I know is that when the stick starts coming down, I shut my eyes, and when I open them, everybody is playing, so I sneak in quietly."[31]

In the early days, the Boston Symphony was often "awfully not togedder!" Partly out of desperation, its members evolved into one of the world's finest ensembles under their astonishing conductor who, by turns solicitous, ruthless, charming, and possessive, was nothing if not passionate. Furiously stopping one rehearsal of Wagner's Prelude to *Tristan und Isolde,* Koussevitzky shouted at the violins, "The first violins is cold! This music must be very appassionato—full of patience! I don't know how you stay married!"[32]

With his imperious manner, his liberally subjective interpretations, his exotic accent, his cape and fur hat, Koussevitzky gave the Boston Symphony a glamour it had not previously possessed. Seats filled, critics purred, the public cooed. One concertgoer approached Koussevitzky after a concert, murmuring, "Doctor Koussevitzky, to us you are god." To which he replied, "I know my responsibility."[33] Therein lay the crux of the matter. This god of culture reigned as a glamourous celebrity, and so, by association, did the composers he conducted. Slowly but surely, Sibelius, once seen as a heroic Viking, was coming to be viewed as a celebrity; in the eyes of America's elite, that would be a tarnishing transformation.

KOUSSEVITZKY HAD POWERFUL CONTEMPORARIES in glamourizing orchestral music in America, the most significant being Leopold Stokowski. Born in 1882 (although he steadfastly denied it), Stokowski had come to the United States in 1909 from seemingly mysterious origins.[34] Marvelously attired, and arrogantly affected (he too had an accent, although his came and went at will), Stokowski took Cincinnati by storm before whirling into Philadelphia. At first he amazed everyone there only by his reasonable behavior and his ultramodern repertoire, including Schoenberg, Cowell, Stravinsky, Hindemith, and Varèse. But gradually he began to put the indelible Stokowski stamp upon the Philadelphia music scene.

He lectured his audiences—about their duty to modern music and especially about their behavior (he particularly hated latecomers, early leavers, chatterers, coughers, and applauders). On one occasion, in order to drive home his lesson, he staged a concert in which the *orchestra* drifted in late and wandered out early. Harold C. Schonberg noted that, before long, reporters began covering Stokowski concerts as routinely as they covered police court and baseball games.[35] On these press reports Stokowski thrived.

Then there were his experiments. He regularly changed the orchestra's seating, putting the violins in the rear, then in the middle, then back on the left. He hit upon the idea of having every one of the players serve a turn as concertmaster, an ordeal that struck terror into many a heart. He decided that music should be heard and not seen, so he commanded that the house lights be extinguished and the players given tiny stand lights. Spotlights, however, played on his own beautiful hands and magnificent head—a necessity, he assured the press, for the players to be able to follow his facial expressions. Forced for a while by neuritis into giving up his baton, he found the experience so freeing that he abandoned it permanently, molding the music with exquisite hand gestures that provoked endless discussion about his showmanship. The net effect of all his dazzling antics was twofold: an orchestra of such silky sound that some (like Rachmaninoff) thought it ranked among the best in the world, and publicity for great music made more titillating by the conductor's exotic ways and glamorous paramours, who included Greta Garbo and Gloria Vanderbilt.

Sibelius shared in the celebrity, again by association. Stokowski regarded Sibelius as one of the Big Four living composers, Strauss, Debussy, and Elgar being the other three.[36] In Cincinnati and later in Philadelphia, he accustomed the public to hearing Finnish symphonies and tone poems regularly. Especially after World War I, when Karl Muck's deportation and replacement by French conductors reduced the number of Sibelius works heard in Boston, Stokowski kept the Finn's music alive in Philadelphia and New York. During the twenties he capitalized on Sibelius: In 1921 he gave the first performance of the Fifth Symphony in the United States and in 1926 of the Sixth, followed later that same year by the Seventh. In one season alone, 1925–26, Stokowski presented no fewer than seventeen performances of Sibelius's works. Stokowski held up Sibelius as an accessible modern. "There is much misconception of modern music," he told Philadelphians. "People say: 'That wasn't modern!' They mean it wasn't ear-piercing. Much modern music is as light, as delicate, as gossamer as the Debussy [*Prelude to the Afternoon of a Faun*]. . . . Today, we have great men working. Men such as Sibelius. Sibelius is talking in a great language. He is a great composer."[37]

In 1924, when the Boston Symphony announced the imminent arrival of Koussevitzky, Olin Downes sensed the publicity potential. Before the conductor had even set foot in America, Downes interviewed him in Paris and predicted that the Russian would "be a formidable rival in America for a conductor whose name also ends with the sound of 'ski.'"[38] Within months of Koussevitzky's arrival, Downes fueled the alleged rivalry with an article headlined "New Musical War Opens Brilliantly—Koussevitzky and Stokowski Strive to Win Favor of New York with Their Batons."[39] Comparisons and competition continued, often with little regard for musical matters. When on April 28, 1930, *Time* magazine featured Stokowski on its cover (the first conductor ever depicted there), the accompanying story called him the best-groomed conductor in America—with Koussevitzky nominated a close second.

According to Oliver Daniel, the rivalry was more friendly than otherwise.[40] Nevertheless, there was the matter of those "firsts." Stokowski had dozens to his credit. Where the music of Sibelius was concerned, he had premiered the Fifth Symphony, the Sixth Symphony, and the Seventh Symphony. Significantly, the correspondence shows that Olin Downes and Serge Koussevitzky began an all-out campaign to procure new works from Sibelius for Boston. And it is hardly surprising that the Eighth Symphony quickly became the focal point of their attention.

In December 1928 Koussevitzky wrote the composer, pleading for a few lines about any new works that had not yet been performed.[41] In June 1930 the conductor wrote again. Reminding Sibelius that he had scheduled the Fourth and Seventh symphonies for the coming season, Koussevitzky asked the composer to reserve something for a first performance in Boston, a request he repeated in December.[42] Meanwhile, a letter Olin Downes wrote to Sibelius following his second visit to Ainola had referred to an unnamed composition then in progress: "God bless you, and also may He, or the Devil, or whoever or whatever produces good music, bless the new work, the great *Mystery,* which you properly keep to yourself, on which you are engaged."[43]

Sibelius himself fanned the flames of desire for the Eighth Symphony. In January 1931 he responded to Olin Downes: "You ask me what I have been occupied with during these two years. It is not only one work but several ones. I enjoy finishing my new works in my head and put off with writing them down—for many reasons, not least on account of my adoration for life an[d] Nature. However I think that there will quite soon be a new Symphony ready for printing—this information strictly private: only for you."[44] That fall Downes cabled urgently:

September 24, 1931

Please ask publisher forward immediately score your eighth symphony my expense.

Koussevitzky wrote, begging to be allowed to premiere the work that very season. He said that he could perform the symphony in both Boston and New York if Sibelius sent the score by March. But 1931 came and went, and no Eighth Symphony appeared. In July 1932 Koussevitzky broached the subject again, offering Sibelius the opportunity to conduct the Eighth himself with the Boston Symphony.[45] The conductor was then planning his Sibelius cycle. He wanted to present the symphonies in chronological order,

86

and he envisioned the Eighth as the crowning finish. Sibelius heard about this plan from both Koussevitzky and from Downes, whose letter announcing the event beseeched: "Will [you] talk with me, for publication, about your music, particularly the 8th symphony, which I understand is now finished. . . . I wish to write about the new symphony in advance of its performance by Koussevitzky." [46]

The pair kept up the pressure. Koussevitzky's New Year's greeting for 1933 begged Sibelius for the Eighth Symphony; one month later he sent a heartfelt wish that the Eighth Symphony still might appear. [47] In April Downes concluded another letter with the plaintive request, "But please, dear master, please give us by next Winter the Eighth Symphony!" [48] In June, Koussevitzky asked if there was any hope of ever premiering the symphony in the New World. [49]

Still the Eighth did not materialize. Instead, Downes had to use a new work by Ernest Bloch to excoriate the Stravinsky cult. In a column for the *New York Times* in March 1934 Downes made it clear that, through Bloch and Sibelius, music's powers of expression and spiritual elevation affirmed the best within humanity. Even Schoenberg's music, with its "sincerity of purpose," stemmed from greater inner depths than that of the shallow, soulless Stravinsky, said Downes, who maintained that Schoenberg's music "has probably done more than the work of any other European of the period to enlarge the boundaries of musical expression." [50]

Yet the promise of the Eighth Symphony still haunted. Nothing would better vindicate his faith, Downes seemed to believe, nothing would better publicize Koussevitzky and the Boston Symphony, and nothing would better affirm the greatness of the human spirit than an Eighth Symphony. In the summer of 1936, as Downes prepared for his fourth visit to Sibelius, Koussevitzky directed him to ask when he could have the Eighth Symphony "for heaven's sake." Downes, in the time-honored fashion of American reporters, badgered and begged the composer for an answer. Could Sibelius tell if it were complete? Well, two movements were written, Sibelius answered nervously; the rest was in his head. Downes persisted. Couldn't he tell how large an orchestra he would call for, how many movements there would be in all, what forms he had designed? Sibelius "recognised my need," Downes reported; he "wanted to do something for a friend, and he was the picture of misery. He mumbled incoherent words. His features worked. Then he turned to me in sheer desperation. 'Ich kann nicht,' he exploded in German, and sighed deeply." [51]

Even then, Olin Downes could not leave the matter alone. In the fall of 1937 he sent Sibelius his *mother's* opinion on the subject:

My mother and I often speak of you and she asked me again about the Eighth Symphony, and I told her that I had decided to spare you any mention of that work, since you were so often annoyed by so many people with questions about it. To this my mother replied by saying to me, "Tell Mr. Sibelius that I am not concerned or anxious so much about his Eighth Symphony, which I know he will complete in his own good time, as about his *Ninth*. He must crown his series of works in this form with a ninth symphony which will represent the summit and the synthesis of his whole achievement and leave us a work which will be worthy of one of the elected few who are the true artistic descendants and inheritors of Beethoven."[52]

Had Sibelius known Louise Corson Downes, this letter might have put the fear of God into him. As it was, he must have felt a terrible frustration over the New World's market forces and relentless publicity machine. Despite diary entries that chart work on the Eighth Symphony and even a copyist's receipt for twenty-three of its pages, with the exception of a few insignificant sketches no trace of it has ever been found.[53] It is of course possible that Sibelius did not subscribe to the Romantic notion that genius never retires; he may simply have claimed for himself a privilege that most of us take for granted. It is also possible that Sibelius's symphony remained in his head, confined there because of the twentieth century's intense musical competition and pressure from such critics and conductors as Downes and Koussevitzky. Or perhaps the spotlight of world opinion that Downes and certain British critics directed toward Sibelius created such anxiety that the composer's creative muse was stifled, an explanation advanced by Erik Tawaststjerna.

There are also Sibelius's own self-imposed standards with which to reckon. It was during these very years when the Eighth was such an issue that Sibelius explained, somewhat defensively:

Let no one imagine that composing is easier for an old composer if he takes his art seriously. The demands one makes on oneself have increased in the course of years. Greater sureness make one scorn solutions that come too easily, that follow the line of least resistance, in a higher degree than formerly. One is always faced with new problems. The thing that has pleased me most is that I have been able to reject. The greatest labour I have expended, perhaps, was on works that have never been completed.[54]

Sibelius's words have the ring of truth. A composer who constantly demanded more of himself, who made regular and far-reaching revisions in his later works, Sibelius may have expended more labor on the unfinished Eighth than on a work such as *Tapiola,* which Damrosch's commission had forced him to release. As for the copied pages of the Eighth, these were almost certainly destroyed in the 1940s when Sibelius burned an entire laundry basket of manuscripts in the dining room fireplace at Ainola—with evident relief.[55] For Olin Downes it was the ultimate tragedy: In the end, Sibelius, like his father, failed him.

FIVE

The Thirties: Sibelius, Downes, and the American People

The world of art is divided in two great currents.
The lower one is that of the masses; their facile taste
is sinking with the love of platitude and the weight
of mechanical inventions—phonograph, radio, cin-
ematograph.*
—Ernest Bloch, as quoted by Olin Downes, 1934

We're the people that live. Can't nobody wipe us
out. Can't nobody lick us. We'll go on forever. We're
the people.
—Jane Darwell's closing words
in John Ford's film *The Grapes of Wrath*

BY THE END of the 1920s two of America's three most glamorous conductors were ardent Sibelians. In December 1930 Olin Downes announced the
"Advance of Sibelius"; conductors Stokowski and Koussevitzky and virtu-
osi such as Efrem Zimbalist furthered the cause, he said.[1] By the following
March Downes was proclaiming "A Belated Sibelius Renascence": Toscanini, the third exotic conductor, had performed Sibelius's Fourth Symphony. Those who had still not seen the light, Downes sermonized, "must
needs bow at last to the encroaching ocean, and here they are, confronted
by the singular, unpretending and profoundly original genius of Sibelius."[2]

That ocean swelled to flood tide during the thirties. In a survey of trends in musical taste reported in 1938, John H. Mueller and Kate Hevner noted that the number of concert performances of Sibelius's music had risen faster than that of any other composer in the decade. A later repertory study drawn from twenty-seven major American orchestras furnished the data to back their claim.[3]

Olin Downes was at that moment an especially high-profile commentator on the rising fortunes of Sibelius; Sibelius, after all, had been "his" musical discovery. As critic for the *New York Times,* Downes wrote for a paper whose Sunday circulation would grow to well over a million by 1950.[4] The *Times,* of course, was located in New York, then musical capital of America if not the world, and its standing as the "newspaper of record," with a reputation for decency and accuracy, added to its prestige and power. There was also its international scope, with a weighty foreign department that gave coverage to musical news. It had been a *New York Times* correspondent who first used the new transatlantic cable in 1876 to flash reports of the *Ring* performances from Bayreuth.[5] In his move from the popular *Post* to the prestigious *Times,* Downes took full advantage of the newspaper's international dimension.

If his wide recognition was enhanced by associating himself with an internationally prominent paper, Downes's success was also the outgrowth of his spirited personality and highly individual style. Virgil Thomson penned an unforgettable description of Downes, whom he called "the last of the music reviewers to enjoy music. He consumed it with delight and described it with gusto. . . . He swam in the full musical current of a great epoch, kept his head up, breathed deeply, clung to the rocks, waved at the fishes, had a wonderful time."[6]

An ebullient writer, Downes took a highly individualistic approach to his work. In his book *The Columnists,* Charles Fisher attributed the blossoming of individualism in American newspapers to the vacuum that writers like Downes rushed in to fill.[7] Gone were the days, said he, when newspapermen dealt with their readers in a personal, almost neighborly fashion; such intimacy had disappeared under the pressures of speed and size. Instead, newspapers took on so neutral a tone that they differed very little around the country—except in their daily weather reports. In place of the owner who passionately wrote his own editorials, a board of directors, guided by the accounting department, now regulated the paper's tone. Few issues in the news engendered blazing rhetoric and few writers challenged the status quo.

Sibelius in 1935. Photograph courtesy of Patelson's Music House, New York.

Into this sterile atmosphere rushed a flood of rich personal opinion from a number of notable columnists.

The columnists of whom Fisher writes are the syndicated columnists. Among them, Dorothy Thompson was perhaps the most extraordinary.[8] Yet Olin Downes, with his exuberant and opinionated personality, his eagerness to win new musical converts, his willingness to embrace causes both political and humanitarian, appealed to many music lovers in America. Harold C. Schonberg has observed that Americans across the country adored Olin Downes, not because he tried to impress them, but because he endeavored to share with them his experience of music.[9] When Downes told the public that Sibelius was "a giant stepping out of an ancient past," the heir to "traditions of a small but heroic people," instinctively employing "their musical idioms without ever having heard a folksong," music lovers recognized a kindred spirit in critic as well as composer.

Around New York, Olin Downes was very much a "personality." His blue eyes, fair hair, and hefty build sometimes prompted friends to describe him as "Nordic." So Lucien Price remembered him. Price further characterized his friend as

> an Elizabethan. Without the alteration of a syllable he would have fitted into the Mermaid Tavern. His conversation was a cadenza, a bravura piece mainly for solo instrument though with an occasional passage of orchestral accompaniment for muted strings; it was a rhapsodic improvisation, sometimes agreeably on the bawdy side, with dazzling bursts of impromptu virtuosity. I love to remember him after some Good Friday matinee of *Parsifal* at the Met, dining in the Hunting Room of the Hotel Astor and discoursing passionately of Wagner with flashing eyes and floating hair, while he waved his fork like a conductor's baton. There was an oyster on the end of the fork.[10]

Price's portrait brings to mind similar stories of the critic's visits with Sibelius, at which no one but Downes had much chance of saying anything at all.[11] Formidable in physique, in appetite, in *joie de vivre,* Downes was a prominent figure in New York's musical life. In 1927 he reversed the roles of critic and performer when, with John Erskine and Ernest Urchs, he staged a Carnegie Hall performance to benefit the MacDowell Colony. As part of the reversal, he assembled for that concert an outstanding array of performers—Hofmann, Barrère, Zimbalist, Gershwin, Damrosch, Gieseking, Casella—as critics.[12] Nor was this Downes's only public performance. He had once played the MacDowell Piano Concerto in concert, and in 1940 he portrayed himself in the film *Carnegie Hall.*

Not surprisingly, the critic's talks about music brought more attention and accolades than his performances. His lecture style was applauded in the *New Yorker:*

> Mr. Downes, you may be glad to know, is not yet eligible to good standing as a lecturer. He works without smirks, he stays within the bounds of the evening's material, he omits the stock anecdotes about pianists, and when he makes an inadvertent reference to "the loud pedal" he immediately reproves himself for a vulgarism and adds a few illuminating remarks about pedaling. He is an enthusiast, happy to share with his listeners the results of his musical explorations.[13]

Americans generally loved his earthy pronouncements, and he was described as "something of a rage" around Brooklyn. Once the child Yehudi Menuhin made Downes forget completely about his cherished ticket to a boxing match at Madison Square Garden. The critic sat spellbound, astonished at the virtuosity of the youngster whom he had planned to dismiss as just another prodigy. He reported to friends, "I don't know whether it's an old soul in a young body. All I know is that the little devil can play like hell."[14]

Above all, Downes made music newsworthy. There were many instances, but perhaps the most famous was Downes's discovery that violinist Fritz Kreisler's "Olden Collection" had actually been composed by Kreisler himself and passed off as the music of early masters. Downes had been preparing for a lecture that would illustrate music for the violin and planned to begin with Kreisler's transcription of Pugnani's *Praeludium* and *Allegro.* He asked Harold Spivacke of the Library of Congress for information on the original Pugnani score. When no such score or any others in Kreisler's so-called "Olden Collection" could be located, Downes became suspicious. One question led to another until finally he cabled Kreisler in Vienna and asked point blank if the violinist had composed these works himself. Kreisler cabled back: Absolutely correct. The music critic seldom kisses but he always tells, Virgil Thomson once remarked, and Downes told—in headlines—around the world. Kreisler's hoax enraged Ernest Newman, who engaged the violinist in a public confrontation.[15] Downes took a more tolerant view. His *New York Times* article of March 3, 1935, entitled "Kreisler's De-

Olin Downes in his New York office. Photograph by Robert Haas, New York. Olin Downes Collection, Hargrett Rare Book and Manuscript Library. Reproduced by permission.

lectable Musical Hoax," concluded: "Mr. Kreisler has added to the gaiety of nations and the violinist's repertory. Shall we begrudge him that? Should the man who has kissed the wrong girl in the dark condemn the practice of kissing?" [16]

In his zeal for pursuing a story at all costs, Downes was indefatigable. A little-known episode, but one that would have profound implications for Sibelius, occurred during his first year at the *Times*. It began with his determination to attend a Mozart opera in Paris the night before the opening of the Prague Music Festival. In order to make them both, Downes rashly hired a private plane, "a superannuated war-plane" as he described it, to fly him through the night to Prague. En route, the plane's engines quit, and Downes and his pilot headed earthward. The pilot bailed out and "marvelously saved his hide," but the critic went down with the plane. Downes later recalled that "peasants sprang from the earth like gophers," pulled him from the wreckage with a slashed scalp, and lugged him to a nearby farmhouse, where a country doctor stitched his scalp while he "yelled as much as he pleased in the grip of two husky Czechs." Undeterred, Downes doggedly made his way to Prague, where he attended the Music Festival and even proceeded to interview Janáček.[17]

One cannot second-guess history; nevertheless, it seems sure that had Olin Downes not survived that crash, Sibelius's fate in America would not have been the same. The force of the enormous wave carrying Sibelius to impossible heights of fame, to which Downes would add his energies during the thirties, would almost certainly have been weakened. And the powerful backwash from that wave might never have occurred. As it was, critics of America's culture industry would eventually argue that the promotion of Sibelius by the critic of an establishment paper, the *New York Times,* and one who resorted to such market-oriented tools as radio and phonograph, caused the composer's popularity to seem manufactured. It set him up as a target for elitists.[18]

Downes was a remarkable combination of an uncannily intuitive listener and a well-trained newspaperman. He responded to music at the most basic, emotional level and then set about to understand his response. When the musician in Downes recognized the profound significance of Sibelius's scores, the newspaperman in him divined the importance of demonstrating to Everyman just how much he and Jean Sibelius had in common. "Hardy Finland" spoke through the "vast heroic music of Sibelius," whose "manly" and "savage" scores resonated with America's own rugged past. Downes's words began to sound from the lips of others. Lucien Price attributed Sibelius's success to his music's ability to awaken the ancestral past that North Americans share with Finns ("Listen, and know thyself!").[19] Harry Rogers Pratt wrote for the *New York Times* that Sibelius "like a man . . . takes the art of musical composition with intense seriousness, but without egotism or self-delusion." And why not? For Sibelius had come of a family line of whom "four were pure Finns, nine were Swedes, eighteen were Finnish citizens of Swedish extraction and one was a German—a genealogical table more American than European in its implications[!]."[20] And, Pratt had added, Finland was not so remote: "One could not help observing how much like America it all was—especially like Maine, Canada and Wisconsin."

Readily divesting Sibelius of any foreign taint, Downes, by virtue of his position with a paper some called the Business Bible and by his many other public activities, was a key figure in situating Sibelius squarely within America's consumer culture. This situation was essentially a matter of perception, but it was a perception with far-reaching consequences.

PHONOGRAPH RECORDS, in the early years of the twentieth century, provided many Americans with their only experience of serious music. By 1920 a phonograph was a normal addition to American living rooms; along with leather-bound books, Victor Red Seal records conferred upon their owner an aura of "taste and property."[21] With the coming of radio in the early twenties, records, with their poor sound and their four-minute sides, began to lose some ground. And when the stock market collapsed in 1929, the record and phonograph business fell off dramatically. It reached an all-time low in 1932, when record sales were only 6 percent of what they had been in 1927. Yet the industry recovered—and powerfully. Figures provided by RCA Victor, which used record sales from 1933 as a base, showed an improvement of 35 percent in 1934, 102 percent in 1935, 238 percent in 1936, 475 percent in 1937, and an astonishing 600 percent in 1938. And symphonic releases played a large part in that rejuvenation. A *New York Times* editorial mentioned two reasons for such a miraculous recovery: the improved record quality and the public's desire to preserve the performance of works heard on radio. RCA's advertising slogans, "Music You Want When You Want It" and "Yours for Keeps on Victor Records," would seem to confirm the *Times*'s theory.[22]

Finland proved itself a pioneer in this industry, while simultaneously putting Sibelius at its forefront. In 1930 the Finnish government entered into financial arrangements with the Columbia Graphophone Company to record Sibelius's First and Second symphonies. The performances were conducted by Sibelius's friend and promoter Robert Kajanus. Harold E. Johnson, in *Jean Sibelius, The Recorded Music,* reported how these recordings were met "with the greatest enthusiasm" throughout the English-speaking world.[23] Olin Downes, however, was greatly disturbed by them. Although he drew widespread attention to the recordings in a lengthy *New York Times* column, privately he wrote Sibelius:

> To my mind the record of the second symphony is the kind of a record that was made ten years ago. Many of the balances are very poor; many of the finer touches of your instrumentation cannot be ascertained from this record. . . . I really think that you or your friends should make some complaint about this, especially if it is true that the Finnish Government is paying to have these things done, because if that is the case I do not think that they are getting the proper return for their money, any more than I think you are getting the proper representation of your genius.[24]

Downes's private reservations showed mainly in his personal correspondence; in the *Times,* although he cautioned that the recordings were not perfect, he praised Columbia's steps to make the music of "one of the greatest figures in music today" accessible to the great public. Meanwhile, he offered Sibelius a proposal: "I am going to suggest to the Victor Company, on this side of the water, that they have some records of your music made by Koussevitzky and the Boston Symphony Orchestra, who have given some excellent performances of your music, not only of the First Symphony, but of the Sixth and Seventh."[25] By 1936 Koussevitzky had recorded the Second Symphony (on eleven sides) with the Bostonians. He also conducted the Seventh with the BBC Symphony Orchestra in a recording for the Sibelius Society.[26]

Downes's attention to the Columbia project prompted the first full-length letter from the composer and one of the longest in the correspondence. Together with the swiftness of the reply, these facts suggest the importance of the recordings to Sibelius. He wrote Downes:

> My dear Friend,
>
> I thank you cordially for your kindly letter, which contained so many things of importance to me. From experience, gained during a long life-time I can say that you certainly have done most for my music.
>
> I was very interested in what you wrote me about the records, though I am rather unacquainted with those things.
>
> Concerning my Symphonies I and II I wish to inform you that the recording was produced on the initiative of Columbia, the costs amounting to $6000, of

99

The jovial Sibelius.

which sum the Finnish Government overtook $1250 for the sake of giving
Robert Kajanus, the grand old man of our music an opportunity to produce
them in London for this purpose. . . . [27]

As the thirties progressed, the number of Sibelius recordings increased
significantly. In June 1932 the London-based company His Master's Voice
began issuing what would eventually be six volumes of Sibelius symphonies,
tone poems, and incidental music; again, Kajanus conducted. Conductors
in America were especially active. In that same year Stokowski made the

first recording of the Fourth Symphony. Koussevitzky in Boston, Ormandy in Minneapolis, and Barbirolli with the New York Philharmonic began recording Sibelius. By 1936 the seven symphonies, the Violin Concerto, *Voces intimae,* and numerous other works were all available on record. In reporting on this phenomenon, Harold E. Johnson observed that the new Sibelius recordings and the public's demand for them were probably mutually influential, at least until the time of World War II.[28]

The widespread appeal of Sibelius's music evident from the success and growing number of commercial recordings would gradually come to be viewed in some quarters with cynicism. Appeal to the people, went the thinking, could be parlayed into financial profit; the wider the advertising, the greater the profit and the greater the popularity, that popularity more apparent than real. And such a "tastemaker" as Olin Downes, known for his anti-Stravinskyisms and for publicizing his opinions through a powerful and conservative newspaper, was a prime suspect in the promotion of such artificial results. Yet the fact that the argument was attached particularly to Sibelius and not to all other composers whose music was recorded indicates its speciousness. Mahler and Bruckner, it is true, were each represented by only a single recorded symphony in 1936, but Sibelius was by no means the only twentieth-century composer well represented on record. *The Gramophone Shop Encyclopedia of Recorded Music* for 1936 lists more than two dozen recordings available that year for Stravinsky, who is described as "one of the two towering musical giants of our day (the other is Sibelius)."[29] In 566 pages describing classical recordings, the number of Sibelius and Stravinsky recordings occupy essentially the same space: slightly less than two pages each.

What dramatically separated Sibelius from Stravinsky was not the number of his recordings but the attitude of Olin Downes. As enthusiastically as Downes promoted the one, he moralistically derided the other—to the detriment of his own hero. Intelligent music lovers were often offended by his shortsightedness. Among Downes's readers, publisher Merle Armitage, goaded by a remark of Downes in the *Times* on November 17, 1946, about "the present sterilities of such a de-raced composer of decadent and sterile leanings as, say, Stravinsky," addressed the critic a lengthy letter on Sibelius's birthday.[30] Armitage spoke for many when he criticized Downes for failing to grant Stravinsky the place he deserved among the moderns, promoting instead a composer who had neglected to add anything really new to the art of music. He expressed the view, by then widely held, that Sibelius was a comfortable traditionalist whose music was a redundancy in the twentieth century and who was being championed by a regressive critic unable to follow the subtleties of new music.

Downes was even viewed by some as a collaborator with the conservative big business and establishment interests. He had once in fact considered venturing into the commercial world of phonograph records. In the early 1940s the critic had formulated an idea he called "Olin Downes's Five-Foot Record Shelf," which he planned in collaboration with friend and business-man Kevie Carmen. The Record Shelf was to contain the greatest music masterpieces in the repertory. Downes toyed with the notion of using mov-ing picture "shorts" to publicize the shelf, which would "undoubtedly be received with great enthusiasm by the public and surely would result in greatly increased sales of records already on the market."[31] The scheme was ultimately abandoned, but it serves to illustrate the blend of high idealism and undisguised consumerism that drew derision from cynics.

Cynics aside, ideas of this kind were common in depression-ridden America. The notion of benefiting the nation during a time of economic distress while uplifting American souls was considered deeply patriotic and even visionary. However naive or self-serving it may appear in retrospect, it was an outlook other leaders in the musical world shared. Almost one year to the day after the Wall Street crash, Leopold Stokowski wrote the critic to suggest that the hard lives of thousands, even millions, of Americans could be made more beautiful if he and Downes joined forces to bring great music to Everyman.[32] Shortly thereafter Stokowski embarked upon commercially profitable ventures in Hollywood. In *Fantasia,* which opened on Broadway in 1940, he created a lucrative blend of technology and art that reached the "thousands, even millions" he had in mind.

ALTHOUGH DOWNES'S INVOLVEMENT with recordings was perhaps not widely known, his association with the radio was another matter. Coincident with his arrival in New York, radio had begun to add a new dimension to music. Many intelligent observers recognized in radio the central musical event of the century. If ever an audience and a medium were made for each other, Irving Sablosky commented,

> it was the American musical audience and radio. This audience had learned hymn tunes, Handel melodies, and folksongs out of the same books; it had seen a minstrel show one night and an opera the next in the same theater; it

had heard Caruso and Sousa on the phonograph, ragtime and Chopin on the player piano, Wagner and polkas, Verdi and quadrilles from the town band. It was an audience without musical prejudices and with a taste for many different things, including the best music. It was, in short, the first mass audience that had existed for professional musical performance. In radio, it found a mass medium to serve it.[33]

Such oft-cited statistics as those of the Chicago Opera Company broadcasts (which elevated the number of radios in Chicago from approximately 1,300 to 20,000 in a single season) and radio audiences estimated in the millions illustrate just how massive the American audience could be. And a far-flung audience it was too. In the late twenties Walter Damrosch's programs were being broadcast from New York to Salt Lake City; by 1940, the NBC and CBS networks reached from the East Coast to the West, as far north as Montreal, and as deep into the South as Miami, Florida, and Weslaco, Texas.[34]

By the early 1930s, radio occupied an essential position in American life. There was a great variety of music, including an enormous number of serious compositions. One significant development was the trend toward broadcasting entire symphonies. In 1931 the *New York Times* announced that 33.4 percent of broadcast time was devoted to serious music; in 1934 CBS announced that its network had presented 444 hours of classical music in 659 broadcasts (up from 368 hours the previous year).[35] The high-minded praised radio for sending the best music to everyone in the nation—the Southwestern rancher, the Southern cotton planter, the middle-American wheat farmer, the Eastern industrial worker. Recreation and education were readily and cheaply available to every American.

There were other benefits. As violinist Albert Spalding explained, "When a man is argued into a stiff shirt and dragooned to a concert, his preoccupation with antagonism tends to handicap the appeal of the music. But broadcasts overtake these unconverted when they are relaxed and comfortable at home—merely by the turn of a dial."[36]

Olin Downes was a highly visible figure in the radio world. Between 1930 and 1933 he acted as commentator for the New York Philharmonic Broadcasts. During the 1936–37 season he did the same for the Boston Symphony, later (1949–51) annotating their rehearsal broadcasts. From 1941 to 1948 Downes chaired the opera quiz held during intermissions of the Metropolitan Opera broadcasts. Then there were special broadcasts: for NBC from Warsaw and Berlin in 1932; with Ignace Paderewski (who offered to give

Olin Downes delivers a radio broadcast. Photograph by CBS. Olin Downes Collection, Hargrett Rare Book and Manuscript Library. Reproduced by permission.

Downes piano lessons) for Polish relief in 1939; for CBS in weekly music talks from 1944 to 1947.

Downes gained a huge following through these broadcasts. By the end of his first season annotating the New York Philharmonic programs, he found himself a celebrity. Fan mail poured in. Newspapers interviewed him. His picture circulated in print. Trying to explain Downes's effectiveness, one reporter mused: "Perhaps it is because Downes can say the word 'exquisite' in reference to a piece of music, and sound altogether masculine."[37] It was certainly clear that Downes made music appealing to American men, who traditionally had relegated music to the ladies. Laning Humphrey observed, "There is a strong masculine contingent of fans. . . . A rancher in Australia writes that he has been pleased to tumble out of bed at 6:30 on his day of rest to hear him. 'Fortunately,' says a Kansan, 'you always make it known just what you are trying to say.'"[38] Downes's correspondence is filled with similar testimony, including that of a New Yorker who wrote that Downes made him feel like the farmer who recognized that Emerson had his ideas; he concluded his letter by offering the critic the best hard cider in the county.

Some examples of the critic's radio remarks have been preserved in printed form, for the talks during the 1930–31 season were subsequently brought out as *Symphonic Broadcasts*.[39] Hearing Sibelius's Fourth Symphony performed that season, Downes was reminded of Edgar Allan Poe, "of the demon who cursed with the curse of silence." And of *En saga,* Downes confessed: "When I hear this music I avow a carnal desire to discard the soft fat ways of life; to set out in oilskins, or something, for somewhere, to discover at least a desperate polar bear bent on conflict! But seriously—who else writes such music today? In these pages Sibelius is the last of the heroes."[40]

Radio disseminated even more widely the heroic conception of Sibelius's music, and it established other associations as well. *Valse triste* was broadcast as the theme song for the radio program "I Love a Mystery"; the composer's *Canzonetta* became the "signature tune" for the Canadian Broadcasting Corporation's symphony broadcast from Toronto.[41] Critics would eventually charge that the radio did far more than bring Sibelius and other great composers into American homes. Its ubiquity helped to mold a particularly American view of the world, they said, and some illusions of popularity—for certain questionable ideas as well as music. Those who did not take to Sibelius scoffed that it was only because of promotion by critics like Downes and radio's "plugging"—the repeated playing of certain works— that listeners to the New York Philharmonic's nationwide Sunday broadcast voted Sibelius a secure first place as their favorite living symphonist in 1935.[42]

There is actually some question as to Downes's effectiveness on radio. In a letter to the *Musical Times,* one listener insisted that "one of the finest discourses I have ever heard on any composer was given on Sibelius by Mr. Olin Downes . . . over the Columbia chain of National Broadcasts." [43] But a different opinion was proffered by Cyrus Fisher; after hearing *En saga* conducted by Toscanini and commented upon by Downes in 1933, Fisher praised Sibelius but complained that "Olin Downes' meaty explanations suffer because he is not a finished radio speaker. He interrupts his sentences with lugubrious 'ahs' and 'uhms' and long, disconcerting pauses." [44] Downes himself would have insisted that, in judging the enduring success of any music, one must leave the critic aside and acknowledge only the power of the works; he himself was increasingly skeptical of men with "reputations." What was not a matter of question, however, was the linking of Sibelius with America's consumer culture. This was an association that would soon prove damning.

"MUSIC APPRECIATION" — another aspect of music in the thirties—was also bound up intimately with records and radio, and thus tainted with the stain of commercial gain. Music appreciation, the effort to acquaint the public with serious music as an aid to artistic understanding, had been evident in texts and public lectures since the nineteenth century. [45]

In the early years of the twentieth century, a few American educators began to experiment with the player piano and with the phonograph. It was Frances Elliott Clark (1860–1958), however, who recognized the profound educational value of the Victor Talking Machine and began using it regularly in her classroom. By 1911 the Victor Talking Machine Company had recruited Clark as director of its newly created education department. At Victor, Clark supervised children's recordings, making about five hundred for educational purposes, and coordinated the printing of associated texts for use in schools. Eventually, she collaborated on a publication entitled *Music Appreciation with the Victrola for Children,* which reappeared in 1930 with the shortened title *Music Appreciation for Children.* Both volumes bore the motto "Learning to Listen, Listening to Learn." Victor stood to gain substantially from the publication of such books; volumes such as *The Victor Book of the Opera, The Victor Book of the Symphony,* and *The Victor Book of Concertos* were usually keyed to Victor records, and so served equally as sales catalogues and textbooks.

Educators also began to capitalize on the instructional possibilities of radio. During the thirties, the use of radios in the schools soared. In 1930 CBS organized a series of programs for the classroom entitled American School of the Air. That June an Institute of Radio Education was held at Ohio State University, at which participants discussed the problems of education by radio. The proceedings were published as *Education on the Air,* the First Yearbook of the Institute for Education by Radio. The following December, members from nine national educational associations formed a National Committee on Education by Radio, whose activities persisted through the decade.[46]

The surge of interest in radio as an educational tool had begun even earlier. With the first regular broadcasts of classical music in 1926, home-study guides organized around radio programs appeared. Although economic difficulties reduced the staff in the Victor Educational Department, its educational efforts were actually extended; Victor was the first to introduce radio music for children.

In 1928 began what was probably the most famous music appreciation program of the century, Walter Damrosch's "NBC Music Appreciation Hour." Broadcast every Friday morning during the school year on NBC network radio, the program was directed toward schoolchildren. "Give me your children," Damrosch had said, "and I will make a nation of music lovers." Schoolroom listeners were estimated in the millions.

The program also reached abroad. A teacher in Santiago, Chile, wrote to express appreciation for the Damrosch program and requested a copy of the instructor's manual accompanying the programs. These manuals included (besides a full-page photograph of Damrosch) an orchestral seating chart, a photograph of the NBC Orchestra, helpful suggestions for teachers, and descriptive notes on each composition performed. There were also student notebooks with questions to test one's knowledge, pictures of instruments to cut out and paste in their correct places, and blank pages for "notes and clippings."

The music appreciators often exhibited what seems in retrospect a naive optimism. Peter W. Dykema, in a little pamphlet entitled "Music as Presented by the Radio," offered as reasons for listening to music on radio the opportunity to increase sympathies, widen the world, foster personal growth, "soar with music," and avail oneself of music's medicinal benefits.[47] More problematic than the naiveté were the fanciful interpretations in which some music educators, especially Damrosch, indulged. The program "Modern European Composers," broadcast on March 19, 1937, included

Sibelius's *Swan of Tuonela*. Listeners were told the following: "The tone poem begins with the majestic but intensely sad swan melody, played by the English horn. Answering phrases in the strings may be interpreted as farewell sighs of souls as they pass to Tuonela."[48] In one of his radio courses in which Beethoven's Fifth Symphony was discussed, students were asked, "What picture did Mr. Damrosch evoke as a possible interpretation of the second movement of the Fifth Symphony?" The *Teachers Manual* directed the reply: a "walk in a lovely garden, in which one finds a statue erected to the memory of some national hero."[49] It was just such whimsical imagery that gave a bad name to music appreciation.

Although Walter Damrosch was the father of music appreciation in America, Olin Downes played a major role in bringing great music to the great public. A fanatical enthusiast about music, Downes was zealously committed to its egalitarian appeal. Representing what was to many an exclusive art, Downes championed his democratic belief that everyone could "be his own critic," and he preached this message widely, using these very words as the title of his first lecture in a series delivered at Carnegie Hall in 1941 before an estimated 1,500 people. Downes endeared himself to Americans all over the continent for the nontechnical, personal way in which he talked about great music and extolled its value to the "plain men and women of the world." One reporter specifically praised him because he refrained from using "fifty-cent words"; another believed Olin Downes to be more influential than the respected Ernest Newman, his counterpart in Great Britain, because Downes spoke as advisor and commentator rather than as if he held a grudge against musicians.[50]

Made known nationwide by his broadcast chats, Downes was also heard on the music appreciation lecture circuit from coast to coast. Indeed, his obituary recorded that his activities as a lecturer almost overshadowed his work as a critic.[51] In Boston, Downes had lectured at Harvard in the summer and at nearby Chatauqua. Upon his move to New York, he initiated a course at the Brooklyn Institute of Arts and Sciences in 1932 called "The Enjoyment of Music," a title well known today as that of one of the century's widest-selling music appreciation texts. The course combined Downes's commentary with performances by such artists as Walter Gieseking, Lily Pons, and Serge Koussevitzky with the Boston Symphony. The following year the Institute doubled the number of courses to meet public demand, and the program continued through 1935. Meanwhile, in 1934 Downes and Walter Gieseking held a lecture-recital series at Town Hall to illustrate the history of the keyboard. With Georgette Leblanc he staged a lecture-performance of *Pelléas et Mélisande.* And in the summer, Koussevitzky usually invited Downes to lecture in the Berkshires, where the critic organized presentations with such musicians as Paul Hindemith and members of the Yale Collegium Musicum.

The name of Sibelius made its appearance in these lectures. A favorite topic was "Finland's Hero, Jean Sibelius."[52] Lecture notes complete with annotations showing when the audience responded with laughter or applause reveal New Yorkers chuckling delightedly when Downes reminded them how unwelcome the "unwashed Viking" had once been in prim Back Bay parlors. In Minneapolis, Downes asserted that Sibelius is "without question the greatest of any living composer."

Yet it was less the number of his talks about Sibelius (for Downes also lectured about Igor Stravinsky, Henry Gilbert, Ernest Bloch, Richard Strauss, Claude Debussy, and many others) than their tone, the insistent emphasis on this symphonist to the detriment of other modern artists—that was the important factor in Downes's representation of Sibelius. For Sibelius's music had nothing fundamentally to do with these music appreciation lectures and their texts, with the commercial growth of recordings, or with radio broadcasts—except by association. And Olin Downes's role in establishing that association was paramount. An enthusiast by nature, Downes had been the first American critic to recognize Sibelius's greatness and hail the composer as a modern musical messiah. His eventual position as "the most influential and best-liked music commentator" in America, together with the length and tone of his crusade, made him in effect Sibelius's publicity agent and leading evangelist. Those who resented being thus badgered were bound to make an outcry. But not before some notable conversions had taken place.

DURING THE POPULIST THIRTIES, many other Anglo-Saxon voices besides that of Olin Downes began to speak out for Sibelius. Many of them praised the composer for not being "difficult"; others maintained that he had taken up the symphony where Beethoven left it and carried it forward into the twentieth century. Moreover, Sibelius spoke with "ancestral memory," a point worth repeating in a decade in which Americans began to value their own traditions.

Within the swelling tide of Sibelian popularity, there began to swim a number of critics who had avoided the waters before. Lawrence Gilman, the same critic who in 1922 had compared Sibelius unfavorably with Stravinsky, wrote Olin Downes in 1936 that at long last he had come to agree with Downes's farsighted opinion—Sibelius was indeed a wonder.[53] The venerated William J. Henderson, one of the so-called Old Guard of American critics, also came around to Downes's view. Like many American men, he appreciated Sibelius's redeeming masculinity, a composer whose symphonies were "food for men whose minds have not ceased to march forward after the age of 40. Comfortable old ladies who were reared in the Kaiserian school of the 3 C's, children, cooking and church, become uncomfortable when they have to sit through such music."[54] Henderson explained how musically intelligent listeners of the thirties had come to understand Sibelius:

> Sibelius composed along novel lines, beginning with thematic fragments which subsequently solidified themselves in a noble structure without the conventionalities of the classic working out. But such treatment was not merely the caprice of the artist: it was a logical evolution of the design of the work and an individual manifestation of the Sibelius mind. It threw confusion into academic cloisters and befogged the public mind. But it is perfectly comprehensible to us now and we all confess that we do not see how that particular first movement [of the Second Symphony] could have been developed in any other way. . . .[55]

The idea of "coalescing fragments" took hold. When American critics left off writing of heroism, nationalism, and virility, it was to the fragment notion that they usually turned. Significantly, the idea seems to have been broached first not by Americans but by English writers, Cecil Gray and Donald Tovey.[56] While Olin Downes had been making Sibelius a hero for Americans, a similar Sibelian fervor had arisen in England, and from time to time the British and American points of view converged or clashed.

Of all the European countries outside Scandinavia, England had given Sibelius the warmest welcome when his music began to spread beyond the borders of Finland. In the first five years of the new century, conductors Granville Bantock, Hans Richter, and Henry Wood had performed Sibelius's First and Second symphonies, *Finlandia,* the *Song of the Athenians* (under the title *War Song of Tyrtaeus*), and the *King Christian II Suite.*

In December 1905 Sibelius visited England at the invitation of Granville Bantock (whom his daughter remembers as the first to perform Sibelius's music in England).[57] Sibelius conducted his First Symphony and *Finlandia* in Liverpool. His performance was made all the more dramatic by his failure to appear there the previous March. Although the March visit had long been discussed, Sibelius vacillated daily and at the last minute canceled, leaving the Liverpool Orchestra to be conducted by Bantock. The abrupt change in plans created the impression that the tyrannical Russians, then ruling Finland, had restricted the composer's freedom to travel. Audiences thus had "the romantic satisfaction of regarding Herr Sibelius as a possible revolutionary, and it was probably this point of view, added to the fact that its performance had been forbidden in Finland, that helped them to so great a display of enthusiasm for his Fantasia on national melodies [*Finlandia*]— an enthusiasm so great that the composition had to be repeated, notwithstanding its considerable length."[58] When Sibelius did arrive in Liverpool late in the year to conduct the same two works, audiences encored *Finlandia* once more; the music critic of the *Manchester Guardian* asserted: "I have never listened to any music that took me away so completely from our usual Western life and transported me into a quite new civilisation."[59]

Less than three months after the success in Liverpool, Rosa Newmarch gave a presentation about Sibelius to the London Concert Goers' Club on February 22, 1906, with musical examples provided by piano and voice. Her lecture, "Jean Sibelius: A Finnish Composer," was published by Breitkopf & Härtel in both German and English—the first publication devoted entirely to Sibelius. Newmarch's booklet reached English readers on both sides of the Atlantic. Olin Downes knew of it when he wrote his entry on Sibelius for the *International Cyclopedia of Music and Musicians* in 1938. Another of the early and enthusiastic supporters of Sibelius, Newmarch found in the Finn's music a "sweeping tide of virile power" and "the spirit of an ancient race lately reborn among the nations." She also clearly perceived that Sibelius would not be confined within the limits of a purely nationalistic style. "If *The Kalevala* is eventually to find its Richard Wagner, there does not seem to be any immediate prospect of his being revealed in Jean Sibelius, who appears to be destined rather to continue the great line of symphonists in which Brahms and Tchaikovsky were his immediate predecessors."[60]

A third English advocate for Sibelius was Ernest Newman (1868–1959). Born William Roberts, this critic, the most celebrated in England in the first half of the twentieth century, devised his pseudonym from his rational outlook, that of "a new man in earnest." As critic for the *Manchester Guardian,* Newman had found himself transported by Sibelius's First Symphony when he heard it in 1905. Consistently impressed by the composer's originality, Newman later contrasted him with Schoenberg, helping to set up the "difficult/easy" dichotomy that undermined Sibelius among many of the twentieth century's intellectuals. And in 1937 the critic compared the composer to Beethoven, a comparison that nearly caused Sibelius's enemies to become apoplectic.[61] Probably because of this comparison, Theodor Adorno gave Ernest Newman the credit for Sibelius's reputation in England.

In the first two decades of the twentieth century Sibelius made a total of five trips to England. Following the 1905 appearance in Liverpool, he conducted the Third Symphony in London in 1908, a symphony he had dedicated to his first host and steadfast friend and champion, Bantock. In 1909 he returned for a third time, a trip memorable for his performance of *En saga* and *Finlandia* at the Queen's Hall concert and for meetings with d'Indy and Debussy. In the wake of this visit, Ernest Newman included Sibelius among the leading modern composers to whom he devoted lectures in his series at Birmingham University.[62]

On his next two trips, Sibelius had something of an uphill battle with the English public for acceptance of his new works. In 1912, in an event again spearheaded by Bantock, Sibelius conducted his Fourth Symphony at the Birmingham Festival (of which Henry Wood was principal conductor). A fifth and last visit took place early in 1921. The world war that had intervened between these visits had disrupted the attention of the English public. Ernest Newman described Sibelius as having to reestablish himself in England. This reestablishment was achieved above all with the well-loved *Finlandia, Valse triste,* and the first two symphonies. As conductors rediscovered the appeal of these early works, Sibelius was again boosted to popularity, and the more demanding compositions made their way into the concert halls. By 1937 Newman could write that there was "no longer any reason to complain that Sibelius is 'neglected' in this country."[63] The change in the music scene abroad was duly noted in the *New York Times.* Correspondent Ferruccio Bonavia wired an account of Sibelius's growing favor among the English in the spring of 1932. Within the space of a few weeks, he reported, Sir Henry Wood, Sir Hamilton Harty, and Dr. Malcolm Sargent had performed the First, Fourth, and Fifth symphonies.[64]

When Cecil Gray published his monograph *Sibelius* in 1931, he described Sibelius's peculiar position with considerable acuity. On the one hand, Gray wrote, Sibelius might legitimately be regarded as one "of the most popular of living composers, if not the most popular of all without exception. His name is a household word, as the saying is; 'Finlandia' is in the repertoire of every orchestra and brass brand, and 'Valse triste' is to be heard in every picture-palace, restaurant, café, tea-shop, and cabaret in the civilized world, from San Francisco to Cairo, and from Stockholm to Capetown."[65] On the other hand, Gray deplored the neglect of "all that is best" in the great mass of Sibelius's work, compounded by a lack of available published scores. This served to misrepresent a composer of signal importance. Gray accused virtually everyone in the world of music when he asserted, "Conductors, critics, publishers, executants of every kind, the public in general—all are equally guilty of having disgracefully ignored and neglected the composer who, I am convinced, will ultimately prove to have been, not only the greatest of his generation, but one of the major figures in the entire history of music."[66]

Gray's enthusiasm for Sibelius, perhaps fueled by the anti-German climate in Great Britain in the thirties, was so great that he maintained Sibelius to be the direct successor to Beethoven. This claim would turn out to be a red rag, even to so sympathetic a Sibelian as Olin Downes. Gray's enthusiasm for Sibelius was shared by Constant Lambert, a member of Gray's circle, who shortly brought forth yet another book with glowing praise of Sibelius, *Music Ho!* Lambert devoted two chapters to the composer ("Sibelius and the Integration of Form" and "Sibelius and the Music of the Future"), as well as part of a third, and ultimately concluded, "Since the death of Debussy, Sibelius and Schönberg are the most significant figures in European music, and Sibelius is undoubtedly the more complete artist of the two."[67]

These British authors were known in America. Olin Downes devoted a review to Gray's biography. He wrote that, having been subjected to "condescension or amusement" because of his enthusiasm for Sibelius, he welcomed a fellow believer. But he did question the heights to which Gray leaped. "'That the symphonies of Sibelius represent the highest point attained in this form since Beethoven' disposes of one Johannes Brahms in a breath, which, after all, is not a light thing to do," observed Downes.[68]

There may have been more than a tincture of professional jealousy here. That jealousy broke open along national lines in 1936. In response to claims in the British press that gave to Englishmen the honor of "discovering" and "promoting" the Finn, Lawrence Gilman retaliated with a caustic article, "Sibelius in America." Gilman, with growing irritation, had read an essay by Alan Frank in *The Listener*. Frank wrote that until Cecil Gray's monograph appeared in 1931, Sibelius's music "had remained virtually unknown out-side of Finland." Was Mr. Frank really so musically illiterate? demanded Gilman in the *Tribune*. Did he not have any idea that Americans had dis-cussed and performed Sibelius's music between 1901 and 1935; that in those years no fewer than 265 performances were given by major U.S. orchestras; that in a single six-month season, one of those orchestras gave no fewer than seventeen performances of Sibelius and not, mind you, *Finlandia* and *Valse triste,* but meaty works, the Fifth Symphony, the Sixth Symphony, the Sev-enth Symphony? Moreover, did Mr. Frank not know that a "penetrating and courageous American critic" had long ago begun "to hammer into the heads of the dull and the obdurate his conviction that Sibelius was a great composer? ... No one in the English-speaking countries," noted Gilman, had done more than Olin Downes "to make the American music-lover ashamed of being deaf and dumb to the presence of the great creative imagi-nation that has finally come to dominate the music of our time." [69]

But if Alan Frank had missed the connection between Sibelius and Downes, the Finns had not. In 1937 they made Downes a Commander of the Order of the White Rose.

Sɪʙᴇʟɪᴜs's ᴘᴏᴘᴜʟᴀʀɪᴛʏ ɢᴀɪɴᴇᴅ in momentum through the 1930s, a de-cade that cultural historian Walter I. Susman has called the heyday of the people. In these years Carl Sandburg penned *The People, Yes;* the Works Projects Administration generated Art for the People as well as the People's Theatre; and John Ford portrayed America's history on film in populist terms. The most appropriate symbol of this populism, the World's Fair, co-incided with the very acme and pitch of Sibelius's popularity in the United States. Held in New York in 1939–40, the event was billed as "The People's Fair" and "Everyman's Fair" and dedicated to "bearing on the life of the great mass of the people." [70] Yet this high-minded title did not completely hide the consumer-oriented appeal, whose purpose was to attract those av-erage Americans to avail themselves amply of the Fair's goods and services.

Olin Downes accepted the chairmanship of the music division of the fair. He described his extraordinary preparations and his efforts to appeal to the populace in a long letter to Sibelius.

> I had devised this program as a sort of a *"Meistersinger finale,"* emblematic of the national, international and communal aspects of the Fair. We opened the

ceremonies with trumpeters in costume, who introduced our performance quite magnificently with the fanfares from the Third Act of Verdi's "*Otello.*" We had groups of trumpeters answering each other from the tops of the buildings of the Fair and, then appeared a procession of representatives of fifty-four different nations in their national costumes and with their national flags, who marched to the top of an open-air stage we had devised for the occasion and stood up there in costume with all their flags waving against the sky. We then had folk dances of six different nations and some American popular music, with both negro and American singers, solo performances by Metropolitan and other artists and a finale which came to its climax with your music.[71]

Downes had seen to it, in fact, that this "preview" had been crowned with Sibelius's *Finlandia.* Six hundred thousand had attended.

This extravaganza, an afternoon event, had been followed by an evening performance that put Henry Purcell, J. S. Bach, and Horatio Parker on the same program as Beethoven's Ninth Symphony. And all this was just a foretaste. Downes was planning programs of religious music that would encompass Catholic, Protestant, Russian and Greek Orthodox, and Jewish music. He set about organizing a special Wagner season with Kirsten Flagstad and other artists of the Metropolitan Opera. He began arranging choral performances, ballets, folk dances, operettas, musical comedies, and American popular songs by as many world bodies as he could arrange. And he envisioned America being represented by at least six of her leading orchestras.

But his consummate wish was to premiere Sibelius's Eighth Symphony at the fair. Elaborating on a theme now old, Downes tried to tempt the composer with assurances that the work would be performed by Koussevitzky and the Boston Symphony Orchestra, "the finest symphonic body in the whole world." It would be broadcast by shortwave radio, he said, over the entire globe. The pinnacle would be to have Sibelius himself present, to supervise the rehearsal and witness the event. "This would crown the music of the Fair as no other event could, if we might stand out in history as the nation and the city which gave your Eighth Symphony to the world."[72]

We know, of course, that no Eighth Symphony ever made its appearance. Instead, with exquisite appropriateness, Olin Downes received from the composer a different score—the music to *Everyman.*[73]

OLIN DOWNES NEVER GAVE UP —on the Eighth Symphony or on Jean Sibelius. Late in 1938 he cabled to ask if Sibelius would make New Year's Day "historical" in America and the world by conducting his music for a round-the-world broadcast. He would be sending, Downes wrote, "creative artists [a] message to a humanity that was never in greater need of your spirit and creation of beauty."[74] To this Sibelius agreed. It was thus at Olin Downes's inducement that Sibelius came out of his isolation to conduct the Helsinki Philharmonic in his *Andante Festivo,* broadcast from Helsinki on New Year's Day 1939.

As the first nation to accept the invitation to participate in the fair, Finland had been invited to launch the fair's dedication, "The Dawn of a New Day." Finland's President Kyösti Kallio would deliver a greeting, after which Sibelius and the Helsinki Symphony Orchestra would be heard on radio, the 150-member Finlandia Male Chorus would sing, and a children's chorus would follow with festival songs. The *New York Times* announced that the composer would lead off the fair's "Salute of Nations."[75] Afterward, kings, queens, emperors, presidents, and statesmen would radio greetings. The exercise was expected to be attended by 6,000, who would gather in Radio City Music Hall.

With its "Dawn of a New Day" theme, the fair was dedicated to an era consecrated to peace, progress, and national optimism. Speakers would discuss America's four cherished liberties—the press, speech, religion, and assembly. An elaborate musical program was to follow: Mendelssohn's *March of the Priests;* the *Sanctus* from Gounod's *St. Cecilia Mass* sung by Metropolitan Opera tenor Giovanni Martinelli and Father Ginn's Paulist choristers; and a benediction and Gounod's *Unfold Ye Portals,* sung by the Schola Cantorum and the Paulist Choristers. At midnight the fair's theme song, George Gershwin's "Dawn of a New Day," was to be broadcast by scores of orchestras throughout the nation. Simultaneously, forty-six steamships on both the Atlantic and Pacific oceans would hold "Dawn" parties.

Finland's exhibit for the fair was a "Symphony in Wood," a pavilion that demonstrated the country's arts and industries and its preparations for the upcoming Olympic Games in 1940. In an official address, Finnish Minister Hjalmar J. Procopé emphasized the ideals of liberty and democracy shared jointly by Finland and the United States, while in his turn New York's Mayor La Guardia, a self-described "great admirer of Finland," hailed the republic's repayment of her war debt (the only one of thirteen to be paid): "Mention the name of Finland," he said, "and every American will admire your one biggest exhibit to the whole world—your national honor."[76] In the politically and patriotically charged atmosphere of 1939, Finnish art and music had a popular edge by virtue of the favorable light in which Americans saw Finland.

Before 1939 was over, the bright optimism had faded on several counts. A letter to the composer shows that Downes—who had worked "all day and night through nearly two years to try and induce those bankers and other idiots to give a really representative program of music"—finally resigned from his part in the fair, disgusted at the pettiness, the dirty politics, and the sheer stupidity he had encountered.[77] And he began to portray Sibelius's music in even nobler tones than before. The mighty Soviet Union once again threatened its tiny neighbor, rolling in on November 30, 1939, with tanks and guns to take over Finland's eastern borders, initiating the Winter War. Downes cabled Sibelius: "Your music fights for invincible Finland we shall raise money by concert of your masterpieces keep safe if you can dear master all America prays for you and your noble country."[78] His Christmas telegram read: "Merry Xmas and victori[o]us new year to you and yours and all the people of the land of heroes."[79]

A picture of Sibelius calmly lighting a cigar appeared in the *New York Times* under the caption "Sibelius Is Safe at Finnish Forest Home; Proud of His People and Grateful to U.S."[80] Pictures of lone Finns, bravely skiing through Arctic snow to engage in guerilla warfare against Soviet tanks, filled the American people with unutterable sympathy.

The war, which Olin Downes repeatedly urged Americans to enter, stirred the critic's crusading spirit and lifted his rhetoric to new heights. He described *Finlandia* (which in 1914 he had termed trivial) as "that hymn to liberty," and *En saga* as a "heroic tone-poem born of the spirit and need of Sibelius's land." They were works "revealed as never before as an expression of universal truthfulness and significance. For art and ethics, music and humanity, had become dangerously separate in the modern world. Allegedly, serious composition had fallen too much into the hands of cliques and snobs. Greatness? Heroism? Sentiment? Oh, go back to Beethoven!"[81]

It was argued, Downes went on, that Sibelius's works were "just music," sentimental, officious, in which only the imaginative could find any hint of Northern nature. Of what, Downes now demanded, *did* these works speak if not of "what is transpiring today in Finland's northern fastnesses, where her warriors are fighting a fight which will go down as one of the mightiest sagas of all time?"

Recalling ruefully the laugh that had accompanied the remark of a Boston composer who, when asked about Sibelius, had quipped that he preferred his symphonies without cod-liver oil, Downes proclaimed: ". . . the cod-liver oil music is to the fore. The symphonies which were too strong meat and too directly human and entirely too odoriferous of uncomfortably primal and elemental things are now reverberating over the world with a song that echoes even farther than Finland's cannon." [82] Whatever hypocrisy and diplomatic pettifoggery reigned in the "civilized" world, "uncivilized" Finns clearly valued honor and liberty and were prepared to die for their beliefs. Those values, according to Downes, were at the core of Sibelius's symphonies and were what could be heard in Carnegie Hall. Whereas Stravinsky was "denying his birthright of poetry, folklore and humanity . . . [a victim of] narrow, self-satisfied narcissism," Downes thundered, Sibelius's music now could be clearly understood. "He meant what he said":

> When the "Saga" is heard again, with the strange flickering and glintings of the orchestra, the flare of the trumpet, the gigantic theme which strides upward in the gloom and the mutterings and premonitions of the instruments—"ancestral voices prophesying war"—and the chants and the sullen rhythms which are of those who dance with knives drawn; and when, after the runic lament of the muted strings, and to the skirlings and poundings of the immense rhythms, the orchestra girds its loins and rises in Berserk fury—then there will be no need for explanations or program notes to remind us of what is happening now in the fastnesses of Karelia and the wastes and glooms and crashing shores of an unconquerable land. [83]

As Sibelius's seventy-fifth birthday approached on December 8, 1940, the momentum of a decade that might have culminated with the Eighth Symphony at the World's Fair now peaked. As early as October, Downes began reporting commemorative concerts. [84] Ormandy conducted the First Symphony, which, though the least mature of the symphonies, "even here speaks with the large voice of the early gods" in its "sincerity, imagination, primeval directness." Koussevitzky selected "caviar to the general," the Sixth and Seventh symphonies, but concluded his program with the Second, to deafening applause. John Barbirolli closed his mostly Sibelius concert with *Finlandia,* in order, he explained, to pay tribute to heroic Finland. Performances continued throughout the season; as late as the following May, Antonia Brico was celebrating the birthday with the Finnish male chorus called Laulu-Miehet performing Sibelius choral works.

A nationwide celebration of the birthday was announced, with the birthday week sparking a National Sibelius Festival. Four hundred fifty orchestras throughout the United States and 5,000 music clubs and societies agreed to participate. The New York Philharmonic, the Cleveland Symphony Orchestra, the San Francisco Symphony, and orchestras in Pittsburgh, Minneapolis, Detroit, and Indianapolis featured Sibelius on their programs. Schools, colleges, and music institutes joined in. Meanwhile, Columbia released new Sibelius recordings to coincide with the celebration: the Second Symphony and *Belshazzar's Feast,* incidental music for a play by Hjalmar Procopé (uncle to the diplomat).

The day before the birthday, Arturo Toscanini conducted the NBC Symphony in an all-Sibelius program. Sponsored by "For Finland, Inc.," an organization devoted to "promoting good relations between Finland and the United States and to assist Finland's recovery from the Soviet devastation," the festival included notable sponsors, many of them influential conductors: Lucrezia Bori, Walter Damrosch, Eugene Goossens, Howard Hanson, Josef Hofmann, José Iturbi, Werner Janssen, Hans Kindler, Dmitri Mitropoulos, Pierre Monteux, Eugene Ormandy, Fritz Reiner, Artur Rodzinski, David Sarnoff, Nikolai Sokoloff, Sigmund Spaeth, Deems Taylor, Lawrence Tibbett, and, of course, Olin Downes.

Toscanini could hardly have been accused of being a promoter of Sibelius's music before 1940. Listeners had actually complained to the *New York Times* that he did not program enough of the Finn's works.[85] Now, however, apparently sensing the wide public sympathy for Finland, Toscanini chose to conduct some of Sibelius's music with the strongest national flavor: the "Liberation" Symphony (the Second), *Pohjola's Daughter, The Swan of Tuonela, Lemminkäinen's Homeward Journey,* and, for a stirring finale, *Finlandia.*[86]

The combination of Toscanini and Sibelius transported Downes to new heights. Never, he wrote, had the indomitable spirit of man shown more brightly than through the Second Symphony's heroic exordium. Never had *The Swan* evoked such poetry and myth. Never had the "immortal" *Finlandia* better demonstrated Sibelius's "immense power to say simple things in a direct and popular way, yet in the way that only a great master and supreme artist could say them."[87] He was the one composer early in the century who was not an escapist, but whose music spoke plainly of the perils to be faced:

> There were the reverberations of what was gathering under civilization's surface. There were to be heard deathless defiance and proclamation of the invin-

cible spirit of man. The cry moved us strangely then, we hardly knew why. Now we understand. And so it is that Sibelius appears today—the one hero and prophet whose music is singularly abreast of the times, the world and its need.[88]

Like Joan of Arc, Sibelius too listened to his voices. He put their prophecies in his scores.

WHILE OLIN DOWNES had been steadfast in his devotion to Jean Sibelius from the very first decade of the twentieth century, events in the critic's personal life almost certainly account for the paroxysms of enthusiasm with which he now responded to the composer. Early in the twentieth century he had considered *Finlandia* and *The Swan of Tuonela* trite; in the 1940s he gave even these works ecstatic accolades.

The correspondence explains a great deal, for Downes confided to Sibelius as to a trusted friend the emotional turmoil of his life. One tragedy was a loss the composer shared: the sudden and completely unexpected death of Arvi Paloheimo, the husband of Sibelius's beloved eldest daughter, Eva. Arvi had taken Downes on more than one unforgettable fishing trip, and Downes repeatedly mourned his death in cables and letters to the composer ("one of my noblest and dearest friends" and "one of the very, very few friends whom I loved").

But the death of Arvi was not all. In letters of utter distraction (pieced together and interspersed with such salutations as "dear Master, you know I am insane"), Downes reported a loss "even dearer" and "more terrible," the death of Louise, his mother, "who was half, or more, of my soul":

Her life had been very tragic, as only I know. Her suffering, her immense and fanatical heroism fed me and made the heroism of your music so dear to me. I took her in my arms that last afternoon while the nurse made her bed and she was so helpless and weak that I could only think as I saw her poor shrunken limbs of Christ being taken down from the cross. Later I went alone with her ashes, and I had to scatter these ashes, with my own hands, upon *her* mother's grave [the grave of the formidable Sarah Jane Corson Downes].[89]

Downes told Sibelius that perhaps Wagner was right, even if he, Sibelius, did not like his aesthetic, and he quoted from *Parsifal:* "*Durch Mitleid wissend.*" He concluded, "Only the departure of those two whom I loved could have made me understand the great wisdom and tenderness of that music" of the early days. But there was more. "I separated from my first wife last

October and re-married last January—I mean—good heavens—not last October and last January, but the October and January of a year before. In other words, I have been remarried since January of 1940. This—the separation—was accompanied with bitter pain, and of course one will never know whether one has done what was right, or—well, never mind . . . dear God, what a confusion!"[90]

Stresses in the marriage had been brewing from near the beginning, especially with the daunting and jealous shadow of Louise ever present. But the actual severance came at a time of other losses and at a time when war deepened his pain. The crusader in Downes was ever ready to battle for a cause, and the war certainly provided one: "We should be fighting. . . . We must also fight, this time, for the peace. . . . I am making speeches at many places about these things just now, especially to the young people at the colleges, and I thank God for our President—the greatest man we have had since Wilson."[91]

Yet, just as surely as he had lost Arvi Paloheimo and Louise, as surely as Americans lost their optimism and their naiveté, Olin Downes would experience another loss: that of Sibelius's "heroic" reputation. While his own extravagant adulation had undoubtedly contributed to that loss, two widely differing events sealed its fate: In the summer of 1940, Finland entered into a pact with Nazi Germany; the following October, the position of music critic for the *New York Herald Tribune* was filled by a former Harvard man, Virgil Thomson.

Sibelius and the Sophisticates

Sibelius is in no sense a naif; he is merely provincial.* —Virgil Thomson, 1940

EVEN WHILE OLIN DOWNES was leading a groundswell of Sibelian popularity, not all American voices steered by the same currents. As early as 1929,
in an article entitled "Sibelius Stripped," Irving Weil castigated those assid-
uous creators of the Sibelius myth for portraying the Finn, minus telling
photographs, as a romantic bard in flowing robes living in isolation beside
the River of Death, gazing interminably with folded arms upon one of Finland's one thousand mysterious lakes (there are always, noted Weil, one
thousand of those lakes).[1] Nothing, said Weil, had done more to make Sibelius's music unacceptable or misunderstood.

Not long thereafter, Paul Rosenfeld, whom Weil had singled out as one
of the mythmakers (along with Mischa Leon, a Dane, and the Englishman
Granville Bantock), embarked on an entirely new tack. Having praised the
virile Sibelius of the vasty open, he now snorted that he was "second-rate,"
calling him that "overstuffed bard Jan Sibelius."[2] In the *New York Times*
there appeared a photograph of a very contemporary-looking Sibelius in tie
and suit with unfolded arms gazing out from a score rather than down at a
lake;[3] and Olin Downes (although nowhere named by Weil) began carefully
noting the number of lakes. Yet Weil's and other warning voices went largely
unheeded as the waves of enthusiasm for Sibelius rolled in to the American
shore. Not until Virgil Thomson appeared on the New York scene did the
tide begin to turn.

Virgil Thomson (1896–1990) is widely known today for his long association with Parisians, from Nadia Boulanger, his teacher, to the expatriate
community of James Joyce and Gertrude Stein, whose poetry he borrowed
for his whimsical music. A witty sophisticate, Thomson established a reputation as an articulate if opinionated critic. ("The way to write American music is simple," he said. "All you have to do is to be an American and then
write any kind of music you wish.") There is another aspect of Thomson's
life, however, that is especially important here. In the fall of 1919, Olin
Downes's thirteenth year at the *Boston Post,* Thomson matriculated at Harvard. He thus became a member of that privileged circle forever closed to
Olin Downes. Thomson's teachers included the Francophile Edward Burlingame Hill and the French-trained Archibald Davison. With them he developed his taste for French music and his enthusiasm for Stravinsky. When
the Harvard Glee Club toured Paris under Davison's direction, Thomson
stayed. There he met Erik Satie and became a devoted disciple. (He once
cited the three *S*'s of modern music as Schoenberg, Stravinsky, and Satie.)
Thomson's ardency for Stravinsky and things French was counterbalanced
by his loathing for Sibelius and things Northern. These ideas reflected his
Parisian world. His teacher, Nadia Boulanger, is known to have made but
one memorable remark about Sibelius: "Poor, poor Sibelius." And French
was the language in which René Leibowitz, a disciple of the Schoenberg
circle, published his monograph *Sibelius, le plus mauvais compositeur du
monde* ("Sibelius, the Worst Composer in the World").[4]

On October 11, 1940, Thomson made his debut as music critic for the
New York Herald Tribune. One paragraph is enough to show that the winds
for Sibelius had changed. "Twenty years' residence on the European continent has largely spared me Sibelius. Last night's Second Symphony was my
first in quite some years. I found it vulgar, self-indulgent, and provincial
beyond all description. I realize that there are sincere Sibelius lovers in the
world, though I must say I've never met one among educated professional
musicians. . . ."[5] Then Thomson addressed the real issue, Sibelius's popularity: "I realize also that this work has a kind of popular power unusual in
symphonic literature. Even Wagner scarcely goes over so big on the radio.
That populace-pleasing power is not unlike the power of a Hollywood class-
A picture. Sibelius is in no sense a naif; he is merely provincial. Let me leave
it at that for the present. Perhaps, if I have to hear much more of him, I'll
sit down one day with the scores and find out what is in them."[6]

The immediate effect of Thomson's piece may best be told by someone who was there. Writing in the *Nation* on October 26, 1940, B. H. Haggin described his experience:

> Friday, October 11, which was to end so extraordinarily, began ordinarily enough: breakfast, the *Times,* headlines about bombings, the Balkans, Willkie, and finally the Philharmonic's opening concert, which I had forgotten about after a glance at the list of works Mr. Barbirolli had chosen for the first weeks of the season. I went on to read Mr. Downes's swollen and muddy flood of words—about Sibelius's Second Symphony, for example, "a paean to the unconquerable spirit that is man," and the performance in which this work "was read, for the greater part, in bardic vein," and "there was breadth and sweep of line"; but in which "a thoughtful reading was distinguished prevailingly by fine proportions and a real sense of form"; in which, however, "this feeling was lost . . . in places where tempo was too suddenly whipped up or slowed down"; and yet of which "the impression was of a too calculated performance, with many fine attributes, one which, had all previous calculations been forgotten, and the music given its head, would have been a complete instead of a conditioned success." Reading this, I felt the mists of New York newspaper reviewing rising about me; by evening, with the reviews in the *Post,* the *World-Telegram,* and *PM,* these mists were suffocating; and then the air was cleared by a piece of writing which a couple of excited telephone calls caused me to look up in the *Herald Tribune.*[7]

Haggin summed up the situation quickly. He thoroughly enjoyed Thomson's review, not because he agreed with it, but for Thomson's outspoken voice and acute musical faculties. In his view, it was the excesses of the Sibelius adherents that had provoked Thomson to counterexcess. Although Haggin concluded that he would as often be irritated by Thomson's perversity as delighted by his penetration, he still rejoiced in the appearance of a fresh voice more in tune with an intelligentsia increasingly sophisticated, skeptical, and confident.

Thomson's outspokenness about Sibelius did not abate or alter during the critic's fourteen-year tenure at the *Herald Tribune.* He never did, it seems, sit down with the scores. He nevertheless pronounced the First Symphony of "inferior" melodic quality, its "harmonic substructure . . . at its best unobtrusive, at its worst corny"; he reported gleefully when Sibelius's Second Symphony received boos while fragments of *Wozzeck* on the same program garnered applause; and he referred to Sibelius, along with Shostakovitch, as "not adult."[8] Perhaps all the talk about Sibelius's "masculinity" disturbed the closet homosexual in Thomson.

As devoted to his Francophile clique as Downes was to his Sibelian cult, Thomson, cleverer by far with words, adroitly chipped away at the myth of the godlike hero. In its place he substituted the image of a provincial dullard, whose music was as superficial as his reputation was manufactured. Yet Thomson had overlooked the same cardinal point as Downes: as critics and cultivators of music appreciation, these "educators" should have endeavored to persuade listeners to give up their dislikes, not their likes. Both men could have learned an important lesson from Koussevitzky, who, by advocating both Stravinsky and Sibelius, put himself in a far stronger position musically than either critic.

As an avant-garde composer himself and one with a Harvard pedigree, Thomson had the ear of the intellectuals, and his articulate jibes shredded Sibelius's reputation with devastating effect among American highbrows. In Thomson's favor too were certain political conditions that began to work against Sibelius. As early as the summer of 1940, Hitler's troops had requested and received transit rights through Finland. Then on June 22, 1941, Hitler issued a proclamation declaring that his German troops stood on the Arctic coast together with their Finnish comrades, "heroes of liberty," ready, jointly, to defend Finland against the Soviet Union. Within weeks, the *New York Times* and other Associated Press papers carried an article entitled "Sibelius Appeals to U.S. to Understand Finn Case."[9] Coming to such an understanding was difficult for the large Jewish population in New York, particularly as Sibelius himself was prevailed upon to make public statements in behalf of the new alliance. Harold E. Johnson alleged that Sibelius greeted visiting Nazi soldiers with the words "I wish with all my heart that you may enjoy a speedy victory."[10] And perhaps some recalled the tiny notice a few years before, when the *New York Times* announced that Chancellor Hitler had awarded the Goethe Medal for Science and Art to Jean Sibelius "in recognition of the love of fatherland that permeates his symbolic compositions." One reader wrote the paper to suggest that American orchestras ban the playing of *Finlandia,* virtually the national anthem of a country fighting U.S. allies.[11]

Along with the political climate, the intellectual one had also begun to change. The year before Thomson left Paris for New York, Olin Downes had contributed his lengthy article "Sibelius" to Oscar Thompson's *International Cyclopedia of Music and Musicians.* In by now wearying and perfervid prose, Downes ceremonially recounted the same phrases he had been honing since 1909. Sibelius, "the next symphonist after Brahms and Beethoven," was "a lonely and towering figure in the music of the early Twentieth Century . . . a gigantic figure striding out of a heroic past either forgotten or existent only in legend."[12] Intellectuals gagged. Many of them suffered further convulsions during what they regarded as the excessive eulogies of the seventy-fifth birthday celebration in 1940. Paul Rosenfeld observed, perhaps a trifle defensively, that while the previous decade had correctly valued Sibelius as a Romantic, the present fetish for Sibelius indicated a dangerous aversion to the new in art; for not only was Sibelius a nineteenth-century anachronism, but much of his music really only derived from Tchaikovsky anyway.[13]

Rosenfeld's article, "The Beethoven of the North," appeared in the *New Republic,* a barometer of sophisticated opinion. It signaled for Sibelius an ominous change in American intellectual currents. The prevailing populist theme of "We the People," heard from figures on the American Left from Aaron Copland to Olin Downes (and even occasionally Virgil Thomson, as in his *Variations on a Sunday School Tune*), was now being challenged from a Far Left populated by European intellectuals and by such Americans as the *Partisan Review* circle.[14] Early in the century both European and American liberals had shared the vision that society's hope lay in the common man, in the masses, who, given the opportunity, could be lifted to "high" culture. Charles Ives, Arthur Farwell, and the young Olin Downes were among the musicians who propounded this democratic view. But World War I, together with the development of film and radio, both of which promoted cultural mass consumption, forced intellectuals to reconsider that vision. As more Europeans immigrated to the United States in the thirties, the Left in America and Europe began to divide. To Europeans, the American proletariat appeared not only nonrevolutionary, but worse, affirmers of the status quo, manipulated by the pervasiveness of radio and film.

This assessment seemed confirmed by the rise of Fascist regimes in Germany, Italy, and Spain in the 1920s and 1930s. The chilling spectre of the charismatic *Der Führer* and *Il Duce* skillfully using radio and film to rally mass support made the critique of populist culture all the more compelling. Thus, while much of the American Left opposed Fascism and promoted art accessible to "the people," an increasingly outspoken Far Left likewise opposed Fascism but condemned art that pandered to popular taste, believing the success of such art to be the result of Fascistic techniques of manipulation. Instead they promoted an elitist view, arguing that only "progressive," "difficult" art could preserve the revolutionary spirit essential to a "true" society. In the thirties were thus sown the seeds of ideas that still flourish. "Art which said 'no' rather than 'yes,' art which refused to assuage distress or give the illusion of social or aesthetic wholeness and completion" [15] seemed the only art with which to resist totalitarianism and sustain creative imagination. The most vigorous advocates of this "high modernist" position in America fell within two groups: the so-called New York intellectuals, a group associated with the *Partisan Review,* who included Dwight Macdonald and Clement Greenberg;[16] and German exiles linked with the Frankfurt Institute for Social Research, who included Max Horkheimer and Theodor Adorno. Of these social critics, it was Adorno who made a specialty of attacking music within the culture industry.

"Music has ceased to be a human force," Adorno wrote in "A Social Critique of Radio Music." It is "consumed like other consumers' goods." [17] The worst effect of this, he concluded disapprovingly, was "commodity listening," a "listening whose ideal it is to dispense as far as possible with any effort on the part of the recipient—even if such an effort on the part of the recipient is the necessary condition of grasping the sense of the music." [18] In an unforgettable analogy to an all-American product (which, coupled with his dislike of jazz, suggests Adorno's lack of sympathy with American culture) he added, "It is the ideal of Aunt Jemima's ready-mix for pancakes extended to the field of music."

Adorno argued that "music was no longer a means, but an end, a fetish" of contemporary society.[19] "Fetishization" to Adorno meant the replacement of the direct relationship between the listener and music with a relationship between the listener and some social or economic value attached to the music or its performers. It took many forms: the cult of the star conductor and performer; the cult symphony; the cult violins; the obsession with sound production equipment; listening that focused on the familiar, promoting listening to "Beethoven's Fifth as if it were a set of quotations from Beethoven's Fifth."[20] Under such circumstances, the reactions of the listeners seem to have no relation to the playing of the music. "Where they react at all," shrilled Adorno, "it no longer makes any difference whether it is to Beethoven's Seventh Symphony or to a bikini." [21]

Adorno was particularly suspicious of radio. "Does a symphony played on the air remain a symphony?" he demanded. "Are the changes it undergoes by wireless transmission merely slight and negligible modifications or do those changes affect the very essence of the music?" [22] Adorno was convinced that American radio, while purporting to bring "culture" to the masses, actually brought them something quite different. However unintended, radio's ideological effect, he insisted, was to reinforce the status quo and create vain self-satisfaction. Rather than confronting social realities, "the ruined farmer is consoled by the radio-instilled belief that Toscanini is playing for him and for him alone, and that an order of things that allows him to hear Toscanini compensates for low market prices for farm products; even though he is ploughing cotton under, radio is giving him culture." [23]

Adorno was convinced that Sibelius's incredible popularity in the United States was a prime example of a musical fetish. In a report compiled for the Princeton Radio Research Project, he devoted an entire section to "The Sibelius Problem":

> One of the most accepted moderns, although famous only in America and England, is the Finnish composer, Sibelius. In the opinion of the writer—and he is prepared to back it by concrete technical analysis—the work of Sibelius is not only incredibly overrated, but it fundamentally lacks any good qualities. Its principle is the interconnection of trivial bits of traditional music into a whole which lacks any logic or continuity, which is fundamentally incomprehensible, and which therefore is regarded as "deep." [24]

In 1948 Adorno wrote in his *Philosophy of Modern Music:* "Twenty years ago the trumped-up glory surrounding Elgar seemed a local phenomenon and the fame of Sibelius an exceptional case of critical ignorance. Phenomena of such a niveau, even if they are at times more liberal in their use of dissonances, are the norm today." [25]

In the same volume he disparaged Sibelius more than once, attacking in particular his exclusive adherence to tonality, that apparently unforgivable symptom of Romantic sentimentality. Adorno could not understand why Sibelius, who in Germany had but "scant resonance," in England and America was accorded high honors:

> The reasons why were never demonstrated in succinct musical terms; it surely was not the great demands of his symphonics that frustrated all attempts to launch him elsewhere. More than thirty years ago I once asked Ernest Newman, the initiator of Sibelius's fame, about the qualities of the Finnish composer. After all, I said, he had adopted none of the advances in compositorial technique that had been made throughout Europe; his symphonies combined meaningless and trivial elements with alogical and profoundly unintelligible ones; he mistook esthetic formlessness for the voice of nature. Newman, from whose urbane all-round skepticism someone bred in the German tradition had much to learn, replied with a smile that the qualities I had criticized—and which he was not denying—were just what appealed to the British. [26]

In 1938 Adorno attacked the composer with all guns blazing in his "Glosse über Sibelius." [27] The Finn's works were "dürftig" and "bootisch"; his themes remain stuck ("Sie bleiben stecken"); worse, "he is a Stravinsky against his will; only he has less talent." Adorno maintained that Sibelius's glory was created solely by technological manipulation:

> It would be very interesting to show: first, to what extent Sibelius is played over the radio, and second, to what influences his popularity is due, and what the public's attitude toward him actually is beyond the superficial applause which his works receive. If his success is really a fact, and not only some sort of manufactured popularity (which is still the writer's opinion), this probably would indicate a total state of musical consciousness which ought to give rise to even graver apprehension than the lack of understanding for great modern music or the preference for cheap light music. . . .
>
> As the author believes that Sibelius really plays a great part in the American broadcasting of serious music, just in the case of the most selective stations it is suggested that a number of interviews be conducted in an attempt to find out what role Sibelius actually plays in the consciousness of the listeners. . . . [I]f Sibelius' music is good music, then all the categories by which musical standards can be measured—standards which reach from a master like Bach to most advanced composers like Schoenberg—must be completely abolished. [28]

Whereas Olin Downes had used the radio to familiarize listeners across the Northern Hemisphere with the lonely music of Jean Sibelius, Adorno viewed the radio voice as an "expert commodity marketer." Where Downes saw in Sibelius and Toscanini heroes of another order, Adorno saw personality cults. Where Downes believed in music appreciation as education, Adorno decried the "name that tune" excuse for real musical knowledge.

Adorno was up against a basic tenet of American life, one that Olin Downes embodied to the fullest and believed in with all his soul, and one that the spirit of the 1930s reinforced: the democratic right of every American to have access to culture. The notion is deeply rooted in American life: Walt Whitman's preface to *Leaves of Grass* states that to be "a bard is to be commensurate with a people," and the image of "the people" abundantly evident in the rhetoric of the 1930s expresses in its own eloquent way this aspect of the American consciousness. Evidence suggests that the populist outlook also coincided with Sibelius's own. In *A Book About a Man,* written by his contemporary Adolf Paul, Sibelius appears as the character Sillén, whose credo is "to give to everybody. . . . It is only a sign of poverty to talk about 'art for art's sake.' All have a right to it. . . ."[29] The deep attraction Americans felt to Sibelius and his music may have arisen in part from their recognition of so kindred a spirit.

Adorno's critique of Sibelius is important today chiefly because it explains how and by whom Sibelius came to be viewed as a superficial if popular conservative, and because it underscores how a personal mission rather than a musical valuation generated that view. Adorno (1903–1969) had come to America by way of England, fleeing Hitler's Germany.[30] Perhaps significantly, he shared a number of traits with Olin Downes—an early talent for the piano, a home with a distant father and a strong mother whose name he adopted; a dislike of Stravinsky; and, above all, a fanaticism about his own opinions. But a crucial difference in Adorno's life was his formal education. Graduated from the Johann Wolfgang Goethe University in Frankfurt, Adorno already possessed, at the astonishing age of twenty-one, a doctorate in philosophy. After hearing excerpts of *Wozzeck,* Adorno aspired to become a composer and persuaded Alban Berg to accept him as a student, whereupon he traveled to Vienna in January 1925 and became a part of Schoenberg's circle. He found himself deeply sympathetic toward their atonal ideas and favored masters, including Mahler. Even after he left Vienna, Adorno championed the ideals of the so-called Second Viennese School—in his musical tastes, in his articles, and in his subsequent editorship of the periodical *Anbruch* during the years 1928 to 1932. He showed himself as staunch an advocate of the Second Viennese composers and their elitist views as Olin Downes was of Jean Sibelius and the democratic attitude toward art.

Returning to Frankfurt, Adorno resumed an old friendship with Max Horkheimer and was gradually drawn into the circle around the Institute of Social Research. There his writing began to demonstrate the Hegelian Marxism that distinguishes his best-known works. In May 1931 he began teaching philosophy at the University of Frankfurt. As the Nazis came to power, Theodor Adorno, son of Oskar Wiesengrund, a Jewish wine merchant, no longer enjoyed a secure academic future. Members of the Institute were among the first to flee Germany. Erich Fromm arrived in America in 1932; Max Horkheimer, Herbert Marcuse, Leo Lowenthal, and Friedrich Pollock came in 1934. These men established a loose affiliation with Columbia University in New York, where Adorno eventually but reluctantly joined them in 1938. First, however, there were three significant years in England.

Immigrating to London in 1934, Adorno arrived in a society where, instead of Schoenberg, Berg, and Mahler, Sibelius was played.[31] Sir Henry Wood was directing all seven symphonies in the Promenade Concerts; Sir Thomas Beecham was overseeing a Sibelius Festival; Cecil Gray was hailing Sibelius as the greatest symphonist after Beethoven; Constant Lambert was echoing Gray. The last straw may have been Bengt de Törne's *Sibelius: A Close-Up.* Publishing his book in London in 1937, de Törne, who tended to invest Sibelius with his own ideas, had the audacity to compare the "Master" to Dante and Velázquez. The infuriated "Glosse über Sibelius" erupted in response to de Törne's book.

On coming to America in 1938, Adorno found the musical scene decidedly similar to England's. The critic of the *New York Times* was extolling that "elemental northern and magnificently ancestral thing in Sibelius's compositions."[32] Koussevitzky and Stokowski and sometimes Toscanini were directing, recording, and touring with his symphonies and symphonic poems. Radio audiences had chosen Sibelius their favorite living composer. And Schoenberg, Berg, Mahler? Few Americans had much use for the first two and Olin Downes was stubbornly and notoriously set against the third. Although in 1908 Downes had ringingly endorsed Mahler as the unlikely successor to Karl Muck as conductor of the Boston Symphony ("Mr. Mahler would be a treasure trove"), Mahler the composer was another matter. On hearing Mahler's Second Symphony in 1919, Downes found it "theatrical, bombastic, and tedious in its reiteration of unimportant themes." By the time he heard the Fifth Symphony in 1926, Downes was pronouncing Mahler "one of the most pathetic figures in the music of the late nineteenth century."[33] His variations on this theme, coupled with his characterization of most music coming out of Vienna as decadent (when not vulgar or foul-smelling or just plain un-American), could hardly have endeared him or his hero Sibelius to Adorno.

It is not without significance that the most heated embroglio of Downes's career concerned Mahler. Although this controversy erupted after Adorno had returned to Germany from America, it serves to point out the extreme positions around which the protagonists argued. The event that sparked the so-called Mahler controversy was a performance by the New York Philharmonic Orchestra in November of 1948 of Mendelssohn's *Ruy Blas*, Poulenc's *Concert champêtre,* and Mahler's Seventh Symphony. In the *New York Times* the day after the concert, Olin Downes made some stinging remarks:

Under ordinary circumstances we might say that the Poulenc music was witty and ingenious but rather superficial; with, however, some delightful folk-tunes, or tunes in the folk-manner, strewn through it. But the context of the program emphasized its distinctions. And as the Mahler symphony went on and on, from one dreary platitude and outworn euphemism to another, one regarded Poulenc with ever-increasing esteem. A composer who does not strut and roar and groan in moods of psychiatric conceit! . . . There is little that this writer cares to say on the subject of Mahler's symphony. . . . It is to our mind bad art, bad esthetic, bad, presumptuous and blatantly vulgar music. . . . After three-quarters of an hour of the worst and most pretentious of the Mahler symphonies, we found we could not take it, and left the hall. Chacun à son goût.[34]

The nontechnical language, the condescending tone, and above all the total dislike, some even called it hatred, of Mahler's music brought swift and heated public reaction. Several readers immediately took Downes to task for judging the work to be "bad music" without any specific references to the score. Another, who described himself as "getting down to Downes," wrote that since the critic was obviously enjoying being the center of attention and furthermore was clearly suffering from heartburn and ulcers, he should confine his criticisms to boogie-woogie and the blues.[35] At least two individuals wrote sympathetically to advise Downes that since the next week's performance of the Philharmonic was to include Mahler's Second Symphony, to be conducted by Bruno Walter, a former student and well-known Mahler champion, the critic should really find someone to take his place. One writer cautioned that by making such violent attacks on Mahler's music, Downes might force uncommitted listeners into the Mahler camp.

In the *New York Times* the following Sunday, November 21, 1948, Downes published parts of two letters that had been written to him about the Mahler review. The first came from a resident of New York who pointed out to Downes that he thought the role of the music critic was to relate how well the musicians played and interpreted a work, not to pass judgment on the music itself unless the work were very new and the audience in need of some insight. He added that he hoped Mr. Downes was polite enough to leave at the end of a movement so as not to disturb other members of the audience. Downes replied first that he saw music criticism's principal value in the discussion of music itself, not in the estimation of a performance. He voiced one of those important ideas that governed his own outlook and that underlies reception history today: that musical discussion should be not just for new works but also for works of the past, since musical values change with the passage of time. Then he turned to the specific work at hand, the Mahler Seventh. "No!" he fairly shouted from the page. "We didn't stay till the end of a movement. We jumped from our seat right in the middle of the third part, as if we had been shot from a cannon. Nerves could hold out no longer. We nearly bowled over an usher in our haste to get to the door." [36]

The other letter Downes published in the same article was marked, "for the defense." A reader from upstate New York wrote, "It is tough to strongly dislike something over the years and yet, with milquetoast diffidence be too inarticulate to voice resentments. How beautifully you have done that for me! I feel like the farmer who recognized that Emerson had some of his ideas. . . . It encourages one to hope that humanity has at last touched bottom in its insatiable pursuit of the tediously obvious."[37]

Numerous letters in Downes's correspondence support the second writer's opinion and reveal how politicized this musical matter really was. The music and film editor of the *Palestine Post* wrote to assure Downes of his one hundred percent support of the criticism of the "malaria malheur." And in one remarkable conglomeration of English puns, phonetic spellings, French phrases, and German exclamations, the letter of another reader emphasized the nationalistic element that many in the highly sensitive postwar atmosphere found implicit in a review in which the Frenchman Poulenc bested the German Mahler. This letter begins: "Bermit me, my dear Olin Downes, to boint out to you vy you are incabable of understanding Mahler, and I'm not afraid of telling you, dis is your malheur. . . . Vat is all dis Hokus-pokus, now you see-it, now-you-don't Heiligum mysticum compared to a Mahler?? Herr Gott! Welche eine offenbarung-Paradoxe von transparency while being solid! . . . I fervently hope that when Bruno Walter dies—and he surely will some day—that il soit enterrées ou enmerdées avec la partition de la 7me de Monsieur Malair [that he be buried or damned with the score of the Seventh Symphony of Mr. Bad Air]."[38]

In the midst of all this public Mahleria came forth none other than Arnold Schoenberg. Schoenberg addressed Downes a three-page letter on the subject of the Seventh Symphony. He staunchly defended Gustav Mahler, quoted musical themes from the symphony (notably from the movements Downes missed by his abrupt departure), and insinuated that Downes was a musical illiterate.[39] Downes printed this letter too in the *New York Times,* on December 12, 1948, prompting another barrage of correspondence at the *Times* office. "Re the Downes-Schoenberg exchange on Mahler," wrote one reader, "goody-goody." Others expressed similar sentiments about the Mahler war, such as "long may it rage."

The Mahler controversy is symptomatic of how difficult it has been to arrive at aesthetic judgments unclouded by nonmusical considerations in the twentieth century. In an age characterized by devastating wars that have often raged over issues of nationalism, political and personal tensions have frequently relegated music's value *qua* music to the background. At one time or another, the reputations not only of Mahler and Sibelius, but also of Wagner and Strauss, Prokofiev and Shostakovitch, Bartók and Schoenberg, have suffered. The controversy also demonstrates with exceptional clarity Downes's position on art. To that position Adorno's equally prejudiced way of thinking was philosophically opposed, and, with the exception of their mutual antipathy for Stravinsky, apparently irreconcilable. Olin Downes's dislike of Mahler and of some music of the Second Viennese composers stemmed partly from his personal dislike of music he called un-American, by which he seemed to mean music that failed to be wholesome or ennobling, or was not to his taste, and partly from the conviction he shared with Sibelius that great music must speak to the "man in the street." That he made exceptions to this view only makes him the more complex and interesting. (On hearing Schoenberg conduct *Pierrot lunaire,* he realized that "if conductors of our great symphony orchestras have come no nearer Schoenberg's real intentions . . . , then we have never heard the major Schoenberg scores."[40])

The composers, students, and friends of the Second Viennese school, among whom we find Adorno, were obviously not concerned with writing "American" music, and they found Mahler, with whose Jewish background a number of them were sympathetic, very much to their taste. Moreover, these individuals generally held to the view that Schoenberg himself stated forcefully and that his adherents disseminated widely: "If it is art, it is not for all, and if it is for all, it is not art."[41] There was a tendency among them to accept this axiom as a fundamental truth, admitting of no relativity. And yet while Adorno decried "relative" judgments, his own judgments were no more objective than any other man's:

> The universal objection that all criticism is relative, a mere special case of mentality whose misuse of the mind depreciates any mind as worthless does not say much. . . . [T]he spot of relativity that stains all judgments about art is not

sufficient to obscure the difference in rank between a Beethoven movement and a medley, between a symphony by Mahler and one by Sibelius, between a virtuoso and a bungler.[42]

Eventually, Adorno had moved to Los Angeles, not far from his idol Schoenberg. There the superficiality of Hollywood life only hardened his cynical views about American culture. He met Thomas Mann, who found in Adorno's writings material that would be essential to his novel *Doctor Faustus*. In 1949 Adorno decided to return to Germany. Active in German intellectual life, he became involved in the academic world's rift over the nature of sociology as a discipline and continued his polemics until the time of his death in 1969.

What was the effect of critics like Adorno and Virgil Thomson? In the concert hall, Sibelius's music was still heard often—even after Finland's political position vis-à-vis the Germans became a question. Statistics from Mueller's *Twenty-Seven Major American Symphony Orchestras* make that clear. The decline in the number of performances of his music after 1940 can be explained more readily as a reaction to the abundance of concerts that celebrated his birthday year.

Among the intelligentsia, however, these critics' opinions had a palpable impact. In the 1940s the intelligentsia were defined as a more or less homogeneous social group, characterized by a need to exhibit independent thought and behavior that debunked the existing hierarchy of values.[43] It is revealing to find that Thomson and Adorno, not usually considered part of the same social circle, not only shared the same opinions but also read one another's writings. Thomson called Adorno a "brilliant author" and spread Adorno's ideas far beyond the Frankfurt School's limited radius through his trenchant journalism. In one column entitled "Radio Examined," Thomson commended to his readers Adorno's evaluation of radio, summarizing in his own succinct manner what Adorno had expressed in turgid, obtuse, and often infuriating prose.[44] The two also corresponded. A letter Thomson addressed to Adorno in July 1942 shows that Adorno had sent the critic an article on Sibelius, presumably for inclusion in the *Herald Tribune*.[45] Thomson praised the ideas in the piece, but rejected it for its tone of indignation, which he feared would create more antagonism toward its author than toward Sibelius.

The attitudes of these men were perhaps inevitable. The sophisticates were driven to an independent position on Jean Sibelius—and that position could only be negative, given Sibelius's enormous popularity in the concert hall, the repeated playing of his music on radio, and the frequent appearance of his name in the pages of the *New York Times* and influential journals. Their opinions show up among others of their social group—composers, scholars, and critics. For example, Aaron Copland, another Paris-educated American, disparaged Sibelius's symphonies and relegated the composer to the world of the 1890s in his book *The New Music*.[46] And Thomson's successor at the *Herald Tribune,* Paul Henry Lang, professor of musicology at Columbia University, gives but passing mention to Sibelius in his huge single-volume compendium entitled *Music in Western Civilization*—and then speaks of the composer pejoratively. Such marginalizing of a major figure continued in American scholarship, reaching its most extreme in the exclusion of Sibelius altogether from an important work on twentieth-century music.[47]

While the American intelligentsia have often followed Thomson's lead, German critics even in comparatively recent years have tended to paraphrase Adorno when writing about Sibelius. Quoting from Peter Bernary's article "Can One Trace the Sibelius Myth?" Erik Tawaststjerna noted that such comments as the following sound decidedly like a rehash of the infamous "Glosse": "One takes the stagnant for Nature, the stammer for the archaic, the immobility for Nordic melancholy, the formal insufficiency for individuality. . . ."[48] The profound influence of German scholars on American musicology in the years following World War II may also account for some of the avenues by which the myth of Sibelius's superficiality has been perpetuated. Paradoxically, while American musicology has long held Adorno in something like contempt, many of its members have fully shared his negative attitude toward Jean Sibelius.

SEVEN

Sibelius and Posterity

There have been those [critics] who thought deeply: "What will posterity say of my opinion?" As if posterity were ever going to give a thought to the matter!* —Olin Downes, 1943

IN THE YEARS after World War II, the images of Sibelius presented by Theodor Adorno on the one hand and Olin Downes on the other calcified. Adorno continued his withering commentary, even after his return to Germany, making disparaging remarks about Sibelius in his *Philosophy of Modern Music* and in lectures delivered at Frankfurt University (and later published as *Introduction to the Sociology of Music*). Downes, meanwhile, although he seems to have grown tired of being identified primarily as Sibelius's champion,[1] still found occasion to feature Sibelius on the pages of the *New York Times,* especially at birthdays, and occasionally for sympathy: In 1950 he began to publicize Sibelius's failure to receive any royalties whatsoever from American performances of his works, the result of having a German publisher in time of war. Much more publicity and behind-the-scenes work eventually enabled Sibelius to receive a $10,000 Christmas gift of back royalties in the winter of 1954.[2]

Both men continued to view Stravinsky as a fraud. Making himself "the splinter in your eye [that] is the best magnifying-glass,"[3] Adorno lectured:

[Stravinsky's] sovereignty and his freedom combined with cynicism in regard to his own self-decreed order. All this is as grand bourgeois as the supremacy of taste, which in the end, simultaneously blind and selective, decides alone what is or is not to be done.

Järvenpää, September 5,1950.

Mr. Olin Downes,
New York 19,N.Y.

Dear Friend,
        My cordial thanks for your letter and
for the interest you have shown my "Kullervo".
Your beautiful words were dear to me particularly
because I still feel deeply for this youthful work
of mine. Perhaps that accounts for the fact that
I would not like to have it performed abroad during
an era that seems to me so very remote from the
spirit that "Kullervo" represents. Though I realise
that "Kullervo" even with its potential weaknesses
has its historical value at least within my own
production I am not certain that the modern public
would be able to place it in its proper perspective.
That was the reason for my negative answer to, among
others, the Polytech Chorus who asked for my permission
to perform it during their tour in America.
        Even in my own country I have declined to
have it produced with an exception made on my last
birthday. Condition here differ from those in the
great world and for that reason I have consented to
the request of the representatives of our government
to produce it on their concert the 8th december.
        I sincerely hope that you, dear friend, will

Letter from Jean Sibelius to Olin Downes, dated September 5, 1950, with the compos-er's extraordinary "old-man's" signature. Olin Downes Collection, Hargrett Rare Book and Manuscript Library. Reproduced by permission.

nderstand my point of view.

I also want you to know how grateful I am for your interest concerning my royalties. That I will never forget.

My whole family has been deeply moved about your kind words of our beloved Arvi and sends you their greetings.

All best wishes to you

Very sincerely yours

Old Friend

Jean Sibelius

By Hindemith, on the other hand, who for decades aped Stravinsky with conscientious craftsmanship, the great gambler is deprived of his savor. The classicistic formulas are taken literally, sought to be fused with the traditional language—with Reger's, little by little—and trimmed into a system of humbly serious bustle. It finally converges not only with musical academicism but with the dauntless positivity of quiet souls.[4]

Downes gave New Yorkers essentially the same message, only identifying Sibelius as the redeeming musical savior:

... It is Sibelius, not Stravinsky with his fake imitations of old masters, nor Hindemith with his modern revival of old counterpoint and pure instrumental forms, who is the neo-classic master in the music of today.[5]

From Paris six years later Downes again fulminated against Stravinsky, writing to Sibelius:

Here in Paris is much music, including a so-called "Masterpieces of the Twentieth C[en]tury Festival," supposed to represent the music of the "free nations" of the western world. There is however no symphony of Sibelius on these programs. There is no symphony by Vaughan Williams, no great work by the greatest composer of the two Americas, Heiter Villa-Lobos of Brazil, and by many many others. But three programs are given Stravinsky. One thing is still young and fresh and unspoiled in Paris—chi-chi![6]

Downes became deeply disturbed by America's course in these years when the actions of Senator Joseph McCarthy profoundly changed the atmosphere in America. On June 22, 1950, a group called American Business Consultants, founded by three former FBI agents for the purpose of publishing their weekly newsletter *Counterattack: The Newsletter of Fact on Communism,* distributed a small but damning book entitled *Red Channels: The Report of Communist Influence in Radio and Television.*[7] Its purpose was to reveal communist infiltration in publishing, radio, and the arts, to call attention to Americans who lent communism their support, and to discourage any association, unwitting or otherwise, with the Communist Party. One hundred fifty of the book's two hundred thirteen pages were devoted to an alphabetical list of actors, writers, composers, conductors, singers, dancers, and radio personalities, together with their allegedly communist activities. Aaron Copland was included for having composed a mass song "The First of May," among many other offenses, and for being involved with the American-Soviet Music Society. Leonard Bernstein made the list for his membership in the same organization as well as the National Negro Congress and the Civil Rights Congress. Ironically, in this "red list" of liberals, which included some two dozen musicians of the likes of Burl Ives and Pete Seeger, Lena Horne, and Marc Blitzstein—Olin Downes, so often viewed as a conservative, had the dubious distinction of receiving one of the longest entries. Running almost three full pages, the list of "subversive" activities in which Downes had participated included sending greetings to the Moscow Art Theatre, supporting communist bookshops, belonging to the advisory board of Films for Democracy, and sponsoring at least a dozen organizations from the Musicians Committee to Aid Spanish Democracy to the Civil Rights Congress. For many artists, the appearance of their names in *Red Channels* was devastating: contracts were canceled, invitations withdrawn. The *New York Times* received letters asking that Olin Downes be replaced. The paper, however, stood by its critic, not because of his politics, but because, its administrators maintained, he was a very good music critic.[8]

Downes, however, was not unaffected by McCarthyism and the fallout from *Red Channels*. In the spring of 1953 he applied for a renewal of his passport in order to travel to the Soviet Union for the purpose of collecting folk songs. The passport request was denied. The letter of denial from the U.S. Department of State alleged that he was a Communist, that he had shown consistent and prolonged adherence to the Communist Party line, and that he had belonged to some twenty-six subversive organizations, including the National Council of American-Soviet Friendship, the American Committee for Spanish Freedom, the American Committee for Yugoslav Relief, the World Congress for Peace, the American Labor Party, and Progressive Citizens of America.[9] Downes's disillusionment, like that of many Americans, was profound.

In these dark years Sibelius's music was a sustaining beacon. "You must surely know," Downes wrote the composer in the fall of 1951,

> that the greatest boon in life, the one sure refuge of the heart and soul, is great art. I, for one, believe less and less in man, and less and less also in God. I do not believe in the man in God. I only believe in the God in man. The God in man finds its greatest, most beautiful, purest and strongest expression in art. As you well know, no other music created in the world during my lifetime, contains this precious essence of art and of what we may call for lack of a better name the truth, than your music, which has sustained me through many a bitter hour.[10]

The appreciation was returned. In an undated letter to their mutual friend Yrjö Sjöblom, Sibelius wrote: "Relay my friendly greetings to Olin Downes,

Olin Downes the music critic. Photograph by Adrian Siegel, Philadelphia. Olin Downes Collection, Hargrett Rare Book and Manuscript Library. Reproduced by permission.

who has penetrated the innermost workings of my art and to whom I owe my reputation in America. What a contrast to our homespun midwives, in their superficiality." [11]

In the summer of 1953 Downes was covering music festivals in Denmark, Norway, and Sweden and was poised to arrive in Helsinki when he changed his plans and returned to New York. He wrote Sibelius from Stockholm on June 16, 1953, to express his great regret not to be able to hear Jussi Jalas conduct the Fourth Symphony, "my favorite of them all." He continued,

"But one great fact is more living than your very presence to me: your music. I am never away from there. I will hope to be back and to you next year. But what are years, or any of the realistic facts of life, beside art and eternity?" [12]

Downes never returned to Finland. In the fiercely hot August of 1955 he suffered a stroke on his way back to New York from lecturing at Brevard Music Center in North Carolina. After a ten-day hospitalization, during which he corrected the proofs of his last work, *Sibelius the Symphonist,* he died. Sibelius's last message came in the form of a telegram to Irene Downes:

> Heartfelt sympathy we loved him as a true friend and shall miss him deeply Aino and Jean Sibelius.

WITH THE DEATH OF OLIN DOWNES, Sibelius lost his most ardent champion. At first, opinion at the *New York Times* remained unchanged. Appraising "Sibelius at 90," Howard Taubman found the composer to be a "Finnish Epic . . . at once the national hero of his country and a creative giant whose music bestrides the modern world." [13] However, with the Carnegie Hall all-Sibelius concert in commemoration of Olin Downes, even the *Times*'s rhetoric began to tone down. At the *Herald Tribune,* Paul Henry Lang labeled the composer merely "genuine." To the special invitation to attend the concert, Virgil Thomson sent his regrets. And from the French quarter, René Leibowitz sent his via his book, *Jean Sibelius, le plus mauvais compositeur du monde.* Most telling of all, the title of *Time* magazine's article on Sibelius's ninetieth birthday showed how far things had gone since the days of worshipful adoration: "Nature Boy at 90," read the tongue-in-cheek headline. A picture of the composer at his piano was captioned, "The kudos is just for the crags." *Time*'s reporter stated that while Sibelius's music had seemed "revolutionary in the 1900s, daring in the teens, peculiar in the twenties, and old-fashioned in the thirties," it had ultimately suffered a kind of "honorable obsolescence." [14]

On September 20, 1957, Sibelius died at Ainola, and it seemed that all Finland attended his passing. Throngs lined the streets of Helsinki for the funeral procession to the Tuomari Kirkko in Senate Square. The reverence well congealed in the composer's old age now became engraved in Finnish granite. Hence the shock and even outrage in Finland on the publication, two years later, of the book *Jean Sibelius* by the American Harold E. Johnson. Johnson maintained that Karl Ekman's earlier biography of Sibelius, of which "it would not be inaccurate to regard Sibelius as its co-author," presented the composer's idealized view of himself from the lofty age of seventy: an isolated, embattled genius. Modesty, wrote Johnson, was a virtue conspicuously absent in Sibelius, as was gratitude—to his early supporters or to the Finnish people, to their government or to the various sources of the financial assistance he had enjoyed over the years. Moreover, Johnson charged that Sibelius had never used his influence to secure pensions or travel grants for younger composers as others had done for him. In Finland, where Johnson had lived for two years and made many contacts (although Sibelius never received him), the book was regarded as a scandal; but it fitted the mood in America. Howard Hanson praised Johnson's "objectivity," while Roland Gelatt entitled his *New York Times* review of the book "Not Beethoven's Successor." He noted that "Sibelius was a major composer of the second rank." [15]

Sibelius remained a hero in Finland, where letters addressed simply "Jean Sibelius, Finland" had regularly found him,[16] but in America the intelligentsia continued to treat Sibelius with a lofty superiority. In 1970 *New York Times* critic Harold C. Schonberg lowered Sibelius to the ranks of minor masters, an opinion he repeated in 1981.[17] His view was shared by another New York critic, Alan Rich, who compared hearing Sibelius in the morning to breakfasting on warm mattress stuffing.[18] Gilbert Chase, in writing *America's Music from the Pilgrims to the Present,* a book about music not only made by Americans but "continuously used by the people of the United States,"[19] made no mention of Sibelius. William Austin, in his *Music in the 20th Century,* did, but he considered the composer naive in his use of modal scales and "baffled by his own adventure."[20] And while Austin devoted seven pages to Sibelius, he gave Prokofiev, Hindemith, and Bartók entire chapters.

Two years before the publication of Austin's book, subscribers to the National Symphony Orchestra, asked to list which symphonies they wished to hear more frequently, voted those of Sibelius in second place (after Beethoven).[21] Nothing points up more dramatically the chasm separating "just listeners" from "intellectual concert-goers and musicians" than that vote. It confirmed to the "initiated" that they retained a mystical knowledge denied "the people," those unwashed masses who remained in the banal universe outside truly great music. It demonstrated clearly what observers of the music scene already knew: that a kind of musical elite had come to view music imbued with any sort of accessibility or spirituality as sentimental and thus contemptible. Antagonism to Romanticism, which Winthrop Sargeant reported circulated at every cocktail party in the early 1950s, brought strongly to mind Stravinskian notions of music as a purely intellectual art—something made up of aural sensations and mathematical relationships only, devoid of emotions and therefore incapable of imparting any. No doubt these ideas also drew sustenance from the enthusiasm of the avant-garde for the abstract serialism of Webern. Led by such figures as Pierre Boulez (who declared Schoenberg dead, however "difficult" his music) and Milton Babbitt (whose mathematical theorizing at Princeton created an American avant-garde), all too many composers in the years after World War II produced mathematically challenging but spiritually sterile compositions. Their audience dwindled, while Sibelius's did not.

It was his appeal to the "great unwashed" that especially rankled the elite. Many in twentieth-century America have subscribed to the high-modernist position that Adorno and others championed. To be validated as great, the contention goes, an artist has to produce music that is inaccessible to the man in the street. And as if being the works of a Romantic nationalist were not bad enough, Sibelius's *Finlandia* and *Valse triste* achieved an enduring popularity that cut across many backgrounds, nationalities, and tastes. These things, along with his cultivation of the no-longer-fashionable symphony, made Sibelius, in the context of the twentieth century, thrice damned.

The interconnectedness of events in the lives of people who have never met is a demonstrable if extraordinary truth, and the present story reminds us that not even great creative spirits are immune. Jean Sibelius's reputation in America hinged largely on three people, two of whom he never knew: Edwin Quigley, whose criminality profoundly shaped his son's outlook on life and art, and Virgil Thomson, whose musical and personal sympathies lay elsewhere. Only Olin Downes's survival of a bizarre airplane crash enabled him to promote Sibelius across the length and breadth of North America. Change any one factor and the story would be different, for while it is possible to consider larger sociological trends, in the final analysis it is individuals who shape the course of history.

For Olin Downes, Sibelius's music and personality filled a deep need—the wish for a hero, unfulfilled since the catastrophic downfall of Edwin Quigley. However comprehensible, Downes's insistence on interpreting the composer as hero and conquering Norseman in a century in which intellect was increasingly valued over emotion seemed more and more anachronistic as the years passed. So too did the intuitive manner in which he responded to music. And there was not only Downes's substance, there was his style. The evangelical tone, undoubtedly his mother's legacy; the grandiose prose with which he made Sibelius into an easily digestible, all-American pablum; and the polemics against such great twentieth-century figures as Mahler, the Second Viennese composers, and Stravinsky—all of this generated heated opposition to his own hero and surrounded Sibelius with a reactionary aura.

Virgil Thomson had a different end in view, or rather, a different axe to grind. None other than Arnold Schoenberg, in a letter to Olin Downes, expressed what happens when a composer turns critic: "Now finally to your question whether I believe composers are as a rule fair or unbiased critics of other composers: I think they are in first line fighters for their own musical ideas. The ideas of other composers are their enemies." [22] Virgil Thomson regarded himself first and foremost as a composer. However brilliantly expressed—and there is no question that his criticism was a literary landmark in music journalism—his repeated slashings at a man whom Americans had voted their favorite living composer suggest envy and anger, a wish that the embarrassing phenomenon of Sibelius would go away.

Yet neither Sibelius's Apostle nor the slings and arrows of a Virgil Thomson or a Theodor Adorno need influence our appreciation of the music of Sibelius. Although current thinking maintains that our own place in history and particular cultural expectations condition our response to a work of art, none of us is obligated to accept others' prejudices or to allow some earlier audience's response to condition our own. If "reception history" is to have any value at all to music (rather than, say, to sociology), it will be in separating received opinions from the musical work itself. By cutting through the agendas, the ideologies, and the polemics—and by weeding out the preconceptions that flourish there—we may hope to interact with Sibelius's music on its own terms, responding out of our own values. As Downes observed in the midst of the Mahler controversy, musical values change with the passage of time. Masterpieces are works to which we return year after year, generation after generation, each time discovering something worthwhile. Face to face with Sibelius's music, acquitted of having to prove our intellectual mettle by distrusting anything of beauty, it is difficult to imagine any but the self-serving denying the stunning originality of the seven symphonies or remaining indifferent to their extraordinary orchestral techniques, many of which have found their way into textbooks on orchestration. That his works have inspired and guided serious composers throughout all the years of the twentieth century is itself an important measure of their intrinsic worth. [23]

While it is true that the critics to a man succeeded in casting the cloud of conservativism over Sibelius, we must remember that today's experiment is tomorrow's orthodoxy; it was ever thus. The intelligentsia eventually denounced even Schoenberg for not being unconventional enough. Only a tragically early death exonerated Mahler from the same charge. And within the cloud of conservatism we may seek the proverbial silver lining. For the arguments thus engendered give us profound insight into the mentality of the twentieth century. They set forth clearly the conflicting positions of those who have supported and those who have denounced Sibelius. They show us how music's very essence has been called into question. And proof is offered of one of the last thoughts Olin Downes expressed to Jean Sibelius: "What are years or any of the realistic facts of life beside art and eternity?" Olin Downes would surely have been the first to endorse a rhetorical parallel to his question: What are critics or any of the realistic effects of their words beside the music of a Jean Sibelius?

Abbreviations used in the Notes

CC	Carbon Copy
CLS	Copy of a Letter Signed by
CF	Correspondence File
GU	Hargrett Library, University of Georgia, Athens, Georgia
JS	Jean Sibelius
LC	Library of Congress, Music Division, Washington, D.C.
LS	Letter Signed by
MS	Manuscript
OD	Olin Downes
SF	Subject File
T	Telegram

Notes to the Introduction

* "On Misreading Meanings into Sibelius," *New York Times,* October 24, 1937; repr. in *Olin Downes on Music,* ed. Irene Downes (New York: Simon & Schuster, 1957), 244.

1. LS Winthrop Sargeant to Olin Downes, July 17, [year unknown: after World War II], GU MSS 688, CF "Sargeant, Winthrop."

2. In 1984 Carl Dahlhaus remarked, "At the moment it is not even clear what, precisely, the history of musical reception means in the first place." His statement appeared in an essay entitled "Problems in Reception History" in *Foundations of Music History,* trans. J. B. Robinson (Cambridge, England: Cambridge University Press, 1983), 161. In that essay, the author articulates various difficulties of *Rezeptionsgeschichte* for the music scholar. Dahlhaus observes that the collecting of accounts and opinions about a musical work, together with evaluating and determining the accounts' relevance according to prevailing norms, constitutes what many consider to be a history of musical reception. Although reception history grew out of a desire to proceed along strictly empirical lines, any position taken by the

reception historian necessarily involves subjective choices and thus carries certain philosophical implications.

Although reception history, or reception theory as it is sometimes called, did not exist thirty years ago (at least as a formalized concept), the quotation from Olin Downes at the beginning of the Introduction (see p. 1) does express one of its tenets: In its "afterlife," a work of art acquires additional meanings; the work may also gradually disclose (to some ideal recipient) its "real," inner meaning. Reception theory arose in West Germany in the late 1960s among literary scholars in response to a methodological crisis in that discipline. Motivated by young intellectuals who questioned the assumptions, both hidden and otherwise, of their predecessors, reception theory subsequently influenced the interpretation of literature and art far beyond German literary scholarship. The movement was shaped by both social and intellectual events, and was especially associated with the University of Constance. Although many individuals were involved, Hans Robert Jauss and Wolfgang Iser were of particular importance in articulating for literary studies a theory that replaced existing approaches for interpreting artworks with models more in tune with twentieth-century aesthetics. The initiators of reception theory considered themselves to be involved in a "scientific revolution," a "paradigm shift," and they were conversant with Thomas S. Kuhn's *The Structure of Scientific Revolutions* (Chicago: University of Chicago Press, 1962; rev. 1970) and Hans-Georg Gadamer's *Wahrheit und Methode* (Tübingen: Mohr, 1965), which had a profound impact on text critics and historians. For further reading, see Robert C. Holub, *Reception Theory: A Critical Introduction* (London: Methuen, 1984).

3. Located in the Hargrett Rare Book and Manuscript Library, the Olin Downes papers, MSS 688, came to the University of Georgia in 1965. Pianist and scholar Jean Réti-Forbes described them in "The Olin Downes Papers," *The Georgia Review* 21 (1967): 165–71. Réti-Forbes, widow of Serbian composer and theorist Rudolf Réti, classified nearly two-thirds of the material, separating the documents into two large categories: a correspondence file, containing personal letters, and a subject file, containing clippings and other materials. Citations of the Downes papers thus bear the designation CF or SF to indicate which type of classification has been consulted. Réti-Forbes also prepared an annotated index of the correspondence file before her untimely death in 1972. The index, a model of its kind, has been microfilmed for wider consultation by Chadwyck-Healey, Inc., in the *National Inventory of Documentary Sources in the United States.*

4. Santeri Levas, *Sibelius, A Personal Portrait,* trans. Percy M. Young (Lewisburg, Pa.: Bucknell University Press, 1973), 28.

5. Erik Tawaststjerna, *Jean Sibelius* (Helsinki: Otava, 1965–1988). The volumes are complete only in Finnish, although volumes 1–4 were written originally in Swedish. Volumes 1–3 are available in English, translated by Robert Layton and compressed into two volumes (London: Faber & Faber, 1976, 1986). The somewhat

complex relationship among the editions is explained in a diagram in the translator's foreword to volume 2, page 11, of the English-language edition. The picture has been complicated further by the recent appearance of volumes 1, 2, and 3 in Swedish: *Jean Sibelius. Åren 1865–1893* (Helsinki: Söderström, 1992); *Jean Sibelius. Åren 1893–1904* (Helsinki: Söderström, 1993); and *Jean Sibelius. Åren 1904–1914* (Helsinki: Söderström,1991). The Swedish volumes are particularly welcome additions to the literature, not only because they preserve the author's original text but also because the quotations from the composer's otherwise unavailable diary (see Chapter 3) appear in their original language. Whenever the English translation has been used in the present book, it is cited as Tawaststjerna-Layton, and the reader should keep in mind that the volume and page numbers are not equivalent to those of either the Finnish or Swedish editions.

6. Otto Andersson, *Jean Sibelius i Amerika* (Åbo: Forlaget Brothers, [1955]). The Finnish translation, *Jean Sibelius Amerikassa* (Helsinki: Otava, 1960), has been used here.

7. Joseph Horowitz, *Understanding Toscanini* (New York: Alfred A. Knopf, 1987).

Notes to Chapter 1

* "The Sibelius Second," *Boston Post,* January 1, 1909; repr. in *Olin Downes on Music,* 13.

1. Useful one-volume biographies either written in or translated into English include Karl Ekman's *Jean Sibelius; His Life and Personality,* trans. Edward Birse (London: Alan Wilmer Ltd., 1936); Cecil Gray's *Sibelius* (London: Oxford University Press, 1931; repr., Westport, Conn.: Hyperion Press, 1979); Nils-Eric Ringbom's *Jean Sibelius, A Master and His Work,* trans. G. I. C. de Courcy (Norman: University of Oklahoma Press, 1954); Olin Downes's *Sibelius the Symphonist* (New York: The Philharmonic-Symphony Society of New York, 1956) [published posthumously]; Harold E. Johnson's *Jean Sibelius* (New York: Alfred A. Knopf, 1959); and Robert Layton's *Sibelius,* 4th ed., The Master Musicians Series (New York: Schirmer, 1993).

2. Downes described Christian thus in a lengthy biographical article entitled "Jean Sibelius" written for Oscar Thompson, editor of the *International Cyclopedia of Music and Musicians.* The critic first wrote the article in 1938, at which time it appeared in the *Cyclopedia*'s fifth edition; the essay has continued to appear in every subsequent volume, including the current, eleventh, edition. Sibelius's objection was made in a letter to Yrjö [George] Sjöblom, a Finnish friend on the staff of the *New York Times.* An undated draft in the composer's hand remains with the Sibelius Family Archives in the National Archives of Finland. This letter may have never come to Downes's attention.

3. *International Cyclopedia of Music and Musicians,* 5th ed., s.v. "Sibelius."

4. "Sibelius's Ancestry," *New York Times,* February 7, 1932.

5. Ibid.

6. An English translation of the *Kalevala* that preserves Lönnrot's poetic meter is that of W. F. Kirby, published in 1907 in the Everyman's Library. This translation has been reissued, with an introduction by M. A. Branch, as *Kalevala, The Land of Heroes* (London: Athlone Press, 1985).

7. Adolf Paul remembers his friend thus in "Zwei Fennonenhäuptlinge: Sibelius/Gallén," *Deutsch-Nordisches Jahrbuch für Kulturaustausch und Volkskunde 1914* (Jena: Eugen Diederichs, 1914), 114.

8. Tawaststjerna-Layton, *Sibelius* 1:89.

9. Among the various accounts of Finnish history, William A. Wilson's *Folklore and Nationalism in Modern Finland* (Bloomington: Indiana University Press, 1976) is particularly useful and the basis for the account given here.

10. Examples of the art of the "Finnish Renaissance" were displayed in an exhibition entitled Dreams of a Summer Night. Scandinavian Painting at the Turn of the Century at the Hayward Gallery, London, July 10 to October 5, 1986. This quotation is taken from the catalogue of that exhibition, edited under the same title and produced for the Arts Council of Great Britain by Leena Ahtola-Moorhouse, Carl Tomas Edam, and Birgitta Schreiber (Uddevalla, Sweden: Bohusläningens Boktryckeri AB, 1986), 108.

11. Ibid.

12. The painting, completed in 1894, is in private hands in Helsinki. Among other places, it has been reproduced in *Dreams of a Summer Night,* 109.

13. Tawaststjerna-Layton, *Sibelius* 1:97. The recently published Swedish edition of volume 1 contains a new supplement entitled "Larin Paraske and Rune Songs," 1:262–72. A statue of the remarkable Paraske stands today in the park beside Helsinki's Finlandia Hall.

14. For a slightly different perspective on this point and an illuminating comparison of *Kullervo* with Wagner's *Siegfried* and Stravinsky's *Oedipus Rex,* see Eero Tarasti's *Myth and Music. A Semiotic Approach to the Aesthetics of Myth in Music, Especially That of Wagner, Sibelius and Stravinsky* (The Hague: Mouton Publishers, 1979), 253–54.

15. For a discussion of the unseemly personal ambitions among the composer's contemporaries that contributed to the awarding of this stipend, see Tawaststjerna-Layton, *Sibelius* 1:190–94.

16. *New York Times,* November 24, 1940; repr. as "Schoenberg Himself Conducts *Pierrot lunaire*" in *Olin Downes on Music,* 295.

Notes to Chapter 2

* Publicity flyer, GU MSS 688, SF "Downes, Olin, Biographical Material."

1. The story broke in the *New York Times* on January 19, 1895; additional articles appeared January 20, 22, 23, and 29.

2. The Downes family history has been documented in Jacob Bentley Graw, ed., *Life of Mrs. S. J. C. Downs; or, Ten Years at the Head of the Woman's Christian Temperance Union of New Jersey* (Camden, N.J.: Gazette Printing and Publishing House, 1892). It is available on microfilm in the series *History of Women,* no. 4252 (New Haven, Conn.: Research Publications, 1975).

3. Ibid., 128.

4. Ibid., 148.

5. There are other parallels between Downes and the man whose name he bore: Downes, like Olin, would be married twice. Whereas Downes would be among the first to champion Sibelius and education through music appreciation, Olin, president of two pioneer Methodist colleges, was one of the first to champion theological education. And a little more than a century before the critic's papers came to the University of Georgia, an institution with which he had virtually no personal connection in his lifetime, Stephen Olin, born in Vermont, spent a period of seven years on the University of Georgia faculty as a professor of "ethics and belles-lettres." See *The Life and Letters of Stephen Olin,* 2 vols. (New York: Harper & Bros., 1853).

6. *Life of Mrs. S. J. C. Downs,* 10.

7. Edward Downes (Sarah Jane Corson's great-grandson), interview with the author, September 15, 1991.

8. *The New Democracy* was a study of social problems in modern society in light of their moral and philosophical backgrounds. This was not her only published work. Earlier, Mrs. Downes had published a poem, *The Sistine Madonna* (n.p.: German-American Publishing Co., [ca. 1901]).

9. Quoted in *The New Democracy,* 295: 37.

10. Louise's grandson, Edward Downes, recalls that on one occasion, finding the adult Olin ensconced in his study with a friend and a drink, Louise emerged shaking her fist to accuse Marion of leading her precious boy down the path to evil.

11. Olin Downes, *Symphonic Broadcasts* (Binghamton, N.Y.: Dial Press, 1931), v.

12. Obituary, *New York Times,* August 30, 1940.

13. Particularly valuable here has been the chapter "The Boston Classicists" in Gilbert Chase's *America's Music from the Pilgrims to the Present,* rev. 2d ed. (New York: McGraw-Hill, 1966), 365–84 et passim. Unless otherwise noted, I have relied on Chase's second edition (rather than the third) for its superior discussion of the Bostonians.

14. Henry James, *The Bostonians* (Boston: 1886; repr. ed., with an Introduction and Notes by R. D. Gooder, Oxford: Oxford University Press, 1984), 13.

15. Chase, *America's Music,* 392.

16. Alan Howard Levy, *Musical Nationalism: American Composers' Search for Identity,* Contributions in American Studies, no. 66 (Westport, Conn.: Greenwood Press, 1983), 23–24. This work is a valuable source on the political climate of the period and its relationship to America's music.

17. Edward Downes, "The Taste Makers: Critics and Criticism," in *One Hundred Years of Music in America,* ed. Paul Henry Lang (New York: Schirmer, 1961), 236.

18. *New York Times,* December 24, 1939.

19. Selections from Hale's writings, together with biographical information, may be found in *Great Concert Music: Philip Hale's Boston Symphony Programme Notes,* ed. John N. Burk (New York: Garden City Publishing Co., 1939); and in John C. Swan, ed. and comp., *Music in Boston: Readings from the First Three Centuries* (Boston: Trustees of the Public Library of the City of Boston, 1977), 87–94. Additional observations and anecdotes are incorporated here from the typescript by John Bradford Gross, "Philip Hale: Gentleman Critic," GU MSS 688, SF "Hale, Philip re."

20. John N. Burk, *Great Concert Music,* vi.

21. Ibid., 1.

22. Among other places Downes's column in the *New York Times,* "As the Years Pass, Bach Grows Mightier," March 17, 1935, expresses the idea that much of what Bach wrote was mediocre. He did, however, admire a great deal of Bach's music.

23. *Boston Herald,* January 6, 1907.

24. The similarities between Hale's writing in such places as the *Boston Herald* of January 6, 1907, and Olin Downes's references thirty-two years later in the *New York Times,* December 24, 1939, seem too close to be coincidental. Downes, like Hale before him, wrote of "the chants and the sullen rhythms which are of those who dance with knives drawn," and described the orchestra, which "girds its loins and rises in Berserk fury."

25. In 1916, after another performance of Sibelius's First, Hale wrote: "The workmanship suggests a well-trained musician who disdaining the smug, conventional thoughts and expression of his colleagues turns toward the conservatory and the professors and exclaims with Whitman:

> The spotted hawk swoops by and
> accuses me—he complains of
> my gab and by loitering.
> I too am not a bit tamed—
> I too am untranslatable:
> I sound my barbaric yawp over
> the roofs of the world."

("Symphony Orchestra's Fifth Concert," *Boston Herald,* November 18, 1916.)

26. Edward Burlingame Hill, *Modern French Music* (Boston: Houghton Mifflin, 1924).

27. Levy, *Musical Nationalism,* 25.

28. "The Art of Romain Rolland," *New York Times,* January 7, 1945.

29. Olin Downes Lectures, GU MSS 688, microfilm, reel 1.

30. *Boston Post,* January 1, 1909; repr. in *Olin Downes on Music,* 14.

31. *Boston Post,* March 2, 1907; repr. in *Olin Downes on Music,* 5.

32. Joe L. Dubbert, *A Man's Place: Masculinity in Transition* (Englewood Cliffs, N.J.: Prentice-Hall, 1979), 31–32.

33. Downes, *Sibelius the Symphonist,* 40–41.

34. Rupert Hughes, *Contemporary American Composers* (Boston: L. C. Page, 1900), 213.

35. Preston William Slosson, *The Great Crusade and After 1914–1928,* vol. 12 of *A History of American Life,* ed. Arthur M. Schlesinger and Dixon Ryan Fox (New York: Macmillan, 1930), 287–319.

36. *Boston Post,* December 15, 1912, and February 7, 1913.

37. "Memories of Olin Downes," *Boston Globe,* August 27, 1955, GU MSS 688, SF "Downes, Olin—Biographical Material."

38. Ibid.

39. This story is related by Howard Taubman in "Olin Downes—I Worked with Him," GU MSS 688, SF "Olin Downes—Biographical Material."

40. Downes later boasted that there had been no professional musicians in his family, thus enabling him to approach music from the standpoint of the man in the street (GU MSS 688, SF, "Downes, Olin—Biographical Material"). There is a striking parallel between Downes's attitude and that of his famous New England contemporary Charles Ives. Both men believed in the vitality of the music of the people, and both abhorred music that smacked of prettiness and preciousness. Both seemed to have taken to heart the advice of the senator from Indiana, Albert Beveridge, who, in a book published in 1906 entitled *The Young Man and the World,* advised the American male to "be a man," to "get out of the exclusive atmosphere of your *perfumed* surroundings . . . [to] mingle with those who toil and sweat" (quoted by Joe L. Dubbert in "Progressivism and the Masculinity Crisis," in *The American Man,* ed. Elizabeth H. Pleck and Joseph H. Pleck [Englewood Cliffs, N.J.: Prentice-Hall, 1980], 311).

41. Walt Whitman, *Leaves of Grass,* Comprehensive Reader's Edition, ed. Harold W. Blodgett and Sculley Bradley (n.p.: New York University Press, 1965), 12–13.

42. Downes eulogized Baermann in his *Boston Post* column, March 23, 1913.

43. Homer Norris (1860–1920) studied in Paris and in 1896 published a book on theory entitled *Practical Harmony on a French Basis.* John Patton Marshall (1877–1941) had studied with Chadwick as well as MacDowell. He eventually became dean of Boston University's College of Music and published various teaching manuals, including one entitled *Syllabus of Music Appreciation.* As Downes did later, Marshall lectured on music at the Harvard Summer School. William Clifford Heilman (1877–1946) was graduated from Harvard in 1900 and five years later became a member of its music faculty. He also studied in Europe, with both Rheinberger and Widor.

44. GU MSS 688, SF, "Olin Downes—Biographical Material."

45. *Current Biography 1943*, s.v. "Downes, Olin."

46. *Boston Post*, November 29, 1908; repr. in *Olin Downes on Music*, 12.

47. Quoted in C. N. Stavrou, *Whitman and Nietzsche: A Comparative Study of Their Thought* (Chapel Hill: University of North Carolina Press, 1964), 64.

48. Whitman, *Leaves of Grass*, 504.

49. Stavrou, *Whitman and Nietzsche*, 26.

50. Downes, *Symphonic Broadcasts*, ix.

51. "Impressions of Sibelius," commissioned by the New York Philharmonic-Symphony Society and printed in the society's program notes for 1945–46.

52. The Allen A. Brown Collection in the Boston Public Library still possesses these and other Sibelius scores. Although the clippings in each are not always identified, they form a useful repository of the reception history of each work.

53. In its melodic contour, the theme somewhat resembles the Finnish folksong *Iso lintu*.

54. Olin Downes, *Sibelius*, ed. and trans. Paul Sjöblom with the assistance of Jussi Jalas (Helsinki: Otava, 1945). Downes's original English introduction has been lost, but a translation from the Finnish back into English by Paul Sjöblom may be found in GU MSS 688, SF "Sibelius, Jean." The quotation cited is from page 4 of that translation.

55. Cecil Gray, *Sibelius: The Symphonies* (London: 1935; reprint, Freeport, N.Y.: Books for Libraries Press, 1970), 17–18; Levas, *Sibelius*, 88.

56. *Boston Post*, January 1, 1909; repr. in *Olin Downes on Music*, 12. "Sibelius' Symphony 'Gloriously Rude'" was the headline for Downes's *Boston Post* review of the work on January 7, 1911.

57. Laning Humphrey, "Olin Downes, Radio Interpreter," *Christian Science Monitor*, May 16, 1931. The music critic was also a boxing enthusiast; during his New York years Downes slipped away as often as possible to Madison Square Garden. (Few knew that, for all his 210-pound bulk, Downes had for a time taken lessons in classical ballet—the better to understand the *Ballets russes* on its first trip to America.) Downes reportedly enjoyed sparring with his musical guests in the foyer of his New York apartment, reliving the Jack Dempsey moves of the evening before, and Howard Taubman relates that when one obnoxious reporter at the *Boston Post* ridiculed his interest in music once too often, Downes invited him outside and began swinging.

58. Olin Downes, "Jean Sibelius," *New Music Review and Church Music Review* 13 (July 1914): 358.

Notes to Chapter 3

* Jean Sibelius to the Danish paper *Politiken*. Quoted in Tawaststjerna-Layton, *Sibelius*, 2: 280.

1. Tawaststjerna reports Sibelius's reaction upon seeing the score of *Mona* (Tawaststjerna-Layton, *Sibelius* 2:243), which Parker delivered during the compos-

er's visit to New England. *Mona* possesses at least an atmospheric connection to the music of Sibelius, even if its chromatic harmony is far more reminiscent of Wagner. Sibelius may have thought that Parker borrowed his opening to *The Swan of Tuonela*, which had also been intended as the prelude to an opera, *The Building of the Boat* (only later did it become one of the four tone poems in the *Lemminkäinen Suite*). Tawaststjerna makes the point that Sibelius's *Swan* itself shows unmistakable similarities to Wagner's *Lohengrin* and *Tristan*. See Tawaststjerna-Layton, *Sibelius* 2:171–72.

2. Biographical information on the Stoeckels may be found in Carl Stoeckel, "Some Recollections of the Visit of Sibelius to America in 1914," *Scandinavian Studies* 43 (1971): 53–88.

3. These letters are in MSS 32, Yale Music Library. See LS Carl Stoeckel to Horatio Parker, August 18, 1913, and LS Jean Sibelius to Horatio Parker, March 10, 1914, March 11, 1914, and April 29, 1914. Parker was exceptionally active in inviting composers and conductors to New England. As early as 1901 he had asked Richard Strauss to appear at the Yale Bicentennial and to receive an honorary degree. Strauss declined.

4. LS Carl Stoeckel to Olin Downes, April 27, 1914, GU MSS 688, CF "Stoeckel, Carl."

5. Oddly enough, the exact date of the composer's arrival is unclear. The confusing situation is explained in Stoeckel, "Some Recollections," 55 n. 2.

6. Bengt de Törne, *Sibelius: A Close-Up* (Boston: Houghton Mifflin, 1938), 30–31.

7. Olin Downes, "Jean Sibelius," *New Music Review,* 444.

8. "Downes on Sibelius/Ovation to Sibelius," Stoeckel Family Papers, Misc. MS 247, Yale Music Library.

9. *Musical America,* June 13, 1914, 3–4. The article is in fact the essay called "Downes on Sibelius/Ovation to Sibelius," preserved among the Stoeckel papers.

10. LS Horatio Parker to the Committee on Honorary Degrees, Yale Music Library, MS 3, Box 1, April 8, 1914. I would like to thank Gayle Sherwood for drawing my attention to this document, which she found in the course of her work on Charles Ives.

11. Stoeckel, "Some Recollections," 81 n. 35.

12. LS Jean Sibelius to Carl Stoeckel, Yale Music Library, MSS 32, Box 27, November 8, 1914.

13. So he wrote his friend Axel Carpelan on June 5, 1914; quoted in Tawaststjerna-Layton, *Sibelius* 2:174.

14. Martin Wegelius, *Länsimaisen musiikin historia pääpiirteissään kristinuskon alkuajoista meidän päivimme,* trans. [from Swedish] Axel Tornudd (Helsinki: K. E. Holm, 1904). A short but relevant passage is quoted in Tawaststjerna-Layton, *Sibelius* 2:49, 50.

15. From a review by Adolf Paul, quoted in Karl Ekman, *Jean Sibelius,* 152.

16. Ekman, *Jean Sibelius,* 155.

17. Tawaststjerna-Layton, *Sibelius* 2:24. Tawaststjerna gives excerpts from reviews of the 1905 concert, as does Ekman, *Jean Sibelius,* 166–68. Busoni, who arranged these concerts, had been Sibelius's teacher and friend since the latter's student days at the Music Institute in Helsinki. Busoni proved himself a steadfast supporter and was almost certainly the most important advocate for Sibelius in Germany in the early twentieth century.

18. *Neue Zeitschrift für Musik* 72 (January 18, 1905): 73.

19. Quoted in Karl Ekman, *Jean Sibelius,* 247.

20. Antecedents to Sibelius's Third Symphony may well include Mozart's Symphony no. 38 (*Prague*), which is also a three-movement work that treats the sonata form in a somewhat unorthodox manner. Sibelius's opening theme even bears a certain resemblance to Mozart's first *allegro* theme in its shape and rhythmic design.

21. Downes, *Sibelius the Symphonist,* 25.

22. Ibid., 26.

23. *Christian Science Monitor,* November 25, 1952.

24. Downes, *Sibelius the Symphonist,* 25.

25. Tawaststjerna-Layton, *Sibelius* 2:92–94. The matter is also dealt with by James Hepokoski in *Sibelius: Symphony No. 5* (Cambridge: Cambridge University Press, 1993). I would like to thank Professor Hepokoski for sharing his manuscript with me before its publication.

26. There are two volumes of the diary (Dagbok 1 and Dagbok 2). The first begins in 1909; the second in mid-1914. Both belong to the National Archives of Finland in the collection called the Sibelius Family Archives. Closed by the family to researchers in 1990, the volumes had earlier been made available to Erik Tawaststjerna, who quotes from them extensively.

27. Tawaststjerna-Layton, *Sibelius* 2:160.

28. Ibid., 2:161.

29. LS Sibelius to Rosa Newmarch, quoted in Tawaststjerna-Layton, *Sibelius* 2:172.

30. Levas, *Sibelius,* 77–78.

31. "A New and Strange Sibelius Symphony," *Musical America,* March 8, 1913, 26.

32. Robert Schumann, *Gesammelte Schriften über Musik und Musiker,* 5th ed., ed. Martin Kreisig (Leipzig: Breitkopf & Härtel, 1914), 1:111.

33. Sibelius's funeral, which took place September 30, 1957, in Helsinki's Tuomarikirkko on Senate Square, was a national event. The music included the Fourth Symphony's slow movement together with *In memoriam* and other works.

34. de Törne, *Sibelius, A Close-Up,* 47.

35. Tawaststjerna-Layton, *Sibelius* 2:159.

36. Some of the critical reactions to the Fourth Symphony have been reported

by Tawaststjerna-Layton in *Sibelius* 2:169–73 and by Harold E. Johnson, *Jean Sibelius,* 145. See also the *Sunday Times,* October 6, 1912.

37. *Die Musik* XI/21 (August 1912): 172.

38. *Die Musik* XIII/4 (November 1913): 195–206.

39. See *Musical America,* March 8, 1913, 26; the *Boston Advertiser,* November 14, 1914; and the *Boston Herald,* November 3, 1917.

40. "A New Finnish Symphony," *Boston Post,* August 4, 1912. In a later article Downes claimed that Sibelius told him the symphony had been composed in a week! The composer's diary proves this to be manifestly untrue.

41. "Sibelius' Fourth by Symphony," *Boston Post,* October 25, 1913; repr. in *Olin Downes on Music,* 45–46.

42. Compare "Sibelius' Fourth by Symphony" with *Sibelius the Symphonist,* 26.

43. Tawaststjerna-Layton reports these frustrations in *Sibelius* 2:205, 210, 213, 218, 231–32, 242.

44. Ibid., 218, 261–62.

45. Ibid., 271.

46. *Boston Post,* October 25, 1913.

47. "Sibelius Symphony Features," *Boston Post,* November 14, 1914.

48. "News of Music," *Boston Transcript,* October 27, 1913.

49. *Musical America,* March 15, 1913, 14.

50. Tawaststjerna-Layton, *Sibelius* 2:271.

51. LS Jean Sibelius to Carl Stoeckel, Misc. MS 247, November 8, 1914. This lengthy and cordial handwritten letter is far more revealing than any of Sibelius's communications to Olin Downes, probably because the composer was writing in German, a language more comfortable for him than English.

52. See Tawaststjerna, *Sibelius* 4 (Finnish edition), plates following p. 176, and Hepokoski, *Sibelius, Symphony No. 5,* 32.

53. *Boston Post,* June 22, 1913.

54. "Jean Sibelius," *New Music Review,* 358.

55. "Schoenberg's Five Pieces for Orchestra in Boston," *Boston Post,* December 19, 1914; repr. in *Olin Downes on Music,* 47–48.

56. *New York Times,* April 23, 1930; repr. in *Olin Downes on Music,* 163–64.

57. "Sibelius no. 4: Its English History," in Ernest Newman, *Essays from the World of Music. Essays from "The Sunday Times,"* comp. Felix Aprahamian (London: 1956; repr., New York: Da Capo Press, 1978), 128–29.

58. Arnold Bax, *Farewell, My Youth* (London: 1943; repr., Westport, Conn.: Greenwood Press, 1970), 62.

59. Some background to this sorry tale may be found in Irving Lowens, "L'affaire Muck, a Study in War Hysteria (1917–18)," *Musicology* 1 (1945–47): 265–74; and James J. Badal, "The Strange Case of Dr. Karl Muck, Who Was Torpedoed by *The Star-Spangled Banner* During World War I," *High Fidelity,* October 1970, 55–60.

60. In an unsigned article with the headline "Finnish Composer Coming: Jean

Sibelius to Be Professor in Eastman School of Music, Rochester," *New York Times,* January 25, 1921.

61. In her biography of her father, Sibelius's great friend Granville Bantock, Myrrha Bantock reports that Sibelius kept his head shaved. (See *Granville Bantock: A Personal Portrait* [London: J. M. Dent, 1972], 126.) Her observation is borne out by contemporary photographs, such as those reproduced by Erkki Salmenhaara in *Jean Sibelius* (Helsinki: Kustannusosakeyhtiö Tammi, 1984), 357, 380, 381, and 395. Pictures taken in 1919 and 1923 show the shaved head, yet in pictures from 1924 the composer has hair again, an indication that Sibelius vacillated on his choice of hairstyle as on so many other choices. Hair loss probably contributed to his decision. In a diary entry on February 15, 1918, recounted in Tawaststjerna's *Sibelius* 4, Sibelius writes, "[I'm] of two minds about my hair. Should I get rid of all the tufts and look like a caricature of Nero + provincial actor?" By the 1930s the decision (and perhaps the hair loss) was irreversible, and a Sibelius image had been ingrained in the public consciousness. The image and its connotations persist. As recently as August 22, 1992, an article in the monthly supplement to *Helsingin sanomat* about the current fashion of shaved heads among both male and female Swedish models mentions that by shaving his head, Sibelius gained credibility and "Finland got her master composer."

62. See Hans Keller's comments on the quartet as symphony in "The New in Review: Symphony and Sonata Today—II," *Music Review* 22 (1961): 172.

63. Paul Rosenfeld, "Sibelius," *New Republic,* December 14, 1918, 189; repr. in *Musical Portraits, Interpretations of Twenty Modern Composers* (London: Kegan Paul, 1922), 245–55.

64. "Sibelius' Third Symphony," *Boston Post,* March 27, 1921.

65. Ibid.

66. "D'Indy Calls Our Musical Taste 'Feverish'—Olin Downes' Comment," *Boston Post,* April 9, 1922.

67. Quoted in Lucien Price, "Portrait of Sibelius at Järvenpää," in *We Northmen* (Boston: Little, Brown, 1936), 359.

68. *Boston Post,* April 8, 1922, and April 9, 1922.

69. Levas, *Sibelius,* 75.

70. See Brian Coghlan's enlightening discussion of *Everyman* in *Hofmannsthal's Festival Dramas* (Cambridge: Cambridge University Press, 1964), Ch. 1 and 2.

71. Ibid., 54.

72. Quoted in Ekman, *Jean Sibelius,* 193.

73. Ibid., 217.

74. Letter of May 20, 1918; reproduced in facsimile in Ekman, *Jean Sibelius,* 238–39.

75. Quoted by Dika Newlin, "Secret Tonality in Schoenberg's Piano Concerto," *Perspectives of New Music* 13 (1974–75): 137.

76. Letter of May 20, 1918.

77. Quoted in Ekman, *Jean Sibelius,* 239.

78. Ibid., 247.

79. Levas, *Sibelius,* 67.

80. "Music," *New York Times,* December 27, 1926; see also Downes's comments in the same paper on December 31, 1926, and November 18, 1932.

81. Lionel Pike, *Beethoven, Sibelius and "The Profound Logic"* (London: Athlone Press and University of London, 1978), 213.

Notes to Chapter 4

* *New York Times,* June 15, 1924; repr. in *Olin Downes on Music,* 90.

1. LS OD April 18, 1927, GU MSS 688, CF "Sibelius, Jean." See Appendix A, no. 1.

2. Quoted in Howard Taubman, Preface, *Olin Downes on Music,* xi. The invitation to join the *New York Times* coincided with the critic's growing frustration at the *Boston Post.* In November 1923, Olin Downes had sent a letter of resignation to C. B. Carberry, the *Post*'s managing editor: "I am told I am expected to go to the opera tomorrow night and write an extensive and favorable article about Miss Gladys Axman's performance. This I refuse to do. . . ." (LS OD, November 23, 1924 [*sic*], GU MSS 688, CF *"Boston Post"*). Subsequent letters in the same file reveal that this was not the first time Downes had felt pressured by Carberry to write a favorable review; when the Axman situation arose, Downes felt he had had enough. *Post* publisher E. A. Grozier responded that Downes was being childish, even though he considered him the best judge of music in Boston. There were also words exchanged over a sum of $3,000 loaned to Downes by the *Post;* it had variously been called a debt, then earnings, then again a debt.

3. "Music of the Month: From Stravinsky to Sibelius," *North American Review,* January 1922, 117–21.

4. "New York Welcomes *Le Sacre du printemps,*" *New York Times,* February 1, 1924; repr. in *Olin Downes on Music,* 80–82. The orchestra was the Boston Symphony.

5. "Paris Preview of the Boston Symphony's New Conductor," *New York Times,* June 15, 1924; repr. in *Olin Downes on Music,* 90. The nontraditional *Symphonies of Wind Instruments,* an "austere ritual" dedicated to the memory of Debussy, came to signify neoclassicism, a term applied to it in a review of 1923. See Glenn Watkins, *Soundings: Music in the Twentieth Century* (New York: Schirmer, 1988), 315.

6. See "Performances of New Music in New York" in Barbara Mueser, "The Criticism of New Music in New York: 1919–1929" (Ph.D. diss., City University of New York, 1975), 224–27.

7. "Stravinsky Visits America at Forty-three," *New York Times,* February 1, 1925; repr. in *Olin Downes on Music,* 95–98.

8. "Stravinsky Introduces His Concerto . . . ," *New York Times,* February 6, 1925; repr. in *Olin Downes on Music,* 100.

9. Gilbert Chase, *America's Music,* rev. 2d ed., 559.

10. *New York Times,* December 6, 1925.

11. T JS, GU MSS 688, CF "Sibelius, Jean." See Appendix A, no. 4. Tawast-stjerna, in *Sibelius* 5:273, reports a diary entry on June 19 mentioning a hopeful message telegraphed to Downes in Paris. This message is not found with the correspondence in GU MSS 688. Downes may have mislaid or discarded it while traveling. In later years Downes would chide himself for his carelessness with correspondence; he particularly regretted discarding a letter from Rachmaninoff in which the composer discussed his *Isle of the Dead.*

12. The embarrassingly full document is given in its entirety in Appendix A, no. 5.

13. "How Downes Came Up," *Times Talk,* vol. vii, no. 5 (January 1954), 5.

14. LS OD, September 30, 1927, GU MSS 688, CF "Sibelius, Jean." See Appendix A, no. 8.

15. *Dagbok* 2, September 12, 1927.

16. Jean Sibelius, conversation with Paul Sjöblom, summer 1933. The composer described Downes with the word *ilmestys,* meaning "revelation" or "miracle."

17. LS OD, August 9, 1929, GU MSS 688, CF "Sibelius, Jean." See Appendix A, no. 15.

18. LS OD, July 18, 1928, GU MSS 688, CF "Sibelius, Jean." See Appendix A, no. 10.

19. See Appendix A, nos. 9, 23, and 37.

20. LS OD, June 22, 1930, GU MSS 688, CF "Sibelius, Jean." See Appendix A, no. 17.

21. Ibid.

22. LS OD, June 18, 1932, GU MSS 688, CF "Sibelius, Jean." See Appendix A, no. 25.

23. Ibid.

24. *New York Times,* November 18, 1932.

25. The incident was reported in several articles in the *New York Times,* December 28, 29, and 31, 1937.

26. According to Harold E. Johnson, *Jean Sibelius,* 208.

27. Biographical sources on Koussevitzy include Harry Ellis Dickson, *"Gentlemen, More Dolce Please!" (Second Movement): An Irreverent Memoir of Thirty-Five Years in the Boston Symphony Orchestra* (Boston: Beacon Press, 1974); Hugo Leichtentritt, *Serge Koussevitzky, The Boston Symphony Orchestra and the New American Music* (Cambridge, Mass.: Harvard University Press, 1946); Harold C. Schonberg, *The Great Conductors* (New York: Simon & Schuster, 1967), 300–308; and David Wooldridge, *Conductors' World* (New York: Praeger Publishers, 1970), 137–52.

28. "Paris Preview of the Boston Symphony's New Conductor," *New York Times* June 15, 1924; repr. in *Olin Downes on Music,* 86–87.

29. Dickson, *"Gentlemen, More Dolce, Please!"* 43, 47.

30. Ibid., 46.

31. Ibid., 51.

32. Ibid., 49.

33. Ibid., 47.

34. Actually, his origins seemed mysterious only when one tried to wrest them from Stokowski. The facts are well documented, and many of them are incorporated into the copiously detailed biography by Oliver Daniel, *Stokowski, A Counterpoint of View* (New York: Dodd, Mead, 1982). The biographical material here is based on Daniel's account, together with information from Harold C. Schonberg's *The Great Conductors,* 309–16, and Paul Robinson's *Stokowski* (n.p.: Vanguard Press, 1977).

35. Schonberg, *The Great Conductors,* 312.

36. Daniel, *Stokowski,* 116.

37. Ibid., 237.

38. *New York Times,* June 15, 1924; repr. in *Olin Downes on Music,* 88.

39. *New York Times,* November 28, 1924.

40. Daniel, *Stokowski,* 806–18. Daniel also includes select correspondence between the two conductors.

41. Copies of the Sibelius-Koussevitzky correspondence, whose originals belong to the Helsinki University Library, may be found in the Hargrett Library at the University of Georgia, MS 634.

42. Ibid., June 21, 1930, and December 16, 1930.

43. LS OD, August 9, 1929, GU MSS 688, CF "Sibelius, Jean." See Appendix A, no. 15.

44. LS JS, January 19, 1931, GU MSS 688, CF "Sibelius, Jean." See Appendix A, no. 20.

45. LS Serge Koussevitzky, July 2, 1932, GU MS 634.

46. LS OD, June 18, 1932, GU MSS 688, CF "Sibelius, Jean." See Appendix A, no. 25. Koussevitzky's letter, MS 634, is dated October 5, 1932.

47. LS Serge Koussevitzky, January 1 and February 1, 1933, GU MS 634.

48. LS OD, April 21, 1933, GU MSS 688, CF "Sibelius, Jean." See Appendix A, no. 28.

49. LS Serge Koussevitzky, June 7, 1933, GU MS 634.

50. "The Artistic Creed of Ernest Bloch Holds True," *New York Times,* March 18, 1934; repr. in *Olin Downes on Music,* 194–97.

51. "With Jean Sibelius in His Realm of the Sagas," *New York Times,* September 20, 1936.

52. LS OD, October 14, 1937, GU MSS 688, CF "Sibelius, Jean." See Appendix A, no. 38.

53. See Erik Tawaststjerna, "Sibelius's Eighth Symphony—An Insoluble Mystery," *Finnish Music Quarterly* (1985): 61–70; 92–101, in which the copyist's receipt is reproduced.

54. Quoted in Karl Ekman, *Jean Sibelius,* 243–44.

55. Tawaststjerna, "Sibelius's Eighth Symphony," 101.

Notes to Chapter 5

* *New York Times,* March 18, 1934; repr. in *Olin Downes on Music,* 196.

1. "Advance of Sibelius," *New York Times,* December 14, 1930.

2. "A Belated Sibelius Renascence," *New York Times,* March 22, 1931.

3. See "A Survey of Trends in Musical Taste," *New York Times,* February 27, 1938, and also Kate Hevner Mueller, *Twenty-Seven Major American Symphony Orchestras: A History and Analysis of Their Repertoires, Seasons 1842–43 through 1969–70* (Bloomington: Indiana University Press, 1973). Mueller's catalog makes it apparent that, although only a handful of works by Sibelius were heard in the first and second decades of the twentieth century (one in 1902, one in 1905, three in 1904, and four in 1903 and 1908), the number began to augment in the twenties; by the thirties, major conductors were programming two and three dozen Sibelius compositions each season (twelve in 1930, twenty-one in 1931, thirty in 1932, forty-three in 1939, and culminating with forty-five in the anniversary year 1940).

4. Edwin Emery and Michael Emery, *The Press and America: An Interpretive History of the Mass Media,* 5th ed. (Englewood Cliffs, N.J.: Prentice-Hall, 1984), 326–33.

5. See Edward Downes, "The Taste-Makers," 235–36.

6. Virgil Thomson, "Olin Downes: A Free Critical Spirit," *Herald Tribune,* January 27, 1957.

7. Charles Fisher, *The Columnists* (New York: Howell, Soskin, 1944), 4–5.

8. For a fine biography of Thompson and one that provides a context for the journalism of Olin Downes, see Peter Kurth, *American Cassandra: The Life of Dorothy Thompson* (Boston: Little, Brown, 1990).

9. Harold C. Schonberg, review of *Olin Downes on Music, Musical Courier,* March 15, 1957, 30.

10. Lucien Price, "Memoir of Olin Downes," GU MSS 688, SF "Downes, Olin—Biographical Material."

11. According to Paul Sjöblom, the Helsinki-based journalist who twice escorted Downes to Ainola.

12. See GU MSS 688, SF "Downes, Olin, re," folder 3. The concert, which took place on January 21, 1927 (and created such publicity that it had to be repeated), featured author John Erskine and his sister playing the Mozart Concerto in D minor, Erskine and Downes playing the Brahms *Variations on a Theme of Haydn,* and Erskine, Downes, and Urchs (of Steinway and Sons) playing the Bach D-minor Con-

certo on three pianos. The "critics," as might be expected, had a field day. Reflecting the general glee at the chance to be the ones to sit in judgment, Ernest Schelling punned, "It might be Urch-some to Downe Erskine, but anyway our chance has come" (*New York Sun,* January 24, 1927), and George Gershwin solemnly noted the presence of some "blue notes." Most reviewed the concert with tongue in cheek. At one point in the Brahms, when "the critic had a severe attack of octaves, Mr. [Josef] Lhevinne [serving as page turner] sprang to his feet like a second about to fling the sponge into the ring, but contented himself with turning another leaf" (*Evening World,* January 22, 1927). Acting as special guest critic for the *New York Times,* Joseph Hofmann called the men "three heroes." Downes especially received praise for his "courage," his "sincerity," and for really "knowing" music. Many rejoiced that such an event, unthinkable in Europe, could take place in America.

13. Quoted in *Current Biography 1943,* 180.

14. Alice S. Plaut, review of *Olin Downes on Music,* in *MLA Notes* 14 (1956–57): 361.

15. This incident is recounted, among other places, by Louis P. Lochner in *Fritz Kreisler* (New York: Macmillan, 1950), 295–308.

16. *New York Times,* March 3, 1935; repr. in *Olin Downes on Music,* 204–5.

17. Confirmation of Downes's plane crash may be found in Janáček's letters (see Charles Susskind, *Janáček and Brod* [New Haven, Conn.: Yale University Press, 1985], 82–84), and in the recollections of Downes's son Edward. Edward recalled being told that his father had been typing a letter to Nancy, Edward's sister, when the plane went down. The critic later concluded his letter with the remark that it was very nearly the last thing he ever wrote. See also GU MSS 688, CF "Bye, George."

18. That a similar phenomenon took place in England would seem to confirm the tendency in human nature to rise against that with which one is overfed.

19. See Price, "Portrait of Sibelius at Järvenpää."

20. Harry Rogers Pratt, "Hardy Finland Speaks Through Sibelius," *New York Times Magazine,* December 8, 1935.

21. See Joseph Horowitz, *Understanding Toscanini,* 198–99, and Robert Huchette Wilkins, "The Role of Serious Music in the Development of American Radio, 1920–1938" (M.A. thesis, University of North Dakota, 1969). The statistics below are provided by Wilkins.

22. Wilkins, "The Role of Serious Music," 190–91.

23. Johnson, *Jean Sibelius: The Recorded Music* (Helsinki: R. E. Westerlund, [1957]), 6.

24. LS OD December 30, 1930, GU MSS 688, CF "Sibelius, Jean." See Appendix A, no. 19.

25. Ibid. Downes's *Times* article appeared December 28, 1930, entitled "The Youthful Genius of Sibelius."

26. The Koussevitzky recording of the Seventh Symphony with the BBC stands

out as a classic. See Robert Lorenz, "Afterthoughts on the Sibelius Festival," *Musical Times,* January 1939, 13–14; and Robert Simpson, *Sibelius and Nielsen, A Centenary Essay* (London: BBC Publications, 1965), 35.

27. LS JS January 19, 1931; GU MSS 688, CF "Sibelius, Jean." See Appendix A, no. 20. Sibelius's private secretary in his later years, Santeri Levas, recorded the composer's continuing concern about the performances of his works. Levas quotes the composer as saying, "Actually I have never been completely satisfied with any single recording." Levas, *Sibelius,* 90.

28. Johnson, *Sibelius: The Recorded Music,* 7.

29. Compiled by R. D. Darrell (New York: The Gramophone Shop, Inc., 1936), 463. If sheer numbers mean anything, then Richard Strauss should be identified as the fair-haired musical idol of the thirties; the *Encyclopedia*'s list of his available works covers five and a half pages, outdoing Sibelius and Stravinsky combined. Strauss in fact was found by two American researchers to be the "early modern" (in a group identified as Sibelius, Debussy, Rimsky-Korsakov, and Franck) whose works dominated the American orchestral repertory; Sibelius, they reported, was the composer with the most rapidly elevating reputation. See Mueller and Hevner, "A Survey of Trends in Musical Taste."

30. LS Merle Armitage, December 8, 1946, GU MSS 688, SF "Sibelius, Jean."

31. Quoted from page 1 of Olin Downes's proposal to McGraw-Hill, GU MSS 688, CF "Carmen, Kevie, re: Olin Downes 5-Foot Record Shelf." The correspondence with Carmen between 1939 and 1941 provides various details about the joint undertaking. The plan for Olin Downes's Five-Foot Shelf adds yet another layer to Downes's deep and complicated relationship with Harvard. One of Harvard's most progressive presidents had been Charles W. Eliot, whose tenure, from 1869 to 1909, had overlapped with the critic's earliest years in Boston. Late in his presidency, Eliot had remarked publicly that a shelf five feet long with the "right" books would contain all that was necessary to make an educated man, provided he read just fifteen minutes a day. Eliot was persuaded to have his book selection published as a set, and these became the Harvard Classics. Eventually a series of lectures was added and published as *Lectures on Dr. Eliot's Five-Foot Shelf of Books* (ed. William Allan Neilson [New York: Collier's Lecture Service Bureau, 1913]). The coincidence of the two shelves hardly needs additional comment. Together with Neilson's introduction to the *Lectures,* further information on Eliot and his idea may be found in Neilson's *Charles W. Eliot: The Man and His Beliefs,* 2 vols. (New York: Harper & Bros., 1926).

32. LS Leopold Stokowski, October 24, 1930, GU MSS 688, CF "Stokowski, Leopold."

33. Irving Sablosky, *American Music* (Chicago: University of Chicago Press, 1969; repr. 1985), 141–42.

34. See Wilkins, "The Role of Serious Music," 23–24, 58–59, and the Map of Networks of the National Broadcasting Company for January 1, 1940, printed in

Broadcasting. Broadcast Advertising, 1940 Yearbook Number (Washington, D.C.: Broadcasting Publications, 1940), 191.

35. Wilkins, "The Role of Serious Music," 83–85, 95, gives statistics and sample programs to illustrate the enormous variety of serious music available on radio. Other useful data may be found in Leon Crist Hood, "The Programming of Classical Music Broadcasts Over the Major Radio Networks" (Ed.D. diss., New York University, 1955). See especially Hood's Table IV, "The Amount of Time Per Week Devoted to Symphonic Music by the Four National Radio Networks, Taken Quadrennially, 1937–53" (p. 39).

36. "The People Now Shake Hands," *New York Times,* December 24, 1933.

37. Laning Humphrey, "Olin Downes, Radio Interpreter."

38. Ibid.

39. The talks were, however, rewritten for the book, which was published in 1931.

40. See Downes, *Symphonic Broadcasts,* 172, 272. The Poe imagery is arresting; it was not until many years after Downes's death that Erik Tawaststjerna documented a musical connection between the Fourth Symphony and Sibelius's projected setting of Poe's *Raven.* See Tawaststjerna-Layton, *Sibelius* 2:195–97. Downes has been twitted for expressing an urge to hunt polar bear on hearing *En saga* (Tawaststjerna-Layton, *Sibelius* 1:130). Perhaps it is worth mentioning, however, that in the Overture in E major, whose composition immediately preceded *En saga,* two of the orchestral parts bear the words *Wolfsjagd in Sibirien* (Wolfhunt in Siberia). See Kari Kilpeläinen, *The Jean Sibelius Musical Manuscripts at Helsinki University Library* (Wiesbaden: Breitkopf & Härtel, 1991), 70. As with his startling understanding of the Poe connection to the Fourth Symphony, Downes was possibly closer to the spirit in which Sibelius composed *En saga* than anyone realized.

41. "I Love a Mystery" began broadcasting in 1939; see Vincent Terrace, *Radio's Golden Years. The Encyclopedia of Radio Programs* (San Diego: A. S. Barnes, 1981), 128. According to Vera Stravinsky and Robert Craft, it was the CBC's use of *Canzonetta* that prompted Stravinsky to arrange the piece for eight-part ensemble (clarinet, bass clarinet, four horns, harp, string bass) in response to being awarded the Sibelius Prize (which he received twice); see Vera Stravinsky and Robert Craft, *Stravinsky in Pictures and Documents* (New York: Simon & Schuster, 1978), 473.

42. "Sibelius, Composer, Leads in Radio Vote," *New York Times,* December 2, 1935. It should be noted that even though it is sometimes stated that Beethoven came in second to Sibelius (as Harold E. Johnson asserted, for example, in *Jean Sibelius,* 209), the *New York Times* reported that listeners cast two votes, one for their favorite living symphonist, another for their favorite from the past. Beethoven placed first in the latter category.

43. W. C. Anthony, "American Appreciation of Sibelius," *Musical Times,* March 1936, 257.

44. Cyrus Fisher, Radio Reviews. "A New Year on the Air," *Forum and Century*

89 (January, 1933): 62. Downes offers some explanations of his own about the conditions under which such talks were given in the introduction to *Symphonic Broadcasts,* vii–viii.

45. James A. Keene's *History of Music Education in the United States* (Hanover, N.H.: University Press of New England, 1982) contains two chapters of particular relevance to the topic of music appreciation: "The Music Educator and Music Appreciation," 227–43, and "Frances Elliott Clark and Music Appreciation," 244–69. See also Richard Lee Dunham, "Music Appreciation in the Public Schools of the United States, 1897–1930" (Ph.D. diss., University of Michigan, 1961).

46. Frank Ernest Hill described the project in *Tune In for Education: Eleven Years of Education by Radio* (New York: National Committee on Education by Radio, 1942). Another useful source for the educational history of radio is Erik Barnouw's *A Tower in Babel,* vol. 1 of *A History of Broadcasting in the United States* (New York: Oxford University Press, 1966).

47. Peter W. Dykema, "Music as Presented by the Radio" (New York: The Radio Institute of the Audible Arts, [ca. 1938]).

48. *Instructor's Manual, NBC Music Appreciation Hour Ninth Season, 1936–1937,* conducted by Walter Damrosch, prepared by Lawrence Abbott (New York: National Broadcasting Company, 1936), Series D, 55.

49. Quoted in Keene, *History of Music Education,* 262.

50. See Virginia Boren, *Seattle Daily Times,* October 26, 1939, and James Davies, *Minneapolis Tribune,* March 29, 1936. Both articles are found among the clippings in GU MSS 688, SF "Downes, Olin, re."

51. "Olin Downes Dies; Times Music Critic," *New York Times,* August 26, 1955.

52. "Brooklyn Academy Lectures," GU MSS 688, microfilm.

53. LS Lawrence Gilman, December 12, 1936, GU MSS 688, CF "Gilman, Lawrence."

54. William J. Henderson, "Klemperer Honors Sibelius," *New York Sun,* December 6, 1935.

55. Ibid.

56. See Tovey's discussion of Sibelius's Second Symphony in *Symphonies (II): Variations and Orchestral Polyphony,* vol. 2 of *Essays in Musical Analysis* (London: Oxford University Press, 1935), 121–25; and Gray's remarks referred to earlier in *Sibelius: The Symphonies.*

57. Myrrha Bantock, *Granville Bantock,* 46. Henry Wood claimed a similar honor, that of being "the first to have helped popularize" Sibelius, in *My Life of Music* (London: 1938; repr., Freeport, N.Y.: Books for Libraries Press, 1971), 156.

58. "The Liverpool Orchestral Society. Jean Sibelius," *Manchester Guardian,* March 20, 1905, 6. The notion that performance of *Finlandia* was forbidden during the Russian occupation is inaccurate, although, according to Harold E. Johnson, Sibelius himself was the source for such an idea. See his *Jean Sibelius,* 92–93.

59. Ernest Newman, "Sibelius in Liverpool," *Manchester Guardian,* December 4, 1905.

60. Rosa Newmarch, *Jean Sibelius: A Finnish Composer* (Leipzig: Breitkopf & Härtel, [1906]), 3, 20, 24.

61. Newman, *Essays from the World of Music,* 127–32.

62. Tawaststjerna-Layton, *Sibelius* 2:106.

63. Newman, *Essays from the World of Music,* 127, 128.

64. Bonavia, "Popularity of Sibelius," *New York Times,* April 10, 1932.

65. Gray, *Sibelius,* 7.

66. Ibid., 13.

67. Lambert, *Music, Ho! A Study of Music in Decline,* 3d ed. (London: Faber & Faber, 1966), 277. Lambert's title comes from *Antony and Cleopatra,* 2.5, in which Cleopatra commands, "Give me some music; music, moody food of us that trade in love," and all respond, "The music, ho!"

68. "A New Sibelius Biography," *New York Times,* January 31, 1932.

69. Gilman, "Sibelius in America," *New York Herald Tribune,* December 6, 1936. Gilman's tirade notwithstanding, it should be noted that between 1960 and the late 1980s British writers devoted themselves seriously to Sibelius where American scholars did not. Dissertations on Sibelius, nonexistent in the United States during the 1980s, include several from British universities. And every Sibelius lover is indebted to Robert Layton for his translations of Tawaststjerna's biography and for his English-language biography *Sibelius* in the Master Musicians Series, now in its fourth edition.

70. See Warren I. Susman, *Culture as History: The Transformation of American Society in the Twentieth Century* (New York: Pantheon Books, 1984), 211–29, in which an entire chapter entitled "The People's Fair" is devoted to this event.

71. LS OD May 15, 1938, GU MSS 688, CF "Sibelius, Jean." See Appendix A, no. 41.

72. Ibid.

73. Downes's manuscript of *Everyman* (*Jokamies* in Finnish, *Jedermann* in German) belongs today to the Robert Manning Strozier Library at Florida State University, in Tallahassee, Florida, the institution that purchased some of Downes's letters together with the critic's scores. The correspondence is not as extensive as the collection at the University of Georgia, and, with the exception of *Everyman,* the scores have been integrated into the music library's circulating collection.

74. T OD December 22, 1938. See Appendix A, no. 42.

75. "Sibelius to Open Salutes to Fair," *New York Times,* December 27, 1938. President Kallio's address was printed in the article "Finland Salutes U.S. in Broadcast," *New York Times,* January 2, 1939. The article "Finland's Voice," in the same issue, praised the "happy choice" of Sibelius to open the fair.

76. " 'Symphony in Wood' of Finns Has Debut," *New York Times,* May 5, 1939.

77. CLS OD, April 8, 1941, GU MSS 688, CF "Sibelius, Jean." See Appendix A, no. 48.

78. T OD, December 3, 1939, GU MSS 688, CF "Sibelius, Jean." See Appendix A, no. 44.

79. T OD, December 25, 1939, GU MSS 688, CF "Sibelius, Jean." See Appendix A, no. 45.

80. *New York Times,* December 3, 1939.

81. "A Composer and His Nation," *New York Times,* December 24, 1939.

82. Ibid. The composer who had made the cod-liver oil comment was Boston-based Charles Martin Loeffler.

83. Ibid.

84. "Symphony Music Honors Sibelius," *New York Times,* October 16, 1940. Other announcements in the *Times* included "Festival to Mark Sibelius Birthday," December 4, 1940; Downes, "Toscanini Concert Honors Sibelius," Howard Taubman, "Records: Anniversary. Companies Observe Birthday of Sibelius with New Disks—Recent Release," Downes, "Symphonic Prophet," all on December 8, 1940; "Barbirolli Pays Honor to Sibelius" and "New Friends Mark Sibelius Birthday," December 9, 1940; Paul Sjöblom, "No Statue for Sibelius," December 22, 1940; "Sibelius Program at Carnegie Hall," January 12, 1941; "Concert Tribute to Jean Sibelius," May 19, 1941.

85. See Richard Leonard's letter to the music editor in the *New York Times,* February 12, 1933.

86. Joseph Horowitz, in *Understanding Toscanini,* 177–80, suggests that Toscanini was shrewdly using the political situation and Sibelius to his own advantage in his rivalry with Stokowski.

87. "Toscanini Concert Honors Sibelius," *New York Times,* December 8, 1940.

88. "Symphonic Prophet," *New York Times Magazine,* December 8, 1940.

89. CLS OD, [undated, 1941], GU MSS 688, CF "Sibelius, Jean." See Appendix A, no. 48.

90. Ibid.

91. Ibid.

Notes to Chapter 6

* *New York Herald Tribune,* October 11, 1940.

1. Irving Weil, "Sibelius Stripped," March 18, 1929, clipping in the score of the Seventh Symphony, Allen A. Brown Collection, Boston Public Library.

2. See Rosenfeld's article on Darius Milhaud, reprinted in his *Discoveries of a Music Critic* (New York: 1936; repr. New York: Vienna House, 1972), 234.

3. Pratt, "Hardy Finland Speaks Through Sibelius," *New York Times Magazine,* December 8, 1935.

4. Harold E. Johnson quotes the Boulanger remark in *Jean Sibelius,* 220. Leibo-witz's jeremiad was published in Liège by Aux Editions Dynamo, 1955.

5. Reprinted in Virgil Thomson, *A Virgil Thomson Reader* (Boston: Houghton Mifflin, 1981), 190.

6. Ibid.

7. Reprinted in B. H. Haggin, *Music in the Nation* (New York: William Sloane Associates, 1949), 52–53.

8. These and other remarks are found reprinted in Thomson's *Virgil Thomson Reader,* 193; Thomson's *Music Right and Left* (New York: Henry Holt, 1951), 6; and Horowitz's *Understanding Toscanini,* 244.

9. July 13, 1941.

10. Johnson, *Jean Sibelius,* 213 n.

11. The awarding of the Goethe Medal was reported in the *New York Times,* "Hitler Awards Medal to Composer," December 9, 1935. Regarding *Finlandia,* see Letter to the Editor ("Would Ban 'Finlandia' Now"), October 20, 1942.

12. *International Cyclopedia,* s.v. "Sibelius."

13. Rosenfeld, "The Beethoven of the North," *New Republic* 104 (1941): 528.

14. A valuable essay on this issue is Richard King's "Modernism and Mass Cul-ture: The Origins of the Debate," in *The Thirties. Politics and Culture in a Time of Broken Dreams,* ed. Heinz Ickstadt, Rob Kroes, and Brian Lee (Amsterdam: Free University Press, 1987), 120–42. I am indebted here to James Dowd, professor of sociology at the University of Georgia, who kindly read my draft of these pages, discussed these matters with me at length, and suggested this and other biblio-graphic sources.

15. King, "Modernism and Mass Culture," 134.

16. Whatever their private thoughts, publicly Greenberg directed his criticism primarily to the plastic arts, Macdonald to literature. Macdonald penned the famous essay "Masscult & Midcult," in which he addressed the vulgarization of high cul-ture. (The essay went through several versions. See the note accompanying it in *Against the American Grain* [New York: 1962; repr., New York: Da Capo Press, 1983], 1–79.) From time to time in his writing about art, Greenberg seemed to indicate his approval of Schoenberg and the twelve-tone method and demonstrated his knowledge of the anti-Sibelian René Leibowitz. See Clement Greenberg, *Arro-gant Purpose, 1945–1949,* vol. 2 of *The Collected Essays and Criticism,* ed. John O'Brian (Chicago: University of Chicago Press, 1986), 219, 224.

17. *Kenyon Review* 7 (1945): 211. Horowitz gives a lively discussion of Adorno's views in *Understanding Toscanini,* 229–37. Adorno's excellent biographer is Martin Jay, whose *Adorno* (Cambridge, Mass.: Harvard University Press, 1984) and *The Dialectical Imagination. A History of the Frankfurt School and the Institute of Social Research 1923–1950* (Boston: Little, Brown, 1973) make mandatory reading.

18. Adorno, "A Social Critique of Radio Music," 211.

19. See "On the Fetish-Character in Music and the Regression of Listening," *Zeitschrift für Sozialforschung* 7 (1938); repr. in *The Essential Frankfurt School Reader,* ed. Andrew Arato and Eike Gebhardt (Oxford: Basil Blackwell, 1978), 284–85.

20. Adorno, "A Social Critique of Radio Music," 214.

21. Adorno, "On the Fetish-Character in Music," 278.

22. Adorno, "A Social Critique of Radio Music," 209.

23. Ibid., 212.

24. Theodor W. Adorno, "TWA Memorandum. Music in Radio," Princeton Radio Research Project, June 26, 1938, Series I, Box 26, Folder 1, 59–60. Paul Lazarsfeld Papers, Rare Book and Manuscript Library, Columbia University.

25. Theodor W. Adorno, *Philosophy of Modern Music,* trans. Anne G. Mitchell and Wesley V. Blomster (New York: Seabury Press, 1973), 7–8.

26. Theodor W. Adorno, *Introduction to the Sociology of Music,* trans. E. B. Ashton (New York: Seabury Press, 1976), 172–73. This work was originally published as *Einleitung in die Musiksoziologie* (Frankfurt: 1962).

27. First published in *Zeitschrift für Sozialforschung,* 1938. Reprinted in *Gesammelte Schriften,* vol. 17, *Musikalische Schriften 4,* ed. Rolf Tiedemann (Frankfurt: Suhrkamp, 1982), 247–52.

28. Adorno, "TWA Memorandum: Music in Radio," 60.

29. Paul's novel appeared in Swedish as *En bok om en människa* (Stockholm: Albert Bonniers Förlag, 1891). It is generally agreed that he portrayed the youthful Sibelius with considerable accuracy in the character of Sillén. Harold E. Johnson in *Jean Sibelius* translates substantial passages from Paul's description of Sillén; the quotation here is taken from page 38 of that work.

30. For biographical portraits of Adorno, see Martin Jay's *Adorno* and *The Dialectical Imagination;* see also the translators' introduction to Adorno's *Philosophy of Modern Music,* vii–x.

31. Erik Tawaststjerna explores this episode in Adorno's life and its significance for his opinion of Sibelius in "Über Adornos Sibeliuskritik," *Studien zur Wertungsforschung* 12 (1979): 112–24.

32. *Olin Downes on Music,* 242.

33. Ibid., 9, 61, 116.

34. "Work by Poulenc Concert Feature," *New York Times,* November 12, 1948.

35. These and other responses to the Mahler review are found in the correspondence files of GU MSS 688.

36. "Mahler Again," *New York Times,* November 21, 1948.

37. Ibid.

38. GU MSS 688, CF re Mahler.

39. The letter, together with Downes's reply, has been reprinted by Egbert Ennu-

lat in *Arnold Schoenberg Correspondence* (Metuchen, N.J.: Scarecrow Press, 1991), 241–47.

40. *New York Times,* November 24, 1940; repr. in *Olin Downes on Music,* 295.

41. See Schoenberg's essay "New Music, Outmoded Music, Style and Idea," written in 1946 and reprinted in *Style and Idea,* ed. Leonard Stein, trans. Leo Black (London: Faber & Faber, 1975; rev. paperback ed., 1984), 124.

42. Adorno, *Introduction to the Sociology of Music,* 148.

43. See Arthur Koestler's essay "The Intelligentsia," originally printed in *Partisan Review* 11 (1944); repr. in *Writers & Politics: A Partisan Review Reader,* ed. Edith Kurzweil & William Phillips (Boston: Routledge & Kegan Paul, 1983), 79–92.

44. *New York Herald Tribune,* February 8, 1942.

45. *Selected Letters of Virgil Thomson,* ed. Tim Page and Vanessa Weeks Page (New York: Summit Books, 1988), 181–82.

46. First published in 1941, the book was revised and enlarged in 1968. See especially pages 38–40 of the revised edition (New York: W. W. Norton, 1968).

47. Glenn Watkins's *Soundings: Music in the Twentieth Century* ignores Sibelius entirely, an exclusion all the more disturbing as it comes from a brilliant and versatile scholar. Yet the lines of force, discernible in early twentieth-century Boston, reached far into the future: Watkins, like Paul Henry Lang, studied in Paris and later became a personal friend of Stravinsky.

48. Tawaststjerna, "Über Adornos Sibeliuskritik," 118.

Notes to Chapter 7

* Quoted in *Current Biography,* 1943, s.v. "Downes, Olin."

1. According to his son Edward Downes in personal conversation and in "The Taste Makers," 241.

2. "Sibelius to Get U.S. Royalties," *New York Times,* December 3, 1954; see also "Plight of Sibelius Confuses Capital," *New York Times,* July 10, 1950, and Downes, "Plight of Sibelius," *New York Times,* July 2, 1950.

3. Adorno's unforgettable description of his role is from his *Minima Moralia: Reflections from Damaged Life,* trans. E. F. N. Jephcott (London: NLB, 1974), 50.

4. Adorno, *Introduction to the Sociology of Music,* 66.

5. "Sibelius at 82," *New York Times,* December 21, 1947. Downes occasionally muted his anti-Stravinskyisms. In a typescript entitled "The Escapist School" and delivered as a CBS talk on May 20, 1945, Downes charged that after Strauss and Debussy ceased to advance the progress of music, the next generation of composers showed a lack of creative direction corresponding to the lack of moral vigor and purpose in the world. His example of this morally depraved group—Stravinsky—has been crossed out. GU MSS 688, SF "CBS."

6. LS OD, May 22, [1952], GU MSS 688, CF "Sibelius, Jean." See Appendix A, no. 70.

7. *Red Channels: The Report of Communist Influence in Radio and Television* (New York: American Business Consultants, 1950). For more on the context of *Red Channels,* the reader is referred to Richard M. Fried, *Nightmare in Red. The McCarthy Era in Perspective* (New York: Oxford University Press, 1990), especially chap. 6; and Edwin R. Bayley, *Joe McCarthy and the Press* (Madison: University of Wisconsin Press, 1981), chap. 6.

8. Edward Downes, conversation with the author, March 31, 1993. It might be noted that the appearance of his name in *Red Channels* did not prevent Downes from being castigated in the *Daily Worker* for his anti-Soviet views.

9. LS R. B. Shipley, Director, Passport Office, May 25, 1953, GU MSS 688 CF "U.S. Department of State, Passport." Shipley informed Downes that he had the right to present his case in person at the Passport Office, but that he would be required to explain the nature and the length of his connection with each organization. Downes responded with a furious letter inviting the passport official to visit him in New York. Edward Downes remembers that it was through the auspices of the *New York Times* that the matter was eventually resolved and the passport granted.

10. LS OD, November 2, 1951, GU MSS 688, CF "Sibelius, Jean." See Appendix A, no. 64.

11. LS Jean Sibelius to Yrjö Sjöblom, n.d., Sibelius Family Archives, National Archives of Finland.

12. LS OD, June 16, 1953, GU MSS 688, CF "Sibelius, Jean." See Appendix A. no. 74.

13. Howard Taubman, "Sibelius at 90: A Finnish Epic," *New York Times Magazine,* December 4, 1955.

14. "Nature Boy at 90," *Time,* December 12, 1955.

15. Howard Hanson, review of Harold E. Johnson, *Jean Sibelius, Saturday Review,* July 25, 1959, 17; and Roland Gelatt, *New York Times Book Review,* July 26, 1959.

16. In one case, a letter from America addressed "Jean Sibelius, Europe" found its way to Ainola! See Levas, *Sibelius,* 113.

17. Harold C. Schonberg, *Lives of the Great Composers,* rev. ed. (New York: W. W. Norton, 1981), 411.

18. Alan Rich, "Whatever Happened to Jan Sibelius?" *New York,* June 9, 1975, 80. ("Jan," incidentally, was never a correct form of Sibelius's name; it was either Jean, Janne, or the seldom used Johan.)

19. So Chase described his goal in each edition of his book (1955, 1966, and 1987).

20. Austin, *Music in the 20th Century* (New York: W. W. Norton, 1966), 103.

21. Fred Blum, "Sibelius and America; A Centennial Survey," Sibelius Museum, Turku, Finland. Typescript, 13.

22. Quoted in Ennulat, *Arnold Schoenberg Correspondence,* 251.

23. To cite just a few composers: Edgard Varèse, who admired the composer's "sense of space" (see Tawaststjerna-Layton, *Sibelius* 2:147), involved himself with his music (see the letter in Appendix A, no. 52) and conducted *Pohjola's Daughter* during his New Symphony Orchestra concerts in New York; Samuel Barber, whose correspondence with Sibelius, preserved in the Helsinki University Library, gratefully acknowledges the composer; Howard Hanson, whose own symphonies owe some of their inspired moments to Sibelius; George Antheil, America's most "ultra" composer, who found in Sibelius a symphonic model; Lukas Foss, whose recording of the *Lemminkäinen Suite* demonstrates his sensitivity to Sibelius; Peter Maxwell Davies, whose four-movement Island Symphony owes a debt to Sibelius; Ralph Vaughan Williams, whose Fifth Symphony is dedicated to Sibelius. Present-day minimalists' slowly changing soundscapes are also directly descended from Sibelius scores. That Sibelius's works have today survived both the grandiose paeans of well-meaning disciples and the barbs and denunciations of the envious is further testimony to their enduring value. Consider, for example, that in the first months of 1992, in such widely scattered centers as Los Angeles, Atlanta, and New York, major orchestras performed the *Kullervo* Symphony, *En saga, Pohjola's Daughter,* the *Karelia Suite,* and the Violin Concerto.

❧ APPENDIX A

Correspondence of Jean Sibelius and Olin Downes

THE CORRESPONDENCE BEGAN in the spring of 1927. Letters and telegrams transcribed chronologically below all belong to the Olin Downes Collection at the University of Georgia. Among the Correspondence Files, one marked "Sibelius, Jean" includes Sibelius's original letters and Downes's handwritten and carbon copies, the only versions known of the critic's side of the communication. In a few cases the file contains xeroxes of letters signed by Olin Downes. These letters are presented here with the kind permission of the Sibelius and the Downes families, and of the University's Hargrett Library.

Throughout the letters Finnish cities are referred to by their Swedish names, as was the custom earlier in the century (hence, Helsingfors rather than Helsinki, Åbo rather than Turku), and the name Leningrad is used rather than St. Petersburg (although Sibelius had conducted in that city before it bore Lenin's name). Wherever possible, individuals discussed in the letters are identified, as are any errors in dates or other facts. In the interest of clarity, dates and places have been standardized at the beginning of each letter and titles of musical compositions rendered in italics or capitals, as appropriate. While a few spelling errors have been corrected and obviously omitted words or letters added in brackets, no attempt has been made to give uniformity to punctuation, to standardize various spellings of names, or to correct awkward grammar.

No. 1 CC. *Olin Downes to Jean Sibelius*

[In GU MSS 688 there are three drafts of this letter. Because each sheds a slightly different light on the past, all three are reproduced here.]

My dear Mr. Sibelius: New York, April 18, 1927

You probably do not remember the writer of this letter who has long been a very great admirer of your music.

We met, however, in June 1913,[1] at the Norfolk Music Festival when you were the guest of Carl Stoeckel. At that time we had a very interesting conversation, and you were so very good as to say you would request your publishers, when I wrote you about it, to send me some of your scores. Soon after came the war, and that is why I did not follow my intention at the time to make a detailed study of every measure of your music.

I am writing you now about two special matters; the first is to ask you whether it would now be possible for your publishers to send me as many Sibelius' scores as they feel that they can, (I have in my personal possession only those of the first, second and fourth symphonies).

The second is a much more important matter and one to which I hope you will give careful and favorable attention.

Could you be persuaded to make a tour as conductor of your own instrumental and choral compositions, next Winter, of the United States? In writing you about this, I am expressing a purely artistic interest of my own; and [at] the same time I am transmitting to you the wish of one of the best and most reputable of American musical managers. He is Mr. William Brennan, manager of the Boston Symphony Orchestra, who feels convinced that he can secure a certain number of appearances for you at the head of leading American orchestras—sufficient, at least, to assure you of a reasonable remuneration and perhaps of a number of engagements that would prove quite profitable.

Any inquiries you choose to make regarding Mr. Brennan, for whose personal integrity and business ability I unqualifiedly vouch, will be certain to be satisfactory to you. The terms, would of course, be matters to be arranged between you and Mr. Brennan. With that part of the arrangement, I have nothing to do and hold it in no personal interest whatsoever, but I am very eager that your music should receive the attention which its greatness deserves in this country.

If you would care to consider such a tour, I will immediately put you into communication with Mr. Brennan and he and I might together make a trip to Finland some time next Summer to see that all preliminary arrangements were properly made.

In this case, also, the opportunity to study your scores would be of use to me in my work.

In any case whether you come to America or not next Winter, I shall try and plan this Summer to visit you in Finland.

I send you my very best wishes and my great esteem of your art, and hope for a favorable reply to *all* of these suggestions.

Sincerely yours,
[Olin Downes]
Music Critic

1. Downes misremembers the date, which was actually June 1914.

No. 2 LS. *Olin Downes to Jean Sibelius*

My dear Mr. Sibelius: New York, April 22, 1927

I am writing to inquire whether you would feel interested in undertaking a concert tour of the United States next season, with a view to conducting your choral and symphonic compositions. In writing you about this I am expressing a purely artistic interest of my own, and at the same time am transmitting to you the inquiry of one of the best and most reputable of American managers. He is Mr. William Brennan, manager of the Boston Symphony Orchestra, who is probably known to you, and for whose exceptional integrity and business ability I ["personally" crossed out] can vouch.

[The following typed paragraph has been crossed out: Mr. Brennan is convinced that he can secure you a sufficient number of engagements with the leading symphony orchestras and choral societies of this country to offer you a fair remuneration for your appearance and also advance the knowledge and appreciation of your music in this country.]

The financial terms and other practical arrangements of your American tour would of course be matters to be ["settled" crossed out] adjusted between you and Mr. Brennan. With them I have nothing to do and I ["have" crossed out] hold in them no interest of any kind. But as a ["very great" crossed out] warm admirer of your genius I would be personally extremely interested to have your art placed in its proper light before the musical public of my country, and would count it a great privilege to be able to benefit artistically by your presence here. I believe that there are many music-lovers in America who feel the same way, and ["to whom the music of yours that they know is very significant" crossed out] I think you would be gratified by your reception.

[The last paragraph is crossed out: Will you please let me know whether this proposal interests you? If it does, Mr. Brennan will communicate with you.]

In any event, I hope to have the pleasure of paying you a visit in Finland in the latter part of this summer.

Sincerely yours
[Olin Downes]

No. 3 CC. *Olin Downes to Jean Sibelius*

[This is probably the letter Sibelius received.]

My dear Mr. Sibelius: New York, May 21, 1927

I am writing to inquire whether you would feel interested in undertaking a concert tour of the United States next season, with a view to conducting your choral and symphonic compositions. In writing you about this I am expressing a purely artistic interest of my own, and at the same time am transmitting to you the inquiry of one of the best and most reputable of American managers. He is Mr. William Brennan, manager of the Boston Symphony Orchestra, who is probably known to you, and for whose exceptional integrity and business ability I can vouch.

The financial terms and other practical arrangements of your American tour would of course be matters to be adjusted between you and Mr. Brennan. With them I have nothing to do and I hold in them no interest of any kind. But as a warm admirer of your genius I would be personally extremely interested to have your art placed in its proper light before the musical public of my country, and would count it a great privilege to be able to benefit artistically by your presence here. I believe that there are many music-lovers in America who feel the same way, and I think you would be gratified by your reception.

I shall sail on the 28th of this month for Europe and shall be in England, France and Germany until the first week in August. About that time, I expect to visit Finland and hope that I can then have the privilege of calling upon you. In the meantime, will you kindly let me know whether the proposal of an American concert tour is of any interest to you? If it is, I will notify Mr. Brennan of that fact and he will then correspond with you regarding conditions. If you will address me, care of the New York Times bureau, 16 Rue de la Paix, Paris, the letter will reach me.

With best wishes, I am

Sincerely yours,
[Olin Downes]

No. 4 T. *Jean Sibelius to Olin Downes*

[received in Paris, August 16, 1927]

Closely engaged with new works regret being unable at present moment decide for tourne stop for kind letter best thanks wishing you welcome to finland.
Sibelius

No. 5 CC. *Olin Downes to Jean Sibelius*

My dear Mr. Sibelius: Salzburg, August 17, 1927

I have been so long answering your kind telegram which I received in Paris, and which I transmitted to Mr. Brennan, because I have been travelling a great deal and very rapidly in Europe, and because I could not know the exact date of my arrival in Finland.

Now I write to say that I expect to arrive at Helsingfors on the 5th or 6th of September, and I hope I may call upon you as soon after that date as is convenient to you.

I am afraid we shall not be able to communicate as readily as I would wish, because I have very little German, and not a word of Finnish. I wish nevertheless once more to shake your hand, which I did when you attended Carl Stoeckel's festival in Norfolk 13 years ago, in 1917.[2] If you have a friend who speaks English, and who can tell me something of your latest works and help our conversation, I would be greatly obliged.

Also I wish to ask if it is possible for your publishers to send me many of your scores—as many as possible, from the early works to the last. When we talked in Norfolk—you have doubtless forgotten this, for it happened long ago as a few minutes of your busy life, you told me that you would speak to your publishers about this. Before another year came the war, and then I knew it was impossible to write you of it. Of course, if it is not possible for the publishers to send me, free of charge, expensive orchestral scores, I shall entirely un[der]stand it. On the other hand, I will study these scores very carefully, and will no doubt have often occasion to write about them, as I have in the past, so that it would not be entirely the publishers loss. In short, I would last [*sic*] every note of your music that I can get, especially the orchestral and choral works, for my library, but shall entirely understand if this is not possible. If I could have them I would like the publishers to mail them to my address in America, since I would not have room to take them with me in my baggage.

I also wish to ask whether your symphonies and other orchestral works have been yet arranged for the piano four hands. I understand very well that the later ones— for example, from the fourth symphony on, are so orchestral that only a little of the effect could be secured on the piano, but I nevertheless wish they were accessible in this form, and I think four hand arrangements—which I suppose as an orchestral composer you detest—help to make music known.

Finally I would ask you whether, after I have seen you, it would be possible to go into the Finnish woods before returning to America, to tramp for four or five days and fish. Please do not misunderstand me: I only ask if you can direct me to some one who can tell me where to do [*sic*], since I am extremely desirous of seeing the Finnish—the real country, the woods and the streams, much more than I am of seeing the cities, and after having listened to a great deal of music—good music and bad music, principally bad, this summer—I am anxious to wash out my ears, and if I could catch a salmon one dream of my life would be fulfilled—two dreams— three dreams—since I have dreamed for many [years?] of Finland—ever since first hearing your music, which came from that land, in 1911[3]—music which I knew could only come from a wonderful, northern country, where there was room to be alone, and a grand nature about, and have also dreamed of seeing you in your own country, and finally have dreamed of catching a large salmon! Or a sturgeon, if there are no salmon running, would do! Or are there sturgeon in Finland? I think so. My dear Mr. Sibelius, don't trouble yourself about this matter, I beg, only, if you know what I should do to get into the woods, away from everything, for four or five days, if possible with a guide who cannot say one word to me, so that he keeps quiet, and we tramp and fish and say nothing for a week, that would be marvelous. Indeed I have even wondered if it would not be possible, in some place in the Finnish woods, where there are few people by a lake with fish in it, to buy very cheaply a small wood cabin, for myself, where I could come every year or every other year for a month, to be by myself, have a few books, a fire, perhaps even, at last a piano, and be completely happy. You may not take this seriously, but I am the man who does these things, and perhaps you can give me a little advice about them when I come. For I cannot bear living only in one country—much as I love my own—and to escape from everyone—perhaps this is my greates[t] dream of all.

Excus[e] my long letter. I take the liberty of speaking to you as a friend. I am frank to say that it is easier sometimes for me to write than to talk. We may not be able to talk much, and since you are an older man than I am, I doubt if my company will interest you. But I have talked to you often through your music; whether we communicate personally or not is without importance. I know best many people to whom I have never said a word; in fact I prefer that kind of company. Therefore, if our meeting is not comfortable or interesting to you, and I realize that it is best to go on quickly, don't misunderstand me. I wish to see you only for a little while, to remember you as a man as well as artist, and there will never be walls between me and you in your music. It is the only great and *noble* music that I hear being produced today.

[Olin Downes]

2. The correct date is still 1914. Inaccuracy persists throughout the correspondence where the year of the Norfolk encounter was concerned. Downes was notoriously mercurial in the matter of dates and times. One friend recalled occasions when the critic had made engagements to eat dinner with three different people at the same hour on the same day; he once arranged lunch in a California town immediately after a morning lecture one hundred miles away; see Leonora Wood Armsby, *Musicians Talk* (New York: Dial Press, 1935), 185–89.
3. Downes's later statements and his own reviews show this date to be off by some seven years.

No. 6 T. *Jean Sibelius to Olin Downes*

Helsinki, August 23, [1927]

Very wellcome to Finland.

Sibeljus[4]

4. An identical telegram, with the composer's name spelled Sibelius and bearing the date August 27, arrived for Olin Downes at the *New York Times's* rue de la Paix address.

No. 7 T. *Olin Downes to Jean Sibelius*

Berlin, September 6, 1927

Have been fearfully delayed arriving tomorrow afternoon hotel kant have only five or six days but hope I can see you and go fishing.

best wishes
Olin Downes

No. 8 CLS. *Olin Downes to Jean Sibelius*

Bord *SS De Grasse,* September 30, 1927

I hope that you, so great a man and artist, will not feel it amiss, Mr. Sibelius, if I address you as my very dear friend. As you see, this is written on ship-board, where I am now, with my wife and children. I feel a great fear and sense of weakness, even dread, in going back to my place of work and living, and the happiness and torture which wait me there. It is really going into battle, and in some ways my summer in Europe, passed a great deal alone, has made me weak and soft, and most unwilling to go back to that place. But I do retain as a priceless memory the strength, the spirit and the *reality*—the marvelous *reality*—which your music, and now yourself, have for me. Neither the man nor the music is a mirage! Both are true, and both have held out to me friendship and courage. After all, it is the grasp of a man's hand that we need most of all. The things you said to me I shall always remember, and they shall always mean to me strength in my life, new hope and faith for the future. You see, I was *not* mistaken, either in Sibelius or Finland. These are not fantasies or dreams or illusions. They exist, and they are my friends. It is quite enough. I expect to return to Finland again, and to shake your hand, either there or when you come over here. But whether we ever meet again or not, I shall know that you are always near, and for that life will be less lonely.

Olin Downes

[Added in the margin of the first page:] Please give my warmest good wishes to Mrs. Sibelius and your daughters.

No. 9 CC. *Olin Downes to Jean Sibelius*

Dear Mr. Sibelius: New York, February 14, 1928

I hope that by the time this letter which I am dictating in considerable haste, reaches you, that you will have received another letter of a more personal kind from me. I have long been intending to write you, but as soon as I landed in America I fell ill with pneumonia and was for eight weeks incapacitated.

This letter is to recommend to your attention my friend Mr. Henry Hadley, the

American composer and conductor,[5] who will next season undertake a tour of various European cities. You may remember Mr. Hadley whom, I believe you met at Mr. Stoeckel's Norfolk Festival when you visited there in 1913.

Mr. Hadley in addition to his high reputation as a composer, has had extensive experience in conducting the New York Philharmonic Society and several American orchestras, and also conducting in Germany where certain of his operas have been produced. But I think you know about him because I seem to remember his speaking in the greatest admiration of your Second Symphony and telling me that you yourself had given him the proper tempi for this score. So I need say no more about that.

Do you think there would be a possibility of Mr. Hadley being extended an invitation to conduct an orchestral concert in Helsingfors—perhaps a concert of American composers? It occurred to me that this might be of interest to the public and I think Mr. Hadley would be glad to accept the engagement.

I need not say that I don't mean this letter as a request but only as a suggestion of an idea which may be of interest to the Finnish public. If you think otherwise, pray do not trouble about it.

With best wishes,
Sincerely yours,
[Olin Downes]

5. Hadley (1871–1937) was a New England native, having come from Somerville, Massachusetts. He studied composition with Chadwick at the New England Conservatory and subsequently wrote five symphonies. Active as a conductor, Hadley helped to found the San Francisco Symphony. During his American visit Sibelius met Hadley several times; the American's symphonic poem *Lucifer* was performed on the first night of the same festival that had featured Sibelius.

No. 10 CC. *Olin Downes to Jean Sibelius*

My very dear Friend: New York, July 18, 1928

I have just found among my letters, the note which I enclose and which I wrote to you on the steamer on the way back to America last fall, from Finland. I wrote this letter on the ship; I could not find stamps on it—it was one of these wretchedly managed French boats, very dirty and disagreeable—and took it to my office where, on the first day of my return to America I was taken ill with pneumonia. The result of this was that the letter to you, sealed but not stamped which I had intended to mail that very first afternoon that I landed, has remained ever since in my desk. It is very much in the nature of a posthumous communication but I send it to you because I would have you know that you were in my thoughts then and that although many months have passed you have been, and are equally in my thoughts now.

With the pleasant memories of the days and hours we spent together and of the very charming and happy and good people of your family, I am sincerely yours— and will you please remember me with especial warmth to Madame Sibelius?

[Olin Downes]

P.S. I have read with the greatest interest the score of your Sixth Symphony, and of course your inscription in it makes it the most valuable musical volume that I have in my library.[6] I have also told two conductors about this work and I think it likely that it will have a performance here next winter.

6. The location of Sibelius's Sixth Symphony score with its inscription to Downes remains a mystery. It has not been found among the critic's papers at the University of Georgia nor is it in the extensive score library that went to Florida State University.

No. 11 CC. *Olin Downes to Jean Sibelius*

My dear Friend: New York, April 24, 1929

Next Saturday, April 27, I am sailing for Europe on the steamship "Minnetonka," reaching Paris May 5th. I shall spend two or three days in Paris and then go to Berlin for two or three more days. After that I shall take an airplane at once for Moscow. I shall be in Moscow and Leningrad for about two weeks. I then plan to return to Berlin via Helsingfors.

In the first place I want to see you again and also Mr. Palloheimo[7] and many other fine people that I came to know in Helsingfors. If I had one or two days to spend there, I should pray for a chance to catch a salmon, but I fear I shall have very little time. This I can tell you better after I get to Leningrad.

Now I want to ask you an important question. Do you know whether the Russian artist Repien is now in Helsingfors as I hear, or does he still live in Åbo as I believe he did when I was in Helsingfors in 1927?[8] In any event, I wish to find him and interview him concerning his memories of the great Russian composers whom he painted, especially Rimsky-Korsakoff and Moussorgsky. I don't know whether he speaks French, although I assume that he does.

Can you possibly find out for me, or ask Mr. Palloheimo if he will do so, where Repien is and if you happen to know him, could you recommend me to him as a serious and responsible critic, much interested in Russian music and art, and ask him if he would give me an audience and give me his reminiscences—not political— of the great musicians whom he has known and painted.

If you can do this, I will be very grateful indeed and if you cannot do this, it will only mean that I will have more time and hope that you will have some time to talk with me again, since I remember with such happiness and gratitude our former conversations. Could you write me a letter to our Berlin office (Kochstrasse 28, Berlin) from where it will be forwarded to me, about these things?

I look forward with the highest anticipations to seeing you all and Finland again, and ask if you will please remember me to Mrs. Sibelius, your daughters and sons-in-law.

Sincerely,

[Olin Downes]

7. Arvi Paloheimo (1888–1940) was the husband of Sibelius's oldest child, Eva, the daughter to whom Sibelius was especially close. The correspondence shows that Downes established a special bond with Arvi, whom he eventually declared to have been one of his dearest friends. The Olin Downes Collection contains a number of letters between Paloheimo and Downes in the Correspondence File labeled "Paloheimo, Arvi." These reiterate and sometimes amplify facts from the Sibelius correspondence.

8. Ilya Repin, as the artist's name is usually spelled, is known both for his portraiture and for his powerfully realistic depictions of episodes from Russian history. Although there is no reply from Sibelius to this request, the critic did find the artist, who was then living near St. Petersburg rather than in Finland. Downes reported his visit in the *New York Times,* July 21, 1929, below a headline that read "The Glory That Was Russia" and the subtitle "Repin, the Artist Who Painted Moussorgsky, Recalls Memories of Dead Composers—A Visit to Sibelius." Downes found Repin none too soon; born in 1844, the artist died in 1930. It is not generally remembered today, but Olin Downes was a first-rate interviewer, a skill he honed from his earliest years as a newspaperman. He won accolades even from those, like Luther Burbank, whom he interviewed.

No. 12 T. *Olin Downes to Jean Sibelius*

Leningrad, May 21, 1929

Greetings please wire me Hotel Europa Leningrad if your music played Helsingfors between twentythird and twentyseventh wish much to see you.

Olin Downes

No. 13 T. *Olin Downes to Jean Sibelius*

Leningrad, May 24, 1929

Delayed arriving Kamp[9] tomorrow morning wonderful to see you.

Olin Downes

9. The Hotel Kämp, located on Helsinki's Esplanade, was a favorite haunt of Sibelius and his artistic contemporaries. The building still stands today, although it has been converted into a bank.

No. 14 T. *Olin Downes to Jean Sibelius*

Leningrad, May 26, 1929

Tonight visiting Repin expect arrive hotel Kamp sometime monday.

Olin Downes

No. 15 CLS. *Olin Downes to Jean Sibelius*

New York, August 9, 1929

Dear Friend and Great Master, whom I love and adore:

I've just received your photograph and its inscription, and indeed this makes me very happy. It is so really *you* and it cheers me to look at it—that *you,* with all you know and have experienced, and with the knowledge of a great spirit, should look so happy—indeed like a boy, and a rather bad one! And I hear you say again all those wonderful things that sometimes made me laugh so, and always gave me happiness and courage. And also I hear you say, "Life is simple!" That's wonderful, you know, and if *you* say it, it's true. Bless you, and thank you a million times for this additional gift, beloved Master.

Yes! I have been foolish at times to bother you with gloomy, selfish and self-pitying thoughts, and I think *this* time, *this* meeting, *this* visit has helped me even more than the previous one, so that I shall remain happier, always, for you—for knowing you and feeling in my heart the clasp of your great hand, and hearing above all your music. And if I ever feel childishly, egotistically sad again, I shall think of "les traditions," and look at your picture, and *laugh,* a very happy laugh, if only in imitation of a great man, with the wisdom and experience of his greatness, who can also laugh.

God bless you, and also may He, or the Devil, or whoever or whatever produces good music, bless the new work, the great *Mystery,* which you properly keep to yourself—on which you are engaged.

I was very sorry, this time, to have no opportunity of seeing Mrs. Sibelius and your daughters,[10] because they are so fine, and I like them so much. I hope next time I shall see them, and I know, in my heart, that that time will be soon. Will you give them all my love and my best messages. But if I could not see the ladies I could see the *men* of the big Sibelius family, and they are winners! Ah, but you should have been at our last supper together—Paloheimo, Ilves,[11] Prof. Virolle, and your humble servant. That was a night for you!

Well, I am here, imprisoned in New York—hot as Hell, and fools and asses as thick as blackberries. But a man is not a prisoner when his mind is free, and when he remembers as clearly as I do—for I remember everything I have seen like a photograph—all the beauty I have beheld in those swift weeks flying over the world, I stored up much happiness and much adventure in that time, and I can *see* it all, *live* it all, over and over again, as much as if it were happening. In fact, I am beginning to think that the true secret of human immortality is simply the continual extension of human memory—that we *remember,* always more clearly, and comprehensively, all that we as individuals, and also all that the race has experienced, that nothing is lost, but that the progress of the race is really like the life of *one* individual, who, the longer he lives, the richer and wiser, and at last, thanks to his knowledge (and its faith he has formed, based on *true* and *great knowledge*), the happier for all he has lived, joyed, and suffered.

But anyhow, I can see Helsingfors this instant, every inch of the streets I walked, my very room in the hotel, and your *beautiful* place at Järvenpää, and the inside of your house, the faces of your family—*all*. And the woods where Aarvi Palloheimo took me fishing, the railroad station, the things we carried with us—the night and the stars as we waited for the train—the woods, the streams, the bridge, or rather raft, on which our auto was hauled by wire ropes over a river—*everything* I remember. I have lost nothing, and I know that nothing of all the immeasurable riches I have collected will ever leave me or die. Nor one note that you have written, nor one word you have said to me. So it is, dear master.

Salute! You have made me proud to live, as I shall be proud to die. Of all the things God has given me, there is nothing more precious, more *happy,* than *Sibelius.*

Olin Downes

10. Sibelius had six daughters in all, but his third, little Kirsti, had died in 1900, not quite two.
11. Eero Ilves (1887–1953) was the husband of Sibelius's daughter Katarina.

No. 16 Copy of Postcard. *Olin Downes and Paul Cherkassky*[12] *to Jean Sibelius*

Dear Master,   Boston, October 2, 1929

Blessings and happiest memories from us, together today in Boston.

Olin Downes

Kära Professor,

Tack för sist. Just har kommit to Boston. Hälsningar.

Paul Cherkassky

[Dear Professor, Thanks for the last time. I have just come to Boston. Greetings.]

12. Cherkassky was a Russian-born violinist who played with the Boston Symphony Orchestra and who, in 1919, had performed Sibelius's violin concerto in Helsinki.

No. 17 CLS. *Olin Downes to Jean Sibelius*

My very dear Master: New York, June 22, 1930

I am writing to you by that awful machine, the typewriter, because only then will you be able to read what I write. I have given letters of introduction to you to two good friends of mine, Mr. and Mrs. Walter Naumburg,[13] whom you may have met years ago when you were in New York. Anyway, they will be in Finland, I think toward the end of July, for a short time, not long after this letter reaches you, and, because I like them very much, I want them to shake your hand for themselves and me. Mr. Naumburg is a banker of this city, himself an excellent 'cellist who plays string quartets once a week in his own home, and a generous patron of music who has instituted a Naumburg musical prize in this city for young and talented musicians. He is a banker by profession, and I believe a very influential one. I know nothing about banking, but we both know about music, and of Mr. and Mrs. Naumburg my wife and I are very fond. If you are not too busy, or occupied, I know they would like very much to see you, and I am very happy that they are going to Finland.

I have not told you, I think, how much Koussevitzky admires your music—now. I think I told you that when he came to America he did not like it. Now he is very enthusiastic, and introduced the Sixth symphony—which I think one of your greatest works—with remarkable effect here this winter. He played the Second symphony and other works, also, in Boston. We were having an argument when he was in this city one day, and I told him how much I disliked the late works of Stravinsky. He said, "Perhaps you do not understand them. You should hear them often before you decide. Remember how at first I didn't like Sibelius!" That is a real conversion, and a useful one too.

Have I ever told you that my boy, now aged eighteen, is determined—God help him—to be a conductor?[14] It is so. He is now, in his young years, an insane Wagnerite, knowing these scores better than I do. He begged to be allowed to go to Europe this year and hear Wagner at Bayreuth, and so he had gone, on a tramp steamer, which will land him at Rotterdam. From there he will go, principally on foot, through Germany to Bayreuth where Toscanini conducts Wagner this season. He has his *Tannhäuser, Tristan, Parsifal,* and *Ring,* in piano and orchestral scores— they were the heaviest part of his baggage. Toscanini has invited him to the rehearsals as well as the performances and I have given him a letter to Baron Frankenstein of the Munich Opera, asking him if he will give my son the same privileges. It will be useful for him to study the two different ways they do Wagner at Munich and Bayreuth.

Well-a-day. I wish I were coming to Finland this year, and at the same time warn you that if I finish my book in time I shall certainly descend upon you next season. I leave now on a lecture [tour] of the western coast, where I shall again try to catch a salmon. And so it goes. May I please be remembered to Mrs. Sibelius and the other members of your family, and may all be well with you, and us meet soon again.

Olin Downes

13. Educated at Harvard, Walter W. Naumburg (1867–1959) was known in New York for his generous patronage of music. With his brother George he continued his father's series of Central Park concerts offered free to the public. Eventually, he created the Walter W. Naumburg Foundation, whose purpose was to select young artists to debut in New York's Town Hall.

14. Edward O. D. Downes (b. 1911), who became a musicologist and critic. Among Edward Downes's many roles, which have included professor, writer, and editor, has been that of quizmaster for the Metropolitan Opera broadcasts.

No. 18 CC. *Olin Downes to Jean Sibelius*

My dear Master: New York, June 22, 1930 [sic]

I am giving two very good friends of mine, Mr. and Mrs. Walter Naumberg, this letter to you and I want you to shake their hands very warmly for me and Finland. Mr. Naumberg who is a man of all sorts of affairs which are incomprehensible to me, is so admirable a musician that if you can furnish three other strings, you can have a performance of your quartet any evening you please while he is in Helsing-fors.

They both look forward very much to seeing you and I can only add that I wish I were there with them. They will bring to you with this, my very warmest wishes and regards to you and Mrs. Sibelius and your family.

Sincerely yours
[Olin Downes]

No. 19 CC. *Olin Downes to Jean Sibelius*

Dear Friend and Master: New York, December 30, 1930

I have been so mortal busy that Christmas greetings which I wished to send to you and your family and relatives have been passed by without my being able to send them. But I do want to enclose herewith two articles which I wrote for *The Times* and which are, in some sort, a Christmas greeting to you and to Finland, from which both you and your music have come.

But there is something else I wish to add, which is not so pleasant. I took the occasion of the recording of your first two symphonies by the Columbia Company,[15] as an opportunity of writing these articles about your music. I refrained from speaking about their poor quality of recording. To my mind the record of the second symphony is the kind of a record that was made ten years ago. Many of the balances are very poor; many of the finer touches of your instrumentation cannot be ascertained from this record. If the Columbia Company had made these records in as careful and modern a way as they should, they would have been very much better, for they are not at all up to the standard to which the American public is now accustomed. I really think that you or your friends should make some complaint about this, especially if it is true that the Finnish Government is paying to have these things done, because if that is the case I do not think that they are getting the proper return for their money, any more than I think you are getting the proper representation of your genius. I play this record of your symphony on my machine quite often, and did so on Christmas night to a group of my friends. I did this because I am so fond of the Second Symphony and because I was able to explain to them to what an extent the record fell short, but I think it would be worth while to insist that the future recordings of your music by the Columbia Company in Europe are properly done.

Next Thursday Toscanini will play here *En Saga,* and today I shall receive the record by H.M.V. of this work, which I expect to find to be better than the records of the symphonies. I am going to suggest to the Victor Company, on this side of the water, that they have some records of your music made by Koussevitzky and the Boston Symphony Orchestra, who have given some excellent performances of your music, not only of the First Symphony, but of the Sixth and Seventh. Incidentally I have meant for a long time to tell you how profoundly I appreciate the copy of the Sixth Symphony which you sent me with a written sentiment which I shall always value very highly and which I personally consider one of the most remarkable of all your orchestral compositions. Yes—and one other thing. Zimbalist[16] gave, with Stokowski, not only the best performance, but the only adequate one of your violin concerto, that I ever heard. This made me very happy because I think that through this performance the public as well as the violinists realised what an extremely interesting and effective work this concerto could be under circumstances of an adequate performance. Very few violinists or conductors whom I have heard interpret it have really understood this composition.

Now I shall stop speaking of these details and shall hope that the New Year has started very well for you and all those whom you hold dear. I wish tremendously that I can see Finland as it is in the Winter time. But, as I once told you, I know something about it through certain pages of your music.

Incidentally, I am extremely curious. Twice within two years you have spoken to me about a large work upon which you are engaged. Is this score finished and could you let me have any news of your latest compositions? Have I been rightly informed that there is now an Eighth Symphony? In America we know only seven.

With best wishes of the Season, I am

Sincerely yours,

[Olin Downes]

15. Originally the English branch of Columbia Phonograph, the company later became autonomous; see Roland Gelatt, *The Fabulous Phonograph 1877–1977,* 2d rev. ed. (New York: Macmillan, 1977), 341 s.v. "Columbia Graphophone Company Ltd."

16. Efrem Zimbalist (1889–1985), Russian-born violinist, composer, and noted teacher, who married the soprano Alma Gluck just days after Sibelius met the singer in Norfolk. Zimbalist eventually took up residence in the United States where, after Gluck's death, he married Mary Louise Curtis Bok, founder of the Curtis Institute.

No. 20 LS. *Jean Sibelius to Olin Downes*

My dear Friend,   Järvenpää, January 19, 1931

I thank you cordially for your kindly letter, which contained so many things of importance to me. From experience, gained during a long life-time I can say that you certainly have done most for my music.

I was very interested in what you wrote me about the records, though I am rather unacquainted with those things.

Concerning my Symphonies I and II I wish to inform you that the recording was produced on the initiative of Columbia, the costs amounting to $6000, of which sum the Finnish Government overtook $1250 for the sake of giving Robert Kajanus,[17] the grand old man of our music an opportunity to produce them in London for this purpose.

You ask me what I have been occupied with during these two years. It is not only one work but several ones. I enjoy finishing my new works in my head and put off with writing them down—for many reasons, not least on account of my adoration for life an[d] Nature.[18] However I think that there will quite soon be a new Symphony ready for printing—this information strictly private: only for you.

I think oft back on your visit here.

Finland is now all snow and waiting for you to come.

My family joins me in my greetings. Arvi is at this time in London.

Yours sincerely,
Jean Sibelius

17. Kajanus (1856–1933), composer, conductor, and contemporary of Sibelius, had founded the Helsinki Philharmonic Society Orchestra. He was an enthusiastic supporter and outstanding interpreter of Sibelius's music. The tone poem *Pohjola's Daughter,* which Downes first heard when Sibelius conducted at Norfolk, was dedicated to Kajanus.
18. Working out ideas in his head seems to have been a long-standing habit with Sibelius. During the year of his study in Vienna, 1890–91, Sibelius had written to Aino: "I stay in bed in the mornings until about 9 or 10 but work out musical ideas in my head for as much as four hours." See Tawaststjerna-Layton, *Sibelius* 1:94.

No. 21 T. *Olin Downes to Jean Sibelius*

New York, September 24, 1931

Please ask publisher forward immediately score your eighth symphony my expense
Best wishes

Olin Downes

No. 22 T. *Jean Sibelius to Olin Downes*

Helsinki, September 26, [1931]

Regret very much having told of my eighth symphony not yet finished most cordial greetings.

Sibelius

No. 23 CLS. *Olin Downes to Jean Sibelius*

Dear Master: New York [1932]

I wish to introduce to you my son, Edward Olin Downes—my son and ambassador! For I am much disappointed that I cannot be present at the festival May 20. But this boy of mine, who wants very much to shake your hand is going to try to reach Helsingfors by that time, and he is now writing a book on opera, and he will also try his hand as *music critic* pro tem, and write an article for the *Times* about the Festival.

So, will you shake *his* hand please, and recognize the great improvement on the father in the son, and, if possible, see that he is admitted to the performances of the festival.

As for me, I hope too to shake your hand before the summer is over.

Olin Downes

No. 24 T. *Olin Downes to Jean Sibelius*

New York, May 13, 1932

Please wire collect times New York date performance your sixth symphony at Helsingfors my son coming possibly also myself.

Regards
Olin Downes

No. 25 CLS. *Olin Downes to Jean Sibelius*

Dear Master: Moscow, June 18, 1932

I am coming to Helsingfors, for one day only, with the wish to see you. My son you saw and I am most grateful for the kindness and hospitality shown him by you and by Aarvi Paloheimo. I met him afterwards in Berlin and he told me of this. I have been, since Berlin, in Warsaw, Kiev, Odessa, Batum, Tiflis, Vladikavkas and this is mailed from Moscow. The trip through the Caucasus was marvelous beyond words, and I heard some very interesting music.

Now I expect to arrive in Helsingfors on the 24th—perhaps the 23rd, but I think the 24th, and I shall ask you a great favor. You know I have never asked you to talk to me about your music or about music. We have talked of other things. But now I ask if you will talk with me, for publication, about your music, particularly the 8th symphony, which I understand is now finished, and your opinions on music, etc. I ask this for two reasons. First I wish to write about the new symphony in advance of its performance by Koussevitzsky, whom I saw in Paris. Secondly, I wish to include this subject, and say something about my visit to you, in a *radio* talk that I will make, for America, probably from either Berlin or Vienna—though possibly, in case I have not time in those cities, from Milan, where I must go for two or three days before sailing for America.

Do you know that Koussevitzky is going to play *all* your symphonies next season. He has greatly changed his opinion about these works since he first came to America. That was in 1924. At that time I asked him how he liked the music of Sibelius, and he said, "But it is so dark." Now he is one of your warmest admirers, and when he tried, a year ago—and in vain—unsuccessfully—to make me admire one of the later works of Stravinsky, he said to me, "Remember how I changed about Sibelius. You must now try to be also open-minded about Stravinsky." To which I replied, "There is no comparison. Stravinsky *was* a great composer. Sibelius *is* a great composer."

Is the 8th symphony in print? And if it is printed, may I have a copy to take with me to America?

Another request. Mr. Hugh Ross,[19] conductor of our leading chorus, the Schola Cantorum of New York, has asked me if I could bring back to him at New York for examination three of your choral works, which he mentions as

Impromptu, op. 19

The Ferryman's Bride, op. 33

"*Oina maa*"[20]

May I take these, too, with me to New York? It goes without saying that the Schola Cantorum would make all the necessary financial arrangements for performance.

Looking forward with the greatest eagerness, dear Master, to seeing you once more, I am

Sincerely yours
Olin Downes

19. Ross (1898–1990) had been trained in Great Britain, where he studied with Ralph Vaughan Williams before coming to North America. In 1927 he arrived in New York to conduct the Schola Cantorum, one of the earliest groups to gain recognition for performances of early music. Ross conducted the first performance outside of a Masonic Lodge of *Onward, Ye Peoples,* part of Sibelius's *Masonic Ritual Music.* The performance, with 500 voices, took place May 1, 1938, as part of the New York World's Fair. The Schola had grown out of the Mac-Dowell Chorus, founded in 1909 by Kurt Schindler, and Ross continued as its director until

the choir's last concert in 1971. During these years he was also a conductor for the Tanglewood Festival Chorus at Koussevitzky's Berkshire Music Center.
20. Undoubtedly the cantata *Oma maa (Our Land)*, composed in 1918.

No. 26 T. *Olin Downes to Jean Sibelius*

Leningrad, June 25, 1932

Leaving Leningrad five oclock twentyfifth arriving Helsingfors twentysixth.

Downes

No. 27 LS. *Jean Sibelius to Olin Downes*

My dear friend,   Järvenpää, October 12, 1932

Madame Hanna Granfelt, famous finnish singer,[21] will give concerts in America, performing finnish music.

My countrymen an[d] I would feel very happy if you, dear friend, could find time to interest you for this esteemed and in my opinion really prominent artist.

With cordial greetings
Yours very sincerely,
Jean Sibelius

21. Hanna Lilian Granfelt (1884–1952) was an operatic soprano who delighted not only Sibelius with her singing, but also Richard Strauss, in whose *Rosenkavalier, Salome,* and *Ariadne auf Naxos* she performed. A tour of the United States in 1930 had been interrupted by an attack of rheumatoid arthritis, and she was forced to return to Finland "wrapped up in cotton."

No. 28 CLS. *Olin Downes to Jean Sibelius*

Dear Mr. Sibelius,   New York, April 21, 1933

I wish to introduce to you my friend, Mr. Lucien Price.[22] He is one of the editorial writers of the *Boston Globe* and author of a number of books. He is not a professional musician at all, but is very fond of music, and intelligently so.

He wishes to talk with you because he has admired your music and been stirred by it as long as I have. It will make him very happy if you will see him and I shall feel that while I cannot come over this Summer, I am communicating with you, through him.

I hope you are very well. I have had a horribly busy and fatiguing Winter and I fear that I must stay during the hot weather in New York and perhaps write another cursed book—although there is nothing I detest more.

But please, dear master, please give us by next Winter the Eighth Symphony!

With best wishes, I am
Sincerely yours,
Olin Downes

22. Price (1883–1964) did visit with Sibelius, and he immortalized the event in "Portrait of Sibelius at Järvenpää." This little-known article was published in the book suggestively entitled *We Northmen,* published in Boston in 1936, in which Price lays emphasis upon a multitude of connections between Americans and other "Northmen."

No. 29 CLS. *Olin Downes to Jean Sibelius*

Dear Master: New York, May 27, 1933

I send you, by the hands of my young friend and your e[a]rnest admirer, Paul Sjöblom,[23] a small souvenir, which he wishes to hand to you himself and which I ask your indulgence for sending to you.

I only send it as token of our mutual admiration of your music, and our veneration for you and you[r] art. You will find in the book two references to your own works, the *Saga* and the First Symphony—works of which I spoke over the radio when Toscanini played them. To this music Paul has listened, and in fact knows all of your symphonies, up to the Seventh well.

He wishes to shake your hand, and look upon you, and hear your voice. His father has been, I believe, in correspondence with you, and is also a friend of mine, and a co-employee of *The Times.* Through him I have met Yrjö Paloheimo, Aarvi Paloheimo's brother, who is here in New York, and we shall all soon dine together and drink American beer (if nothing more!) in your honor.

Through my young friend, then, Paul Sjöblom, I salute you, whose music is for the youth of today and tomorrow. I commend him to you, and with every good wish to you and your family, remain

Sincerely,
Olin Downes

23. Paul Sjöblom is the journalist who would later escort Downes to Ainola. His Finnish father, Yrjö (usually called George), a member of the *New York Times* staff and referred to earlier in these pages, founded America's first Sibelius Society at Menassen, Pennsylvania. The younger Sjöblom made his way back to Finland as a young man and covered the Winter War, some of Finland's darkest hours. He has often written about Sibelius for both Finnish and American publications. The "small souvenir" that Paul Sjöblom was taking to Sibelius was Downes's book *Symphonic Masterpieces.*

No. 30 CLS. *Olin Downes to Jean Sibelius*

September 12, 1934

Alas, dear master, it is a great disappointment, indeed a tragedy to me, that I cannot come to see you. I have received news I fear will force me to return Saturday to America. My stay in Europe has been short—very short and hurried—and I so *wanted* to see you! And Aarvi Paloheimo, and Ilves.

Well, please keep a warm place in your heart for me, and I shall surely return next summer, when we can, I hope, talk long and happily. May you be always well and happy, and producing for the world wonderful music.

Sincerely yours,
Olin Downes

No. 31 LS. *Jean Sibelius to Olin Downes*

My dear friend,   Järvenpää, November 10, 1935

I want to recommend to you Miss Marian Anderson,[24] who has had very great success with her concerts here in Europe. She has performed also some of my songs in an admirable way, and it would please me much if you would acquaint yourself with her art.

With cordial greetings
—always sincerely yours
Jean Sibelius

24. Marian Anderson (1897–1993), contralto, became the center of national controversy in 1939 when, because of her race, she was denied the use of Constitution Hall in Washington, D.C. Downes's articles on Miss Anderson's belated debut at the Metropolitan Opera, some twenty years after the letter reproduced here, are reprinted in *Olin Downes on Music,* 428–30, 432–34.

No. 32 CC. *Olin Downes to Jean Sibelius*

Dear Mr. Sibelius,   New York, June 3, 1936

I wish to introduce to you herewith, one of my very best friends, Mr. T. R. Ybarra,[25] long a writer for *The New York Times,* now an international journalist of wide experience and reputation, who wishes very much to shake your hand for the personal pleasure of this, and *not* for an interview, although he may well at some time write an article about you. I have often spoken of you to my friend Ybarra, and he has a great desire to call upon you. If it is perfectly convenient for you to see him I know he would very deeply appreciate it.

Since Mr. Ybarra may present this letter to you before I can hope to reach Helsingfors, I would like to add that in a few days I am sailing for Europe, to return to

America in early August, but that I hope very much you will allow me to go to Helsingfors some time in July and see you once more.

Sincerely yours,
[Olin Downes]

25. Thomas Russell Ybarra, who, despite Downes's assurances here, did interview the composer; see "Music Maker" in *Collier's,* April 17, 1937, 26, 46–48.

No. 33 T. *Olin Downes to Jean Sibelius*

New York, June 6, 1936

Arriving Berlin thirteenth hope can see you sixteenth.

Olin Downes

No. 34 T. *Olin Downes to Jean Sibelius*

Berlin, June 16, 1936

Taking plane arriving Hotel Keampf tomorrow in evening hope i may see you then or on thursday best wishes to all.

Olin Downes

No. 35 T. *Olin Downes to Arvi Paloheimo*

New York, November, 1936

Colliers extremely desirous new photograph Sibelius by world famous photographer Roger Schall[26] now travelling Helsingfors via Riga stop recognize Sibelius very reluctant about photographing and if impossible I understand but Ybarra and I would consider it very great favor if new Sibelius photograph could illustrate his forthcoming Collier interview stop please cable if you think this can be done.[27]

Downes

26. Roger Schall, b. 1904, was prominent among the "human interest" photographers of his day. Associated in the thirties with *Vu* magazine, the foremost illustrated weekly in France, he adapted a style of depicting workers as heroes from Russian photographers.
27. The *Collier's* interview (see note 25 above) did appear with a photograph, one of the most morose pictures of Sibelius known, attributed to Klinsky-Pix.

No. 36 T. *Arvi Paloheimo to Olin Downes*

Helsinki, November 16, 1936

Sibelius greeting agrees condition he approves photos awaiting information arrival roger.

Paloheimo

[Added by hand:] Hälsningar [Greetings] Arvi

No. 37 CLS. *Olin Downes to Jean Sibelius*

Dear Mr. Sibelius,   New York, June 29, 1937

I want herewith to introduce Miss Antonia Brico,[28] conductor of the Women's Symphony Orchestra of New York, a very serious, gifted and enterprising musician who has scheduled your Second Symphony for performance next year and who wishes to ask you particularly some questions concerning the interpretation of your own works.

She would greatly appreciate an audience with you. I am glad to give Miss Brico this letter because I know how industrious and ambitious she is and how much genuinely good work she has done for music in New York.

With best wishes, I am
Sincerely yours,
Olin Downes

28. Brico (1902–1989) aspired to be a conductor from a young age and studied with Karl Muck. She moved to New York and for a time was something of a rage as the conductor of an orchestra for unemployed musicians that had been founded by Marion Downes, Olin's first wife. Eventually, the novelty of a woman conductor wore off, and Brico, deprived of an orchestra, moved to Denver, where she conducted the Denver Businessmen's Symphony. A prizewinning film by folksinger Judy Collins, her student, and Jill Godmilow, entitled *Antonia: A Portrait of the Woman,* depicts her life and work. In New York Brico had become friends with Olin Downes, who urged her to study Sibelius's music. Introduced by the letter transcribed here, she spent much of a summer at Ainola. Her subsequent letters to Jean and Aino, preserved today in the Helsinki University Library, address the composer and his wife (in German) as "Beloved Papa and Mama." Brico's personal papers, containing notes, interviews, and many other materials, some relating to Sibelius, belong to the Colorado Historical Society in Denver, classified as Collection no. 1457.

No. 38 CC. *Olin Downes to Jean Sibelius*

Honored Master: New York, October 14, 1937

I wish to write you briefly of two rather personal things.

One is that Antonia Brico has returned here overjoyed and tremendously inspired by the hospitality and the assistance as a conductor that you gave her when she came to see you last Summer. I think that that meeting will have a permanent effect upon her character and her art, especially since, as I think you saw, she is very serious and ambitious and idealistic. It touched me very much to hear from her about you and Mme. Sibelius, and to greatly regret that I could not have come to Finland last Summer.

The second thing is this, and I think it is very important. My mother and I often speak of you and she asked me again about the Eighth Symphony, and I told her that I had decided to spare you any mention of that work, since you were so often annoyed by so many people with questions about it. To this my mother replied by saying to me, "Tell Mr. Sibelius that I am not concerned or anxious so much about his Eighth Symphony, which I know he will complete in his own good time, as about his *Ninth*. He must crown his series of works in this form with a ninth symphony which will represent the summit and the synthesis of his whole achievement and leave us a work which will be worthy of one of the elected few who are the true artistic descendants and inheritors of Beethoven." And, dear Master, I beg you to take these words, though they come from one not personally known to you, very seriously. It may seem impertinent for me to offer such a suggestion, but I do feel that this is really necessary and right. I would feel this if only because of the fact that I know well that your spirit requires more than one more symphony for it to complete its creative course. More than ever was I impressed with this when Koussevitzky played your Seventh Symphony—superbly—with the Boston Symphony Orchestra last Summer at the Berkshire Music Festival. At that time, and prior to the performance, I made a fresh study of this marvelous score. I cannot tell you what serenity and elevation this contact with this music and Koussevitzky's noble performance gave me.

I feel more than I ever felt before that the world and the future must have at least two more Sibelius symphonies and so, with my mother, I beg you to look forward, not only to the completion of the Eighth but to the culminating Ninth.

With best wishes, I am
Sincerely yours,
[Olin Downes]

No. 39 T. *Olin Downes to Jean Sibelius*

New York, December 24, 1937

Merry xmas to you mrs. Sibelius and family and best wishes arvii Paloheimo am writing.

Olin Downes

No. 40 CC. *Olin Downes to Jean Sibelius*

My dear Master: New York, March 1, 1938

May I introduce herewith two of my old friends, Mr. and Mrs. Frank La Forge,[29] who will be in Finland this Spring and who greatly desire to pay you their respects.

Mr. La Forge is one of the leading musicians of New York City, the teacher and coach of many of our most representative singers. More than that, he is a real musician, who desires to have better knowledge of your compositions.

I wish that I might be able to present my friends to you personally, but for the present, this must be enough.

With best wishes to you and Mme. Sibelius, and all your family, I am

Sincerely yours,
Olin Downes

29. Frank La Forge (1879–1953), pianist, teacher, and composer, was greatly in demand as an accompanist because of his fine musicianship and his habit of memorizing his music in order to watch the soloist at all times. He trained and coached many singers, including Marian Anderson. La Forge was one of those fortunate musicians to whom death came while performing—in his case, while playing piano at the New York Musicians' Club, of which he was president.

No. 41 CC. *Olin Downes to Jean Sibelius*

Dear Master: New York, May 15, 1938

I think you would have been thrilled if you had heard your hymn sung at the close of our afternoon Pageant of the "Preview" of the World's Fair. It came at the end of a ceremony that had been distinguished by much pageant and color, which my colleag[u]es and I had devised and your work, by its very breadth and simplicity, concluded our program in a very noble and impressive way.

I had devised this program as a sort of a *"Meistersinger* finale," emblematic of the national, international and communal aspects of the Fair. We opened the ceremonies with trumpeters in costume, who introduced our performance quite magnificently with the fanfares from the Third Act of Verdi's *Otello*. We had groups of trumpeters answering each other from the tops of the buildings of the Fair and, then appeared a procession of representatives of fifty-four different nations in their national costumes and with their national flags, who marched to the top of an open-air stage we had devised for the occasion and stood up there in costume with all their flags waving against the sky. We then had folk dances of six different nations and some American popular music, with both negro and American singers, solo performances by Metropolitan and other artists and a finale which came to its climax with your music.

We had devised this afternoon Pageant, witnessed by 600,000 people, as an exhibit of the popular and democratic and "folk" aspects of the Fair. We followed this in the evening with a Concert, in which there were performed a short work of Henry Purcell, the Englishman; three chorales of J. S. Bach; a really fine choral piece—the opening chorus of your old friend Horatio Parker's *Hora Novissima,* after which Dr. Damrosch conducted Beethoven's Ninth Symphony.

I intended this occasion as a foretaste of what I hope we may do (if I can be given the money!) for music at the Fair. I have planned, at least, a very elaborate program for 1939 of religious music, from the plain chant period, to the present day of the Catholic, Protestant, Russian, Greek Orthodox and Jewish faiths; a special Wagner Season with Mme. Flagstad and other artists of the Metropolitan Opera Association, which is a "fait accompli;" choral performances by great choral bodies of American and foreign nations, with which I am already negotiating through George Sjöblom; ballets from many nations, performances by at least six of the leading symphony orchestras of the U.S. and one or two from Europe—I hope—such as the Conzertgebiouw from Amsterdam; our very rich literature of American folk music and folk music and dances from practically all of the foreign nations participating in the Fair—there are now about sixty-two—and all other aspects of our American musical life, including operetta, musical comedy, the popular songs of American composers, which have become part of the life of our people.[30]

Excuse me for writing you at such length, but I have a special purpose which is the dearest wish of my heart.

I want to know if we may not have, for the first performance in the world, Sibelius completed Eighth Symphony.

If you should complete the Eighth Symphony by that time, Dr. Koussevitzky, who will visit the Fair for two weeks with the Boston Symphony Orchestra, is very agreeable to giving it its world premiere here. You know from this that the symphony will have very careful preparation and will be played by what, in my opinion, is the finest symphonic body in the whole world. If we can have this premiere, it will be shortwaved over the entire world and, we should, of course, make special preparations in regard to public announcements for the performance.

My final and consummate wish, dear Master, would be if it could be performed in your presence, with you here as our honored guest. If you could come, I would also wish that you could be here in time for the rehearsals of the symphony so that, in the course of the preparations, Dr. Koussevitzky would have your precise wishes to the smallest detail, which no doubt he would anticipate anyway, with the sympathy and insight of the great musician that he is. I would regard this as the supreme pinnacle of the music program of the Fair and I would ask you, if you will take my request most seriously. This would crown the music of the Fair as no other event could, if we might stand out in history as the nation and the city which gave your Eighth Symphony to the world.

With best wishes to you and to all your family and to Paloheimo and Ilves and all their lovely wives and children and the farm, where I pray I may some day again dig in the garden and have a good Finnish bath.

Sincerely yours,
[Olin Downes]

30. Downes, an early enthusiast of jazz, was also a great lover of American folk music. In 1940 he collaborated with composer Elie Siegmeister on *A Treasury of American Song* (New York: Alfred A. Knopf, 1940), a collection of tunes harmonized by Siegmeister and annotated by Downes and Siegmeister together. The book was revised and enlarged in a second edition three years later.

No. 42 T. *Olin Downes to Jean Sibelius*

New York, December 22, 1938

Dear Master this is to ask if you will make new years day historical in America and the worlds by yourself conducting your music as Finlands greeting to humanity made by radio and t[h]rough agentry of New York Worlds Fair on that day when president of Finland will also honor us by representing your great republic i know this is asking very much of you but please realize you are not appearing as virtuoso in concert but from the quiet and seclusion of radio studio will be talking in your own [illegible] language to your friends all over the world and that in so doing you are sending creative artists message to a humanity that was never in greater need of your spirit and creation of beauty with the warmest personal regards and hopes that you will find it in your hear[t] to and on this occasion.

Olin Downes

No. 43 T. *Olin Downes to Jean Sibelius*

New York, December 25, 1938

Dear master you cannot know what joy your consent to conduct for us and finland and the world gives me[31] i thank you with all my heart and wish you madame sibelius and aarvi and all the sibelius clan the merriest of christmases.

Olin Downes

31. A letter to Downes from Paloheimo describes the journey to the studio to make this broadcast. A terrible snowstorm swept through the countryside that day, causing Sibelius and Paloheimo, who was escorting the composer into Helsinki, many delays and giving Sibelius a great deal of anxiety. On the return to Ainola, Sibelius grumbled: "Does Olin Downes know how much I really did for him and that I only did it for his sake?" GU MSS 688, CF "Paloheimo, Arvi," January 5, 1939.

No. 44 T. *Olin Downes to Jean Sibelius*

New York, December 3, 1939

Your music fights for invincible Finland we shall raise money by concert of your masterpieces keep safe if you can dear master all America prays for you and your noble country.

Olin Downes

No. 45 T. *Olin Downes to Jean Sibelius*

New York, December 25, 1939

Merry xmas and victori[o]us new year to you and yours and all the people of the land of heroes.

Olin Downes

No. 46 T. *Olin Downes to Jean Sibelius*

New York, March 22, 1940

Cannot express loss and shock to me of arvis wholly unexpected death[32] he was for me one of my noblest and dearest friends in finland please give his dear wife my utmost sympathy and my thanks that you and madame sibelius and all others of sibelius family are still alive now we must all work for arvis memory and for finland.

Olin Downes

32. The bitter cold that made the Winter War of 1939–40 so terrible also killed the trees of the Paloheimo apple orchard, a loss Arvi took very hard. In this stressful time (March 1940) Paloheimo apparently suffered heart failure and died at the age of fifty-one.

No. 47 LS. *Jean Sibelius to Olin Downes*

My dear Friend,   Helsinki, December 17, 1940

Please accept my heartfelt thanks for your friendly thoughts and kind congratulations on my 75th birthday.

I was *very* glad to receive your message and we all send you our most cordial greetings and best wishes for the new year.

Yours,

Jean Sibelius

No. 48 CLS. *Olin Downes to Jean Sibelius*

New York, [1941]

[Handwritten at the top of a typed page numbered I:]

Alas! This was a beginning, dear Master, of a letter to you which I began to write, I think last January [substituted for October]. I am going to just put this and its continuation in an envelope right now, and send it to you. Otherwise, God knows when one of my constant thoughts about you will reach you. You, who are a very part of my life and strength to me.

O.D.

[In typed copy:]

Dear Master and Friend, [crossed through]

For long, very long, I have wanted to write you, and you know how constantly you are in my thoughts. There is so much I have wanted to say, and which, in a letter, takes so long and perhaps makes much too long a communication for you to read without fatigue. But I have talked with you on two occasions, and we said more then than can ever be said in a letter—or you said it. The first was when you gave the grace of your music and yourself to me and to America and the world when you yourself directed the performance for us at the New York World's Fair. The second was when Toscanini gave a concert of your music at the time of your birthday, a concert in which I had the honor of a small part as commentator, and when, as I then cabled you, your music gave me such comfort and when I realized anew how wonderfully you had written as the young poet of death in the *Swan of Tuonela.* That was only one of the experiences of that evening but I can tell you that I never realized so profoundly as I did then the genius of that little piece, and its holy truth. You spoke to me, and I thought never more wisely or truly in that piece, and I was better able to understand, for within a short time I had lost two people who were very dear to me. Aarvi I saw but seldom, yet he was one of the very, very few friends whom I loved. When I got your letter[33] that his heart had ceased to beat it was with the knowledge that one part of the living life had gone—not that I feel he is absent, for without the slightest theory or belief of any definite kind I know very well that the organic life is not the end at all, and that everything Aarvi was to me is still with me—in as great fullness as before, or greater. That is something *additional* that death brings to us who continue, temporarily, the organic life. Death brings *addition,* not *subtraction.* It is the last mortal gift that those who precede us give, and it is the greatest, of course, of all. We understand so much more, we live with them so much more, and they are more than ever ours, just when they are in the place and at the time when they can—when life can—give us that last priceless heritage. The savage that ate the heart of a brave enemy that he might be braver still—that is us, when our true friends set out on the next great voyage of the mysterious and wonderful journey. So it was of Aarvi that I was thinking, as I listened to that particular music (*Swan of Tuonela*). And of one even dearer, and a more terrible loss to me—my mother, who died last September, and who was half, or more, of my soul. I lived through that, dear master, and she helped me so much when she left me so lonely. In her last moment of consciousness I held her in my arms. The day before that she braced herself high on her pillow, and listened eagerly as I read her a paper which was a denunciation of modern literary men of America who are escapists and who write of unrealities because they dare not face the realities, so terrible, of the world of today. I was very much moved by that. My mother listened with her eyes shining, and said, "You must try to put every word of that in your music page"—although it was not directly about music. But it *was* about music. Perhaps, today, *only* about your music. And *The Swan of Tuonela* spoke to me of all that, very profoundly. Just imagine that I had dismissed that composition as a small, inspired, and beautiful piece, but not as of any great importance in the sum total of your works! What a fool I was. But sometimes, you know, Wagner was right, even if you [substituted for "we"] do not like his esthetic: "Durch Mitleid wissend." Only the departure of those two whom I loved could have made me understand the great wisdom and tenderness of that music of you, the young poet "sans peur et sans reproche," wrote in your early days, with the true wisdom of your own people, your own myth, your own genius—intuition, not knowledge. That is music of great beauty and great comfort, and not of silly weeping, or maudlin tears. But I won't dwell upon that, for who knows the truth that you spoke there better than you? Still, I return again and again to the joy which that deep truthfulness and that knowledge that the music contains. It is so innocent and so profound. There is such love and knowledge, that there is no sorrow—only beauty, understanding, compassion [substituted for "and great comfort"] for us all, and great knowledge of eternity.

[Here the consecutively numbered pages, III to IV, jump to a new topic: Toscanini as conductor.]

The tempo is sometimes too fast, and the orchestral tone too light, bright, and clear, for what I personally believe to be the true character of the music. But that is Toscanini. His sincerity and his heroic and passionate devotion to his art are the things, after all, that matter most. He is the only interpreter I know who will compromise at nothing, who fights every day the most furious fights for what he believes, and who will kill anybody who does not unite with him in making the best possible interpretation. In addition to this, he is the most adorable character in the world, with a voice which is husky and quite sweet, and away from his music the most lovable and irresistible of all people. But with the baton—to the transgressor— *really* terrible, really insane—an avenging demon. The players do not dare when he becomes angry, as he very often does, to say one word, to move. Nor would I dare to do so if I were present! But otherwise—he wants any idea, any opinion, which is sincere and could possibly be well founded. Even I have had arguments with him, to which he does me the infinite honor to listen attentively, and always, as I am perfectly sure, to think it over, and in all probabil[i]ty reject. But he gives the sligh[t]est idea, the smallest note, the consideration of a god. I must tell you, too, that on the occasion of the Sibelius program I sat in the broadcasters box, which was at the back of the orchestra, so that, through a very transparent window, I would see very clearly his every gesture and expression. It was genius at play, and then I can give you no idea of the sculptured magnificence of the face, its imperiousness and fire, and mobility; the beat which is wholly unconventional, and the most effective and expressive I have ever seen; the eyes that cannot see four feet away from him, yet fairly blaze their instantaneous message to the players; and with all this fire and mobility such a concentration that there is at once something absolute[ly] masterful and inscrutable in the countenance. And then a native gesture that only an Italian artist would make: when he wishes the utmost intensity of a melodic phrase, the left hand goes to his heart. Ah, but this man, this artist, is a king. If you have not met I wish you could, because he would most humbly ask you, with a directness to which he would expect the most direct answer, whether this or that was right, or wrong, and he would be at your feet in his search for that secret. I say, again, that to know, as musicians, Sibelius the composer, Toscanini the interpretive genius and high priest of his art, is enough for a life-time.

[The letter breaks off here, and then continues on a fresh sheet, which begins with the following message scrawled over an otherwise typewritten page:]

This is "communication No. 2"—Please forgive me. But there is so much I want to say. How could I *ever* say it?

[Typed:]

Dear Master,

For so long I have wanted to write you. But have not known how to do so—what to say. What can one say, of those things concerning which one would wish to say only something real, and that one thing desired, that something real, is the one thing which never can [be] said—certainly not said by any word of mouth or on paper. My own thoughts, wishes, and sorrows are so much less than yours, and Finland's, that I fe[el] a[l]ways like an interloper in dreaming to address you. I shall try not to fatigue you too much with too long a l[e]tter now, but perhaps, if it is too long, Mme. Sibelius or the person who pleases you both the most will read you parts of it at a time, or something like that. I could say nothing about Aarvi's death, for the reasons I have said. And I cannot now. I always lived, so to speak, near him, and though I might not see him, or you, in years, it did not matter. I am not injured by his loss, and I do not see death as a tragedy; only as a mystery. And that is what I understood, and knew so well that you understood, even as a very young man, when you created *The Swan of Tuonela.* At the concert Toscanini gave, and played that piece among others, it was to me like a word with Aarvi. You see the only words are the music, so that you can say the necessary things and I cannot. But I think you knew this, and heaven knows you had enough sorrow not to be burdened with another letter of regret of mine at the départe of Aarvi. I had very, very few friends that I had grown to love as I loved him.

Now let me tell you a little of the Toscanini Sibelius concert. As you probably heard this concert broadcast to Finland I need tell you nothing about the performances, but I will tell you something else which touched me greatly. It was at the rehearsal. Toscanini took the score of *Lemminkäinen's Homecoming,* which he had memorized in about one day after re[c]eiving it and was rehearsing from memory with the orchestra—he took the score from a desk on which it was lying by him, and he roared at the orchestra: "I *love* this music. *Don't forget.*" It was a most passionate declaration—and warning. I of course shall not ask you what you feel about Toscanini's interpretation of your music, which, to me, is sometimes more Latin than Northern. But his passion for music, and the purity of his soul where music is concerned is beyond any description. If you do not know him—I mean now as a man— I only hope that you do, or will. For I think he would mean much to you. He does to me, because as a conductor he is as honorable as you are as a creative musician! He has no price, and every rehearsal is a battle to the death for his ideal of the interpretation. If he had been a soldier at your side at the front, and you had been prostrate and wounded and [at] his feet, and he fighting to save you, he would not fight more furiously than he fought that afternoon, and every afternoon of rehearsal, for the best, the very best, he could do with your music. I seldom hear him without this realization. On the night of the concert, after having made a short speech in the intermission about you, I was seated where I was facing him as he conducted, and could see him clearly through the glass observation room of radio manipulators. It was the face and the m[ie]n of a god—a most imperious god, and a god intent only on one thing—the music. I never saw a more inspiring face, or witnessed any artist so intent, terrifically intent, on his task. Perhaps it was the effect of his face and his personality, but it seemed to me that this time he came nearer what is to me the secret of your music than ever he came before. And his modesty is so true. He played last winter your Fourth Symphony, and I could not go. I wrote him a note, asking him if there was any lik[e]lihood of him playing the work again, soon. He answered that he hoped so, but greatly regretted that I could not be there, "because," he said, "I had the illusion that this time I had understood the symphony." It was in the same tone that he said two years ago, after a performance of Beethoven's Ninth, "When I played it last in London I thought I had found it. But no! it was only *last night* that I found it." He said this to David Sarnoff, who told me, and Toscanini is like that, always.

I could have wished that he had played some of your later as well as earlier works on that occasion. On the other hand, it was very good for me to hear the earlier scores again. I must tell you this: when I was young I under-valued those scores, and thought them more important as formulative than as mature compositions. But now I think differently. The *Lemminkäinen* music—the whole suite—will I believe endure as long as the later pieces. It is the young poetry of your people and land, and if I may say so to you, I am still astonished, again and again, at some detail of instrumentation which is so simple but so unique. But I will not trouble you with my ideas of your music.

There is, however, a question I have meant to ask you for years. It is a small detail, and this, I suppose, just not the time to ask it. But when Toscanini played the second symphony I asked myself the question I am now going to put [to] you. It concerns the place in the first movement of this symphony, when the kett[l]edrums emphasi[ze] the D which is the pedal point of the passage after the *poco largamente* of the development section. You have simply a trill-mark over the quarter-note Ds of the drums. And all the conductors play it so—simply with a sustained trill for five quarters of the measure. But is not a good strong *accent* on each of these Ds intended? I have this feeling as being the nature of the music, and also from the fact that where the Ds are doubled by the basses they have each a dash over them, indicating also an emphasis. The ["kettle" is deleted] drum passage is written like this: [there are spaces but no examples to illustrate Downes's questions in the GU MSS 688 copy]. Should it, by any chance, be intended, like this:

And [should] there not be a little cres[c]endo and *zurückhaltend,* like this:

Or [am] I, dear maestro, merely an idiot, or behaving like a virtuoso conductor, who wants to make something where nothing of the kind was intended? And anyhow, don't bother to answer! I just want to get this little question off my mind!

Did you know that Procopé[34] and some of his friends asked me if, in celebration of your 75th birthday, I would prepare, in book form, a sequence of some of the newspaper articles I had written about you and your various works? In case you heard of this, I want to explain why I did not do it. When I first heard that some new literary material about you was coming over-seas, to be published if we could find a publisher in book form, and was asked if I would be willing to write a short introduction to this material, I told them I would be very glad to do so. But when the material reached me, I found it ["very" deleted] incomplete and containing practically nothing that had not already been published in earlier English books or magazine articles about you. So I wrote this to Procopé and told him that I doubted if an American publisher would want such incomplete material. Then Procopé wrote me and begged me to write something myself. I did not want to do so, for two reasons. First, it might appear that I, intentionally and conceitedly, had disparaged the material about you from Finland, because I wanted to write it myself. Second, because I do not like to republish articles hastily written for newspaper consumption in book form. Least of all would I wish to write such superficial material about the music of Sibelius.

But they begged me, for the sake of the celebration. They told me I could say in an introduction that these were simply a sheaf of newspaper articles which I had put together for purposes of a birthday celebration about you, and that a little could be made, with pictures, that would sell, and the funds from it be devoted to money for Finland.

On this basis I tried, but, dear master and friend, I *could not* do it. I tried till the last possible day. My old material, i.e., the newspaper articles, se[e]med to me so poor that I could not stand them. I then began to change the articles and try to connect them. Nothing came out right. So, after a month of effort, in every available hour, I simply told the publishers I could not do it. Some day I would like very much to make as careful and thorough a subject as I could of your music, and then to come to Finland and ask you only a few questions, but make an investigation there that would provide a volume on this subject with really complete and authoritative information. Such are the only terms on which I would be so impert[in]ent as to make a book on this subject. I have a strange reputation, I find, here-abouts— that of being an "authority" on Sibelius!!! You and I both know how ridiculous that is. It was my good fortune, as a young critic, that I was fascinated by your music, heard it, and also studied it, to a certain extent, wh[en]ever I had the chance. But that is not being an "authority." I have a very funny and quite exalted position, dear Master, in this country, because I have happened to like the music of Jan Sibelius. I tell them all the truth, which is that I know very little about your music. But I cannot stop them. This furnishes an excellent idea of the way reputations are gained, and certainly, the older I grow, the less I believe, either in "reputations," or most of those who have them! I say these things because, in case you might hear that I refused to write the book about your art—a book I would have been only too glad to write if I felt I could do so—you will know why I declined, and also why I told Procopé I really did not think there was any use in my attempting such a book. Though God knows I would have been only too happy, if I could have completed this, to have been in this way accessory to the sending of small funds to Finland.

[handwritten date:]   April 8, 1941

Master—you know, I am sure, that I am insane. These are all letters I have been trying to write you for months. There is not time to repeat them in some complete way, so I have clipped off the parts in the accompanying two letters which repeated themselves, and now I add, before my day of insane work and hurry, hurry, hurry begins, one more shorter word.

I want you to know that I live in your music more than ever, and perhaps still more in the knowledge of you. This knowledge grows all the time upon me, particularly since my mother's death, and hearing, after that, *The Swan of Tuonela*. And that is not the only thing I have heard. Excuse me if I say that I have been only with you, very often, when I hear or take before me the score of the slow movement of your Fourth Symphony. And so many other pages. The Seventh I heard only two nights ago, given, on the whole, the best interpretation I have yet heard of it, by Thomas Beecham.[35] Koussevitzky's has certain classic and tonally beautiful qualities which Beecham's had not. But there is more of the essential grandeur and strength of this work, which is so noble and so consoling to me, in Beecham's reading.

But no more of that now. I have had some great sorrows and great joy since we last talked. My mother died as I have told you. I did not know how I would endure it, but she helped me. She helped me by not telling me that she knew she was going, and perhaps I helped her by not letting her know that I knew her end was near. I saw her, of course, every day, and read to her that last day before she fell asleep and passed through the portals to the other side without again waking. Her life had been very tragic, as only I know. Her suffering, her immense and fanatical heroism fed me and made the heroism of your music so dear to me. I took her in my arms that last afternoon while the nurse made her bed and she was so helpless and weak that I could only think as I saw her poor shrunken limbs of Christ being taken down from the cross. Later I went alone with her ashes, and I had to scatter these ashes, with my own hands, upon *her* mother's grave. It seems to me that perhaps one only truly lives and feels life—the life visible and invisible which is the whole universe, when those really a part of us have led the way. Do you know the line of our great poet, Whitman: "Superb vistas of death." He means, life after life, many existences, states, transformations—endless vistas of infinity.

Now please excuse me. I fear it is not appropriate to dwell on this to anyone in Finland, where there has been such tragedy. God knows—so confused thoughts go t[h]rough my head. And then there is the other thing—I separated from my first wife last October and re-married last January—I mean—good heavens—not last October and last January, but the October and January of a year before. In other words, I have been re-married since January of 1940. This—the separation—was accompanied with bitter pain, and of course one will never know whether one has done what was right, or—well, never mind. The point is, at least, that I am very happy with my present wife, who is very dear to me and extremely helpful. I won't go into more of these personal matters, but dear God, what a confusion! And that terrible World's Fair! I worked there all day and night through nearly two years to try and induce those bankers and other idiots to give a really representative program of music. And I got part of it done, but much not done, and this because of such pettiness, dirty politics and intrigue and st[u]pidity,—as I had expected!! I felt proud of what I did, and then resigned. But at what a cost of time and strength. I want to see you and Finland, and I shall. There is a better day—I did not say a perfect one—but a better day, for the world, if we in America fight hard enough for it. We should be fighting in the war. We must also fight, this time, for the peace, and know that all our lives we must continue to fight for that peace—every man— not just the philosophers who are not heard and the politicians who deafen everyone and dest[ro]y the faith of humanity. I am making speeches at many places about these things just now, especially to the young people at the colleges, and I thank God for our President—the greatest man we have had since Wilson. But no more of that either. I am late already, dear master. I shall write you shorter letters more often in the future, and you need not answer one of them. You are answering them always with your spirit and your art. And now, when I stand before my mother's grave, as I did only a few days ago, on her birthday, and I looked at the evening sky, I can talk to her of you, and you can talk to both of us—let us say, in the final pages of the infinite beauty and consolation of the Seventh Symphony. May I please be remembered to Mme. Sibelius, and I think I must try—a thing I want to do, yet shrink from—to write some letter to your daughter and the widow of beloved Aarvi.

Olin Downes

33. This letter is not with the Sibelius correspondence in the Downes Collection.
34. Hjalmar Procopé (1889–1954), the Finnish diplomat referred to in Chapter 5.
35. Another Sibelius enthusiast and an important interpreter of the symphonic works, Sir Thomas Beecham (1879–1961) also gave a memorable tribute to Sibelius over the BBC on the composer's ninetieth birthday.

No. 49 LS. *Jean Sibelius to Olin Downes*

My dear Friend,   Järvenpää, May 8, 1941

With great pleasure I have received your kind letter and I have read it over and over again.

Many cordial thanks for all that you write about my music and about our dear Arvi whom we shall never forget. He was a real friend of yours.

It was kind of you to tell me about your marriage. We were very glad to hear it and we wish you much happiness.

I hope you will not forget your promise to write me then and again though my own letters to you by known reasons always must be somewhat stereotypic.

With friendship.
Yours
Jean Sibelius

No. 50 T. *Jean Sibelius to Marcus Tollet[36] and Olin Downes*

Helsinki, December 28, 1943

Hearty thanks and best greetings.

Jean Sibelius

36. Tollet was a diplomat who had met Sibelius as early as 1921 in London, where Tollet was in the Finnish Embassy; see Tawaststjerna, *Sibelius* 5:64.

No. 51 LS. *Jean Sibelius to Olin Downes*

My dear Friend, Järvenpää, January 2, 1946

I may sincerely assure you that among the many congratulations I received across the Atlantic yours was one of the most welcome. You know: only few critics in the world have understood the spirit of my music as you have done and there is scarcely a single [one] who has done so much for it as you.

When today, in the age of eighty, I look backwards and search for my real friends, you surely are one of the first among them. So accept, my dear friend, my heartfelt thanks for all that you have done for me, for your courage and sincerity and for your great heart.

With cordial greetings and all best wishes for the New Year.

Your real, grateful friend
Jean Sibelius

No. 52 CC. *Olin Downes to Jean Sibelius*

Dear Master: New York, December 15, 1948

I should have been among the hundreds who sent you birthday greetings the other day. But I don't believe that you ever need greetings from me to know how much in my heart and my life you are. Perhaps I observe this greeting better than by a formal telegram to add to the overloaded deskful that you doubtless have received.

I had occasion to do some radio work with Koussevitzky and the Boston Symphony Orchestra, to describe to the audience the music that they were to play. The week before Koussevitzky did not know whether he would work with your Sixth Symphony or your Seventh Symphony. Therefore to prepare myself and refresh my mind I re-studied both scores. I cannot begin to tell you with what happiness I found myself getting a little deeper into this wonderful music than I ever had. I was sorry indeed that he was not going to play both scores, because on again reading through, and really doing some more work on the score of the Sixth Symphony which I especially treasure because you sent me this with your autograph years ago, it seemed to me that in that work perhaps more than ever before, you conversed so marvelously with what I would call "your voices," meaning the voices of nature that speak to you so truly in your music, as the voices of Jeanne d'Arc spoke to her in her hour of trial, and that your music was getting constantly simpler and constantly more profound and constantly more original in the profoundly simple ways which you are using in achieving your expressive ends. The wonderful things that you have done with the strings in both of these symphonies, the secrets of development which become always more unique, as it seems to me, always more direct, dispensing with all superfluities and clichés of the past, and always more authentic in their approach to the great mysteries of life and of beauty.

You may know that years ago on the occasion of your seventy-fifth birthday, Pro-copé and others begged that I would issue a brochure on the music of Sibelius. When I told them that I was not sufficiently prepared to do this, or sufficiently profoundly versed in your art to attempt this, they suggested then that I just use a series of newspaper articles that I had written and put them together in a book, as that nice young Sjöblom has done in Finland with my articles.[37] But I found my articles altogether repetitious and in most respects superficial on the subject of your art, and after vainly attempting something I gave up the proposal. Only now am I beginning to feel that I might some day write a real book of examination of the Sibelius symphonies. Perhaps in another ten years, if I am alive then. You may well have forgotten saying something to me that I never can possibly forget, namely, that in a future day, perhaps after you had gone, I would find myself doing creative work. Perhaps that creative moment may come when I turn with adequate time to do the job to the real study of your music.

At any rate, what I must now tell you is that Koussevitzky finally decided on the Seventh Symphony. I thought I knew this score fairly well, but as I turned back to it I discovered that I knew but the superficial quarter of it. I read the music, I even copied out some passages before going up to Boston to hear the rehearsal, and again I knocked myself on the head and said to myself, "You ass. So you thought you knew something of the music of Sibelius." I said to Koussevitzky then that if you had written only the Seventh Symphony you would be among the greatest of the musical immortals. I added that in order to write the Seventh Symphony you had to write all the earlier six, but not one of the six could possibly be spared from the literature of modern music. And again I had the unspeakable purification and ec-stasy that I have when I succeed in the midst of the distraction that surrounds m[e] here in New York, in really immersing myself again in your art. It is so far and away the highest and purest art that music knows today that I sometimes feel it is my only spiritual refuge that is left. I think it is impossible to pay it sufficient homage, just as I could find no words for the respect and the love in which I hold you, not merely as a personal friend whose hand it has been my privilege to shake, but as the great friend of humanity and truth, and the eternities, as you speak of these things in your music.

Do you know I did not even start this letter with the intention of speaking of these things, but they came irresistibly to my mind and I had to write them before I came to the practical purpose of the present note. I have a record here of an aria of yours *Arioso,* sung by Aulikki Rautawaara,[38] and recorded by Telefunken. There is a good singer here in New York, a Mrs. Goerll, a friend of my good friend, the musician and composer Edgar Varèse.[39] She wishes to secure the orchestral score of this aria because she wishes to perform it through America. Neither she nor Varèse have been able to find who publishes the parts or where they can be secured. So Varèse asked me if I would write you and ask you if there is any way or any place from which Mrs. Goerll can secure this music, in the orchestral version. If you have time to send me this information, he and I and Mrs. Goerll will of course be very grateful. Send it to me if you have the time to spend on such a minor matter, dear master. But don't even bother with it if by neglecting to do this you can write one more measure of Sibelius music.

With warmest greetings to you and to Madame Sibelius and your daughters and their respective families, I am

Sincerely,
[Olin Downes]

37. Downes is referring to the volume *Sibelius*, a collection of the critic's articles translated into Finnish by Paul Sjöblom and published in Helsinki just after World War II.
38. *Arioso*, Sibelius's op. 3, is a setting of a Runeberg poem for soprano and string orchestra. The singer Aulikki Rautawaara (1906–1990) was a Finnish soprano who achieved international recognition. A fine interpreter of Sibelius's songs, Rautawaara was married for a time to Finland's "Bad Boy of Music," composer Erik Bergman.
39. The little-known and seemingly unlikely friendship between Edgard Varèse (1883–1965) and Olin Downes is borne out by their correspondence in GU MSS 688, CF "Varèse, Edgard."

No. 53 LS. *Jean Sibelius to Olin Downes*

My dear old Friend,   Järvenpää, January 16, 1949

A few days before Christmas came your letter which, needless to say—I was delighted to receive. Please accept my cordial thanks for all your kind thoughts. As I said [to] you at the Torni in Helsinki I have always been sure that some day you will write something exceptionally good about my music, original and to the point. And I am happy that a man of your measures will interpret my works.

My thoughts are often with you. I have heard that you are the very health and work like a giant. I was glad to hear that.

As for the orchestral score of *Arioso* you will please write to Westerlunds Musikhandel, N. Esplanadgatan 37, Helsingfors, mentioning the number of parts.

With kindest regard from my family and myself I send you in old friendship my warmest wishes for the new year.

Yours sincerely,
Jean Sibelius

No. 54 CC. *Olin Downes to Jean Sibelius*

Dear Master: New York, April 15, 1949

May I take occasion with this letter to introduce Mr. Yousuf Karsh,[40] a photographer who is not a mechanician but a true artist. He has been so highly recommended to me, as also the nature of his intention as an artist, that I feel confident in asking if you would permit him to take some photographs of you which he would like to prepare in the most careful fashion, and to submit to you for your approval for any further use he might wish to make of them. My friend, Mr. Leopold Mannes[41] of the Mannes School of Music of this city, has thus spoken to me of Mr. Karsh and I am glad to follow Mr. Mannes's recommendation in this matter, and to present herewith to you Mr. Karsh, who expects to be in Helsinki next July 5th to 8th inclusive.

I need hardly say that my last wish would be to submit you to any photographic process which might not be to your desire, but should you be inclined to oblige Mr. Karsh he would greatly appreciate this courtesy.

As you well know, there go to you with this letter, and all the time, regardless of any letters, my gratitude and deepest esteem for your art.

Sincerely yours,

[Olin Downes]

40. Karsh of Ottawa (b. 1908), as this artist is known, took some of the most magnificent photographs in existence of the old Sibelius. One was published together with a memoir of the portrait sitting in Karsh's *Portraits of Greatness* (London and New York: T. Nelson, 1960), 182–83. (A copy of the photograph, autographed by Sibelius, is among the pictures in the Olin Downes Collection.) Although born in Armenia, Karsh spent his apprenticeship years in Boston, where he arrived in 1928, which happened to be when Koussevitzky began conducting Sibelius's works with great frequency. Karsh recalls that a London official helped him to contact Sibelius in 1949, but the letter here indicates that Olin Downes also had a hand in paving his way to Ainola.

41. Leopold Damrosch Mannes (1899–1964), music educator, pianist, composer, and scientist, was also an administrator, directing the school founded by his parents from 1940 until his death. Under his direction, the Mannes School became the first in the United States to incorporate the teaching of Schenkerian analysis into its curriculum. It was also the first to offer a degree in early music performance. Mannes's extraordinarily varied interests included photography, and his scientific experiments with Leopold Godowsky led to the invention of the Kodachrome color process in 1935.

No. 55 CC. *Olin Downes to Jean Sibelius*

Dear Master: New York, August 31, 1950

I do not have to tell you how constantly I think of you these days and indeed all days. Our old friendship, very dear to me, has been strengthened in these recent months in the very best way. I have had reason to re-study a number of your scores, and although I thought I knew most of them well, I am working on them now with a host of new realizations, some of them matters of musical craftsmanship— harmonic and contrapuntal details—but most of them merely a deeper realization of the integrity and the profundity of your music.

Now I am writing with a special and most earnest request in view.

I note that the Polytech Chorus of Finland is coming to America to tour the country this coming season. And I recall, first, an evening when Aarvi Paloheimo, my dearly missed friend, loaned me the M.S. score of your *Kullervo* symphony to examine as much as I might in a few hours late one night in his apartment. I must say that in examining this early work of yours, while I could only do so in the most hasty and superficial way, my anticipations of the beauty and freshness of the music and its nature moods, was more than fulfilled. Secondly I discover that you permitted a performance of three movements of the *Kullervo* Symphony in Helsinki, I think in 1945.[42]

Now I wish to propose the following. Would you be favorable to a performance of these three movements or the *Kullervo* Symphony in its entirety, with the Finnish Chorus, for an American premiere of the work next winter in America?

If you are agreeable to this idea and permitted me to do so, I would like to suggest it to Toscanini and the NBC Symphony Orchestra for a first radio performance over America and the whole world. And then, without doubt many leading American orchestras would be interested in further performances in various cities with the Finnish Chorus, which would come over here with your precise directions as to its interpretation of the choral part of the symphony.

There enters here a further consideration, namely, that a leading American music publisher would be granted the contract to publish this score under arrangements which at last would insure you not only American royalties, but also European royalties accruing to you from each performance of the symphony. This would at least be a first approach to a publishing arrangement which had some justice to you in the matter of royalties, while I also believe that the performance of your early music would be of the greatest artistic interest and significance in bringing this work to the attention of the world.

I have a premonition that you may be apprehensive of the performance of *Kullervo* as representing an early and comparatively immature representation of your art. But is it not true that an artist's early and youthfully inspired production may have in it a certain precious thing which reflects the utmost honor upon him and which speaks to humanity in a way to which a highly developed technic or stylistic sense is of quite secondary importance?

I write, dear master, in great hope that you will give careful consideration to this proposal, which I believe could readily be developed here in such a way that those who asked the privilege of the performance and publication of your music would be in a position that would enable you to impose upon them exactly the terms and the conditions in the matter which would be most acceptable to you.

If you are favorable to this idea, might I hope for an early reply because a thing of this kind should be set in motion as soon as possible. I hope this letter finds you and Mme. Sibelius and your children happy and well. As for myself, I have been talking with you lately very much, with your scores.

Sincerely,
Olin Downes

P.S. That fine young man whom you and I both know, Paul Sjöblom, has, I learned from his father, just recently returned to Finland. It was he who told me of the performance of the *Kullervo* symphony in 1945, and if it would be of service to you, he might be of aid in some aspect of this matter.

42. Sibelius had permitted a single performance of *Kullervo's* third movement in 1935 in conjunction with the celebrations of the one hundredth anniversary of the *Kalevala*.

No. 56 LS. *Jean Sibelius to Olin Downes*

Dear Friend,   Järvenpää, September 5, 1950

My cordial thanks for your letter and for the interest you have shown my *Kullervo*. Your beautiful words were dear to me particularly because I still feel deeply for this youthful work of mine. Perhaps that accounts for the fact that I would not like to have it performed abroad during an era that seems to me so very remote from the spirit that *Kullervo* represents. Though I realise that *Kullervo* even with its potential weaknesses has its historical value at least within my own production I am not certain that the modern public would be able to place it in its proper perspective. That was the reason for my negative answer to, among others, the Polytech Chorus who asked for my permission to perform it during their tour in America.

Even in my own country I have declined to have it produced with an exception made on my last birthday. Condition[s] here differ from those in the great world and for that reason I have consented to the request of the representatives of our government to produce it on their concert the 8th December.[43]

I sincerely hope that you, dear friend, will understand my point of view.

I also want you to know how grateful I am for your interest concerning my royalties. That I will never forget.

My whole family has been deeply moved about your kind words of our beloved Arvi and sends you their greetings.

All best wishes to you.

Very sincerely yours,
Old Friend
Jean Sibelius

43. It is not at all clear what Sibelius means, since no performance is known of *Kullervo* either in 1949 or in 1950. Professor Erkki Salmenhaara kindly provided the following dates for the performances of this work between its premiere and 1958:
April 28, 1892   first performance
April 29, 1892   matinée performance
April 30, 1892   fourth movement only performed
March 1893   three performances
March 1, 1935   third movement performed together with two movements of the *Lemmin-käinen Suite* (see note 46 below), Georg Schnéevoigt conducting

June 1957   "Kullervo's Complaint," an extract from the third movement
June 12, 1958   entire *Kullervo* Symphony, Jussi Jalas conducting

No. 57 CC. *Olin Downes to Jean Sibelius*

Dear Master: New York, October 4, 1950

Your last letter, in which you have told me so clearly the reasons, which are profound and right, why you do not feel that you can permit the performance of the
Kullervo Symphony in America this Winter, was in that particular a great disappointment to me. And yet I feel that you are eternally right. It is all too true that
these are not the times when the spirit of the *Kullervo* Symphony would be entirely
appreciated. I did not know that the Polytechnic Chorus had already asked your
permission to have this work performed in America, or I would not have bothered
you with the question about it. I think they still hoped that perhaps my wishes added
to theirs might move you to change your mind. But in this they should have known
that they would be mistaken, because I know enough of you and of your spirit and
your mind to know that you do not change such grave questions once you have
decided about them. May I say, that I feel in the sure knowledge that you show in
making this decision not to have the work performed in America, the same verity
and the same inner wisdom that I feel in your music.

But now I have a most urgent wish to express to you, and I wonder whether you
could possibly grant it?

Could you possibly permit the *Kullervo* Symphony to be photostated, at my expense of course, and allow me to have that material in the most sacred confidence
in my study? I would promise never to show it to a single conductor or even a single
musician if you will permit this to be done. I would never in any article quote a
theme from this symphony. But there is one thing that I wish to do very much. That
is to study the score carefully in order to make known to myself its contents and
character, and to speak about it in an article in a book which I am writing, in which
I discuss most of your important orchestral compositions.[44] The *Kullervo* Symphony,
with which I was fairly enchanted through beloved Aarvi Paloheimo, I was able to
spend a few hours with him one night in his house in Helsingfors, is in my opinion a
most important and inseparable link in your progress as a composer, and profoundly
related to the modern orchestral repertory, which I hope, will be a far more mature
and complete affair, at least in its approach to the compositions which I will tell
about, than that early and rather childish volume which I issued on this same subject
many years ago, and of which I even had the effrontery to send you a copy.[45] I
suppose everyone commits youthful indiscretions, and I was rather alarmed than
pleased when you actually showed me this book in your library shelves, and assured
me with a smile that it was there, and inferred, which I rather feared, that you had
even some knowledge of its contents. I sincerely hope this isn't so, although, cer-

tainly, I said nothing about you which did not indicate your greatness and your verity as a creative artist. But I want this new book of mine to be as representative as possible on its subject. It is intended to be a book for the great public and not the small one, but there shall certainly be no foolishness in it, if I can prevent that, and it will be at least a more scholarly examination of its subjects than the one which appeared some twenty years ago.

I would like to put some pages about the *Kullervo* Symphony in this book, in a general and indicative manner. For this I would like to examine the score, aside from the fact that of course it would be by far the greatest treasury that my musical library holds—and as I have said, one that I would hold in the completest confidence, as you may be assured.

Now along exactly these same lines, I am trying to get a hold of those two first numbers of the *Lemminkäinen Suite, Lemminkäinen and the Maidens of Saari* and *Lemminkäinen in Tuonela.*

Is there any way in which I could locate the material of these scores and also have them photostated, at my expense and for the purposes of my book?[46] George Schnéevoight,[47] as probably you know, played them here in New York ten years ago, and then proudly told me that he had these manuscripts exclusively in his possession, and implied that nobody else but he would ever see them or conduct them while he lived. I understand he has now died, and I wrote Mr. Jalas[48] asking him if he had knowledge of the whereabouts of the music. But he does not seem to know just where they are now. To me these movements are among the most beautiful and wonderful of your early music. They should of course be published and accessible to everyone. But would it be possible, that by the same process of photostat, and by some search which you would direct, if you do not know where these scores are now, I might have copies of the same in this matter for my study and examination, and critical remarks thereupon?

I have three more months' time in which to finish my book, and I need hardly say that if I could get any part or all of this material at the earliest possible moment, I would be eternally grateful and obligated to you.

Sincerely yours,
[Olin Downes]

44. Downes is probably referring to his essay *Sibelius the Symphonist,* which was not completed until 1955. It was published posthumously by the New York Philharmonic-Symphony Society.
45. The "childish volume" is *Symphonic Masterpieces.*
46. The scores Downes seeks are two of the four movements of Op. 22, the *Four Legends,* often called the *Lemminkäinen Suite.* Although Breitkopf & Härtel had published two of the movements in 1901, *Lemminkäinen's Return* and the famous *Swan of Tuonela,* the two sought by the critic were not published until 1954.
47. Schnéevoigt (1872–1947) was the Finnish conductor who shared with Robert Kajanus the leadership of the Helsinki City Orchestra; he eventually succeeded Kajanus as sole director.

48. Born Blomstedt, Jussi Jalas (1908–1985) changed his Swedish name to a Finnish one. He married Sibelius's daughter Margareta and became a well-known conductor and interpreter of Sibelius's music. A number of his scores in the Sibelius Academy Library bear performance annotations made during conversations with the composer.

No. 58 LS. *Jean Sibelius to Olin Downes*

My dear old Friend,   Järvenpää, October 26, 1950

I have received your last letter and was glad to see how well you have understood the reasons why I cannot permit the performance of *Kullervo* in America. Much could be said about that but I just thank you and go to the main point. It shall be a pleasure for me to send you a copy of the *Kullervo* Symphony. To my great regret I cannot have it photostated as the whole work then must first be written on thin transparent paper which, of course, cannot be done. In its stead, however, I have had the Symphony photographed and the film will be sent to you in a week or so. It will be a simple thing to you to have enlarged copies made of any page you wish or of the whole work.

As for *Lemminkäinen and the Maidens of Saari* and *Lemminkäinen in Tuonela* I can tell you that these works according to a letter which I recently received from Breitkopf & Härtel in Wiesbaden will be printed this autumn by the British & Continental Music Agencies, 125 Shaftesbury Avenue, London, W.C.2. I have today written to the firm and asked them to send you a copy of each score as soon as they are printed.

I am indeed happy that you write a book about my development as a composer, a subject that nobody else has written about yet. I am sure you will do it with real understanding so that the book will cause admiration. And I need not tell you how grateful I am to you for the kind interest you always have taken in my music.

With warmest regards and all best wishes from my family and myself,

Yours very sincerely,
Jean Sibelius

No. 59 LS. *Olin Downes to Jean Sibelius*

Dear Master: New York, November 9, 1950

I cannot describe to you the joy I felt on receiving your letter of the 26th with your consent to send me a copy of the *Kullervo* Symphony. I think this is the most precious gift that I have ever received in music, and it will mean so much the more for me because I am certain to find in it some of the secrets of a great spirit unfolding the beauty and mystery of life and precipitating that vision in the sovereign language of the tone world. Excuse me if this sounds extravagant or theatrical, but it is the truth and it is an aid to one's own being that I particularly crave now, in these most tragic days of the world. I also am delighted to hear that you have asked Breitkopf & Hartel to send me the scores of the two missing numbers from the *Lemminkäinen* Suite, which will really be wonderful.

I am saying these things purely from my personal side, and I cannot expect you to hope too much from the results of my fresh studies of your music and my endeavor within a comparatively limited compass to give the public some small conception of the manner and the matter of your artistic development. In the first place I am becoming more and more bitterly discouraged with my own work and perceive more and more that I have not the equipment or sufficiently creative capacity to write in a way that really would be an illumination, much less a revelation, of the profound secrets of the musical art. I do not consider that the work of an analyst, however learned and clear-sighted, can ever represent the province of interpretive criticism. And I do not consider that a representative interpretive critic, who at the proper level of his functioning would also inevitably be a great creative artist, can be accomplished by anyone so limited in experience as I now discover with the passing years, of such second-rate mentality as myself. Furthermore I discover that whatever I have done so far toward acquainting the public or that portion of it which reads what I write, with the import of your work, is anything more than the most superficial journalism.

I don't know whether you know that on the occasion of your 75th birthday Procopé and other representatives of the Finnish government here did their best to induce me to get out a brochure about you which would be based upon and perhaps consist mostly in a succession of the articles that I had written about your music. So I had a number of these articles dug out—articles which I almost never keep of any of my writings about music, and which I quite logically realize are mainly material for the morning waste basket—and from these sat down to assemble some kind of a book upon this great subject. When I did so I was absolutely devastated by the realization of what I had done. I had merely written and largely repeated a number of rhetorical phrases of an impressionistic or perhaps merely journalistic sort, which were only of a most exterior kind, about your creations. I doubt if I can do much better than that even now, but at least what I undertake will be a slightly sounder study and assessment of what I am able to discover and to express, while the gift of your *Kullervo* Symphony will be something else. It will be a means of communing with the beauty that you have discovered and created in the world, and that will be quite aside from and far above any of my routine efforts to partially inform readers about it.

I still live in the very great hopes that I may see you again and shake your hand again before all the years have passed. I doubt at this moment if I would even be permitted a passport to Finland, because my political ideas which I have at times publicly expressed are distinctly at odds with those of my government and have caused me apparently to be suspected of Red-ish views and affiliations which are charges recklessly made in these days against any liberal thinker in our national politics. When this American "iron curtain" will be lifted, who can tell? But I am still hoping that circumstances will change, and also that my personal circumstances will permit me a trip to Finland within, let us say, the next 365 days, and that I will be able to clasp your hand again. On the other hand, you know very well, and I know very well, that our personal contact is of comparatively little importance by the side of the degree of communication with you which your music has made possible to me. The great personal pleasure and inspiration it would be to see you, great as that is, would never be my first necessity. Whether I am in America and you are in Finland, whether you precede me by a few years to the other side of existence, is something which I am certain concerns neither of us very much. There is a longer existence and a closer relationship than all that, and the truth which I have felt in your heart and which is quite imperishable, is a great rock and stronghold.

With best wishes, I am
Sincerely
Olin Downes

No. 60 T. *Olin Downes to Jean Sibelius*

New York, November 23, 1950

Kullervo photographed arrived hurrah million greetings and thanks.[48]

Downes

48. "That fine young Sjöblom" was the instrument by which the *Kullervo* Symphony was placed in Downes's hands. On Sibelius's instruction, this journalist retrieved the *Kullervo* score from the Helsinki University Library and carried it across the city's Esplanade to have the copy made. Today the copy is among the Downes materials in the Robert Manning Strozier Library at Florida State University.

No. 61 CC. *Olin Downes to Jean Sibelius*

Dear Master: New York, April 18, 1951

I wish very much to attend the Sibelius Festival this June in Finland, and to see you again and shake your hand, and listen to your music. But to my great regret, this will not be possible. In one sense, from the personal point of view, this is not an inescapable necessity, for I live and I know you in some part through your music with which I am acquainted, which is a nearer means of communication between us than even a conversation could be. And whether we are thousands of miles apart or in the same room with each other is no real difference. I always feel that you are near, near at least to the best part of me, and insofar as I am capable of it I am permanently near you. I will greatly miss the opportunity of seeing you personally this summer, a thing upon which I had rather counted, and of hearing in arranged order any of your most representative scores. But we are never really apart, and your spirit will never die.

Sincerely yours,
Olin Downes

No. 62 LS. *Jean Sibelius to Olin Downes*

Dear Friend, Järvenpää, May 18, 1951

Many thanks for your kind letter which I was very pleased to receive. It was indeed a disappointment to me that you cannot attend the Sibelius Festival in June. I would have liked to shake hands with you after so many years. Of all the guests that could visit me during the Festival you would have been one of the most welcome.

You are often in my mind and I am always happy when I hear that you have written something about me.

With my kindest regards and best wishes,

Cordially
Your old friend
Jean Sibelius
The best wishes from my family.

No. 63 LS. *Jean Sibelius to Olin Downes*

My dear old Friend, Järvenpää, October 12, 1951

You cannot think how glad I was when I received your kind souvenir through Antonia Brico. Thank you for recalling in my mind those wonderful times when you were in Helsinki. It is said that times change and we with them and that holds good also for the old good Hotel Kämp which I nowadays hardly ever visit. The room where we used to be together does not exist any more. It is but a memory as so much in this world. When I remember it my heart is filled with gratitude for all that you have done for me.

A firm hand shake and my warmest regards,
Your grateful friend
Jean Sibelius

No. 64 LS. *Olin Downes to Jean Sibelius*

My own dear Friend: New York, November 2, 1951

Your letter which I received of October 12th gave me the greatest pleasure. It gave me some sadness too. First for the fact that I was unable to get to Finland to see you this summer, and second for the news that the old Hotel Kämp, which is so deeply and everlastingly associated in my memories with our first meeting in Helsingfors, was changing, and that it seems that you and I shall not see it any more. I have, however, hopes which I refuse to abandon that I may get over to Helsingfors again and if there was anything left of that hotel, I would wish that I may take you back there for a moment and drink a glass again to one of the great nights of my life—one of many wonderful hours that I have had the privilege of spending with you. But what I can never forget is the little room and you and Aarvi, whose loss to me, instead of decreasing gets greater with the years—how we began the feast that night, and all the other splendid fellows who came in and made the hours fly by till the early morning. I remember on that occasion that I drank a whole quint of the best Hague and Hague Scotch liquor, and everybody talked about everything in the world, and time stood still and I for one, sensed that wonderful sensation in which one realizes that really there is no such thing as time, that the great and eternal things of life are timeless, and that there I was with the greatest musician in the world, and with other wonderful men, including that prince Aarvi—, for a while, in Olympus. But alas, I now see on re-reading your letter the statement that the room where we were together then does not even exist any more. Perhaps it is best that we shouldn't see it again or have any change in our memory of that evening. I have always felt that there was a divine goodness and rightness in the decree of destiny that one of the greatest musicians who ever lived, Mozart, when he died, was flung into the earth into an unknown grave. His body should have met just such a fate, and been flung aside as being important only as long as it embraced his soul.

But never, my dear Master, speak to me of gratitude from you "for all that you"—meaning me—"have done for me." You must surely know that the greatest boon in life, the one sure refuge of the heart and soul, is great art. I, for one, believe less and less in man, and less and less also in God. I do not believe in the man in God. I only believe in the God in man. The God in man finds its greatest, most beautiful, purest and strongest expression in art. As you well know, no other music created in the world during my lifetime, contains this precious essence of art and of what we may call for lack of a better name the truth, than your music, which has sustained me through many a bitter hour. The gratitude for this is all mine, and I would say this of you if you were my bitterest enemy, and even if your character were not what I know it so well to be—know it through our personal contacts, but know it even more through your music. I admire this all the more, because so often in that music I feel not only the solitude of nature but also the solitude of the man and the artist who knows that he is eternally alone and faces and even welcomes that supreme test and liberation of the spirit. Please excuse me if I am getting too personal, especially getting too personal in cold type. I started this letter with no such intention, but now I'll not change it. I find life getting shorter and shorter, with always less time to waste on anything but the truth. Please accept at any rate my salutations to the great and lonely Sibelius, and my eternal gratitude for all that you are and all that you mean to me. One thousand handshakes—for all eternity.

Sincerely,
[Olin Downes]

No. 65 CLS. *Olin Downes to Jean Sibelius*

Dear Mr. Sibelius:[50]   New York, December 27, 1951

I herewith enclose a copy of a letter which Mr. Carleton Smith,[51] director of the "National Arts Foundation," an organization little known to me, is evidently sending out to various prominent artists regarding contributions by them to Mr. Smith's campaign which he seems to be actively pursuing for contributions in your interest. At least this seems to be the gist of Mr. Smith's letter.

The enclosed letter was given me by the wife of Alexander Brailowsky, the well known pianist.

You will note that the last paragraph promises every contributor to this fund a personal letter of appreciation from you.

Will you kindly write me to the Music Department of *The New York Times* if you endorse this appeal of Mr. Smith's and the terms of the letter, which no doubt he is sending to a number of prominent artists, as he has written them. *The Times* wants to be sure that this communication meets with your approval.

With best wishes,
Sincerely yours,
Olin Downes

50. The formality of this letter is explained by document no. 68 below.
51. Carleton Smith (b. 1910), journalist and entrepreneur, interested himself in Sibelius after the war and was eventually awarded Finland's Order of the White Rose. He is not to be confused with Carleton Sprague Smith (b. 1905), the champion of Latin American studies and for many years chief of the New York Public Library. A letter from Sibelius's daughter Eva (GU MSS 688, CF "Paloheimo, Eva") dated January 7, 1952, tells Downes how distressed her father was on discovering that the hundreds of fine cigars he had received as a birthday gift had been solicited by Carleton Smith rather than being spontaneous gifts from music lovers.

No. 66 T. *Jean Sibelius to Olin Downes*

Helsinki, January 5, 1952

Many thanks for kind letter and information given answer follows by airmail cordial greetings Sibelius.

No. 67 LS. *Jean Sibelius to Olin Downes*

My dear old friend, Järvenpää, January 8, 1952

I hope you received my cable concerning Mr. Carleton Smith. Mr. Smith who is known to me since long time has made on me a very favourable impression. Since the war, during the times when conditions here were very hard I have frequently received from Mr. Smith cigars and coffee which were very much appreciated here. These gifts were usually accompanied by letters from friends of my music.

Now it seems to me however that Mr. Carleton Smith has adopted rather unusual methods for his activity on my behalf without my approval. I am quite convinced that Mr. Smith himself upon closer consideration realizes this.

Yours sincerely,
Jean Sibelius

No. 68 CC. *Olin Downes to Jean Sibelius*

Dear Master: New York, February 8, 1952

It was such a pleasure to hear from you, even in such an unpleasant connection as that of Mr. Carleton Smith. But I think I should add one more word about that gentleman. Greatly as I dislike to do anything which might affect the friendship, or which might affect unfavorably upon someone who had genuinely acted toward you as a friend and admirer, I feel I should tell you that over here Mr. Smith is regarded with a good deal of distrust, as being something between a very prominent self-advertiser and an adventurer of sorts. He is constantly seeking to get himself in the paper, and I was obliged to warn members of an English opera company at Glynd[e]bourne, who cam[e] over here to inquire into operas that Mr. Smith was making them, or professed to make them, that no arrangements in which he took part should be accepted seriously unless they were accompanied by very solid contractual arrangements and money in the bank.

I am very averse to saying unpleasant things about anyone, but I am very much more concerned about your interests and the protection of you and your ideals than I am about any effect that these remarks of mine might make upon the fortunes of Mr. Smith. In the meantime I shall not publish anything in the papers of the information that you have given me or the letter that you sent him, because I am certain you would not like to have this matter made public, but if Mr. Smith continues his misrepresentations we would be prepared to direct them publicly in this or other matters—providing always we had your permission to do so.

I do imagine, however, that the letter you have written him will deter him from further misrepresentations, so uncharacteristic of you in every way, that he has been making. I even heard of this from Sir Thomas Beecham, the conductor, and his wife, who have been in New York. I shall not hesitate, personally, if any musicians mention this matter again, to say that I happen to know that it is absolutely abhorrent to you and that you would never have dreamed of having your name put in such a way before the public or any of your colleagues, composers or executive musicians either.

By the way, you will be interested to know that Beecham gave the finest performance of your Sixth Symphony that I ever heard three days ago here, on the 5th, with the Philadelphia Orchestra. And I myself, in reviewing this performance,[32] had occasion to tell Sir Thomas that he had increased my understanding of the symphony as no other conductor before him. I think I have told you that I very seldom hear performances of your works which are satisfactory to me. Even our great and enthusiastic friend Koussevitzky, never wholly satisfied me, even with the Second Symphony. Toscanini's first performance of the Fourth, years ago, seemed to me to miss much of the depth and the fantasy, and the sombre power of that work. For that reason I did not go to his second performance of it several years later. But the same friend who heard the first with me told me that it was immeasurably a development and growth over Toscanini's first reading. I then wrote Toscanini, and told him that I had not heard his second performance of the Fourth, and expressed the wish that he might do this the following season. He answered me with characteristic modesty. "I am sorry," he said, "that you did not hear my last performance of the symphony. For I had the illusion that this time I had penetrated to the secret of the score!" I do not feel that I know enough about orchestration, or, that I am sufficiently expert in score reading, to be able accurately to calculate precisely what the color and instrumental course of a given passage should be. But I have the feeling that in the middle of the Seventh Symphony, and again in its final pages, there was not quite the force of the one passage, or the melancholy grandeur and revery of the last pages. I myself dream of the second appearance of the trombone theme, over the chromatic scale, this time in a minor tonality, being projected with more power, more wildness, by the brass instruments answering each other in imitation, than conductors usually give this phrase. I hope I am not talking like a fool to you, the composer of the symphony! But I feel that if this middle part were given more salience and power than is usually the case, that the whole symphonic fabric would be better balanced.

The opening of course is one of the most beautiful and ideal passages in symphonic music, and when the entrance of the trombone, like a heavenly messenger of the skies, is properly announced, it seems to be of a breath-taking beauty and spirituality. But I want the re-appearance of that theme at the central part of the symphony, to sound out with something of a suggestion of wildness and, let us say, with a suggestion of the lightning and grandeur of a passing storm. It seems to me that this way one would have the proper preparation and the proper balance for the grand sunset conclusion of the symphony. But there are a hundred details that I would ask you about, if I had the courage to do so. I never hear them treat the development section of the first movement of the Second Symphony with enough savage power. It is just possible that I may be able to go abroad for a few weeks this summer, and if I do I shall certainly hope that you will receive me, and if that takes place I must ask you a lot of little questions about details of this score.

Antonia Brico and I have talked over some of these details, and I was very pleased to see that you supported me in my conclusion about a certain measure in the finale of the Fifth, of which the true nature, I thought, was foretold in earlier measures, and I was very happy to find that she had ascertained from you that this was the case—as I thought it should be.

Ah me! If only I didn't have to waste my time writing for the waste-basket and tomorrow's newspaper, and could have some months and periods when I could sit down and really study your masterpieces, and really lay myself open to penetration by them in all parts of my mind.

With very best wishes, dear master, to you and yours, I am

Sincerely yours,
[Olin Downes]

52. "Beecham at Best in Concert Here," *New York Times,* February 6, 1952; repr. in *Olin Downes on Music,* 402–4.

No. 69 CC. *Olin Downes to Jean Sibelius*

Dear Master: New York, April 24, 1952

I expect to sail t[o]morrow, the 25th of April, on the New Amsterdam for Europe, although there are so many things to be done that I may have to wait two or three days and fly in the same week. But as arrangements are now I expect to reach the Paris office of *The New York Times* on May 2nd, and have to report much music thereabouts and also serve as one of the judges of the Ysaÿe Piano Contests in Belgium until just about June 6th. By present plans I shall thereupon fly to Helsingfors and to you, and I can assure you most sincerely that about the one real attractive [thing] which this quick and crowded journey is going to have for me, is at last the opportunity of seeing you once more and shaking your hand, and hear some performances of your music by the nation and the musicians to which that music preeminently belongs.

May I please be remembered most warmly to Mrs. Sibelius and to all the other members of your family.

Sincerely yours,
[Olin Downes]

No. 70 CLS. *Olin Downes to Jean Sibelius*

Dear Master: Paris, May 22, [1952]

I am now planning to come to Helsinki for three days of the Sibelius Festival—June 10, 11, and 13. I would like to hear the program of the 10th of Finnish music besides your own. I wish I could hear the whole festival, but cannot for reasons of an over-crowded schedule of reporting music all around Europe—a thing I detest to do.

Here in Paris is much music, including a so-called "Masterpieces of the Twentieth C[en]tury Festival," supposed to represent the music of the "free nations" of the western world. There is however no symphony of Sibelius on these programs. There is no symphony by Vaughan Williams, no great work by the greatest composer of the two Americas, Heitor Villa-Lobos of Brazil, and by many many others. But three programs are given Stravinsky. One thing is still young and fresh and unspoiled in Paris—chi-chi! There are the same affectations and hypocrisies I found here when I first came here in 1924 after the first world war. I am very tired with it.

I am also physically tired. I am a member of the jury for the Queen of Belgium piano competitions—the Ysaÿe competitions is the more honorable title—and have to sit on this jury five hours a day then air-plane back to Paris in late afternoon, hear a performance and fly back by early morning plane to get to the competitions in Brussels which begin again at 10 AM the next morning. It is a terrible job but the double task I was forced to undertake for various reasons. It will be finished by the first week in June.

I have never had so much work to do over here and this is the last time I will ever come to Europe as a newspaper correspondent. I came principally with the wish to see you, and hope that you will not be too tired or busy to see me when I get there. If you should not be able to see me I would of course understand. In any case, it will be wonderful to be in the same place with you again. (Although, entre nous, I do not admire too much Ormandy's readings of your symphonies!)

Aufwiedersehen, dear Master,
Olin Downes

No. 71 T. *Jean Sibelius to Olin Downes*

Helsinki, June 6, 1952

Very pleased to see you cordial greetings = Sibelius

No. 72 T. *Olin Downes to Jean Sibelius*

Paris, June 7, 1952

Much joy at your message arriving helsinki plane 13.50 june 11 anticipate greatly shaking your hand again at such time and place as convenie[n]t to you regards to madam and all your family.

Olin Downes

No. 73 CC. *Olin Downes to Jean Sibelius*

Dear Master: New York, May 25, 1953

This is to say, that I expect to be in Helsinki for the last two days of the Sibelius Festival on June 16 and 17, and look forward immensely to hearing authoritative interpretations of your music by Mr. Jalas, and I hope the music of some other Finnish composers. And I also hope that I may come out and shake your hand if you are not too busily engaged to see me, and ask if you will kindly tell Mrs. Sibelius and Mrs. Pal[o]heimo and Mrs. Jalas[52] too, how much I hope to see them again.

This is written in hot haste, before I fly tomorrow for Copenhagen, from whence I shall cover some festivals in Denmark, Sweden and Norway before coming to Finland. I shall go to the Kemp Hotel as usual.

With much love to all,
Sincerely,
[Olin Downes]

53. Sibelius's daughters Eva Paloheimo and Margareta Jalas.

No. 74 CLS. *Olin Downes to Jean Sibelius*

Dear Master: Stockholm, June 16, 1953

It now seems that after all I cannot hope to see you, or to hear Mr. Jalas's interpreta-tion of your Fourth Symphony, my favorite of them all, and the very one which I seldom hear adequately interpreted.

My letter to your daughter explains all this, and if you are interested she will explain it to you.

But one great fact is more living than your very presence to me: your music. I am never away from there. I will hope to be back and to you next year. But what are years, or any of the realistic facts of life, beside art and eternity?

Olin Downes

No. 75 CC. *Olin Downes to Jean Sibelius*

Dear Master: New York, July 13, 1953

I wish to introduce to you with this letter two old and dear friends, Mr. and Mrs. Hans Kaltenborn.[54] As you probably know, Mr. Kaltenborn is one of our most dis-tinguished editors and radio commentators, but do not fear! He is not a musician or a critic anxious to get copy. But he and Mrs. Kaltenborn would deeply value, as I know, the privilege of meeting with you if this possibility develops in a way mutually convenient, and I am sure that you and Mme. Sibelius would find pleasure in them.

With best regards to all,
Sincerely yours,
[Olin Downes]

54. Hans von Kaltenborn (1878–1965) was the "suave Voice of Doom" who first brought the sounds of live battle to American radio audiences during the Spanish Civil War. Associated with CBS from 1929 until 1940, Kaltenborn then continued producing his controversial newscasts at NBC. As editor and author, he wrote various books, including *We Look at the World* (1930) and *Kaltenborn Edits the News* (1937).

No. 76 T. *Aino and Jean Sibelius to Irene Downes*

Helsinki, August 25, 1955

Heartfelt sympathy we loved him as a true friend and shall miss him deeply.

Aino and Jean Sibelius

APPENDIX B

The Writings of Olin Downes on Jean Sibelius

THERE ARE MANY REDUNDANCIES among Downes's writings about Sibelius: radio talks were recycled into articles; articles were combined into books and sometimes served several different editors; portions of books in turn appeared translated into Finnish bearing new titles. Thus, each entry in the rather long list that follows by no means represents an original contribution about Sibelius. Nevertheless, the quantity, the variety of formats (newspaper articles, music encyclopedia entries, music appreciation lectures, and so on), and the period over which they appeared are an indication of the kinds of audiences the critic reached and the number of people who heard his opinions.

Only articles signed by Olin Downes are included in this list. Those marked with an asterisk have been reprinted in *Olin Downes on Music.* It should be noted that some of the articles reprinted there are abbreviated, and most are supplied with new titles.

Articles in the Boston Post

January 5, 1907	"Rehearsal for 11th Symphony" [Symphony no. 1]
January 1, 1909	"The Sibelius Second"*
March 5, 1910	"Symphony Orchestra" [*En Saga*]
January 7, 1911	"Sibelius' Symphony 'Gloriously Rude'" [Symphony no. 2]
August 4, 1912	"A New Finnish Symphony" [Symphony no. 4]
November 10, 1912	"New Programmes and Performers to Entertain Great Public—Sibelius and Moussorgsky Growing in Popular Esteem" [Symphony no. 1]

November 16, 1912   "Master Work by Symphony"* [Symphony no. 1]

April 19, 1913   "New Sibelius Work Played" [Symphony no. 5]

October 19, 1913   "Sibelius' 4th Symphony"

October 25, 1913   "Sibelius' Fourth by Symphony"*

October 26, 1913   "Sibelius' Symphony Rich in Modernity" [Symphony no. 4]

November 2, 1913   "Liszt and Anisteldt" [new Sibelius compositions for violin; comments on the Violin Concerto]

November 14, 1914   "Sibelius Symphony Features" [Symphony no. 4]

January 23, 1915   "Strauss and Muck at Odds" [Symphony no. 1]

January 5, 1916   "Kniesels Play New Sibelius" [*Voces intimae*]

March 5, 1916   "Composers and Conductors" [Symphony no. 2]

November 8, 1916   "A Splendid Symphony Program" [Symphony no. 1]

January 13, 1917   "Sibelius' Pieces by Symphony"* [*Pohjola's Daughter; Oceanides; Night Ride and Sunrise*]

October 24, 1920   "Not Far from Symphony Hall" [Symphony no. 1]

March 27, 1921   "Sibelius' Third Symphony"

October 23, 1921   "Musical Comment" [comments on the first five symphonies and various tone poems]

November 12, 1921   "Symphony Glorifies Sibelius" [Symphony no. 2]

April 8, 1922   "Siloti as Symphony Soloist" [Symphony no. 5]

April 9, 1922   "D'Indy Calls Our Musical Taste 'Feverish'—Olin Downes' Comment" [Symphony no. 5]

Articles in the New York Times

February 1, 1924   "'*Sacre du Printemps*' Played" [with the Violin Concerto]

December 6, 1925   "The Sixtieth Year of Jean Sibelius: His Contribution to Modern Music" [includes portrait]

December 27, 1926   "Sibelius and Gershwin Mingle" [comments on *Tapiola*]

December 31, 1926   "Dusolina Giannini Soloist" [comments on a repeat performance of *Tapiola*]

January 29, 1928   "The New Metropolitan" [comments on the lagging fortunes of Sibelius at the hands of U.S. conductors]

July 21, 1929   "The Glory That Was Russia" [comments on a visit to Sibelius]

March 9, 1930   "Novelties Given by Koussevitzky" [Symphony no. 6]

December 5, 1930   "Stokowski Gives Sibelius Symphony" [Symphony no. 1, with cuts]

December 7, 1930   "Sibelius' *'Finlandia'* " [comments on the Violin Concerto]

December 14, 1930   "Advance of Sibelius"

December 28, 1930   "The Youthful Genius of Sibelius" [Symphonies no. 1 and 2]

March 22, 1931   "A Belated Sibelius Renascence"

June 7, 1931   "Original Musical Comedy" [comments on Sibelius's evolution]

January 31, 1932   "A New Sibelius Biography" [Cecil Gray's]

November 9, 1932   "Brilliant Concerts Thrill 2 Audiences" [Symphony no. 4]

November 18, 1932   "Koussevitzky Gives a Sibelius Program" [Symphony no. 1, *Swanwhite,* and *Tapiola*]

November 17, 1933   "Audience Cheers for Koussevitzky" [Symphony no. 2]

April 5, 1934   "Berezowsky Work Has First Hearing" [Symphony no. 3]

November 19, 1934   "Sibelius Symphony Given by Janssen" [Symphony no. 5]

January 4, 1935   "Spalding Soloist in New Concerto" [Koussevitzky conducts a Sibelius symphony]

February 8, 1935   "Janssen Returns to Conduct Here" [Symphony no. 4]

May 5, 1935   "Philharmonic's Plans" [advances idea of Sibelius as conductor]

December 8, 1935   "Sibelius at Seventy"

December 11, 1935   "Stokowski Pays Honor to Sibelius" [Symphony no. 4]

January 15, 1936   "Unusual Program by String Quartet" [the Musical Art Quartet plays *Voces intimae*]

February 16, 1936   "Biography of Sibelius" [Karl Ekman's]

April 3, 1936   "Boston Symphony Arouses Audience" [Symphony no. 2]

August 23, 1936   "Berkshire Symphonic Festival"* [Symphony no. 2]

September 20, 1936   "With Jean Sibelius in His Realm of the Sagas." [Illustrated; parts of this article were translated into Finnish for *Uusi Suomi,* appearing under the title "Olin Downes kirjoittaa Sibeliuksesta" (Olin Downes Writes about Sibelius)]

October 24, 1936   "Chicago Symphony Gives 2d Program" [Stock conducts Symphony no. 2]

October 24, 1937	"Sibelius 'Readings'; Gentle Admonition to 'Early Erroneous Commentators' on the Symphonies"*
December 1, 1937	"Symphonies Given by Women's Groups" [Antonia Brico conducts *Oceanides*]
January 7, 1938	"Boston Symphony Here with Chorus" [*The Captive Queen* and *Origin of Fire*]
January 9, 1938	"Sibelius in Life and in Music" [review of Karl Ekman's and Bengt de Törne's biographies]
February 8, 1938	"Sibelius Songs Given by Theodate Johnson—The Iturbis Play at Carnegie Hall" [a varied program of songs in English, German, and Swedish]
August 7, 1938	"Where a Composer Works" [on Sibelius's surroundings in Järvenpää]
September 24, 1939	"Program Devoted to Sibelius; Government of Finland Honors Its Greatest Composer with New York World's Fair Concert—Schneevoigt in Debut Here"
September 29, 1939	"Sibelius Concert at Carnegie Hall" [*Lemminkäinen Suite*]
December 24, 1939	"A Composer and His Nation; Music of Sibelius Conveys Spirit of Finland—Concert for Benefit of Country Stresses His Work" [*Finlandia, En saga*]
January 12, 1940	"Boston Symphony at Carnegie Hall" [Symphony no. 2]
October 11, 1940	"Season Is Opened by Philharmonic" [Symphony no. 2 "seen as sign of unconquerable spirit"]
October 16, 1940	"Symphony Music Honors Sibelius" [Symphony no. 1]
December 8, 1940	"Toscanini Concert Honors Sibelius" [Symphony no. 2, *Pohjola's Daughter, Swan of Tuonela, Finlandia*]
	"Symphonic Prophet"
December 9, 1940	"New Friends Mark Sibelius Birthday" [*Voces intimae*]
January 12, 1941	"Sibelius Program at Carnegie Hall" [Symphonies no. 2, 6, and 7]
May 19, 1941	"Concert Tribute to Jean Sibelius"
November 17, 1941	"Paul Morel Leads Unusual Program" [Violin Concerto]
February 15, 1942	"Boston Orchestra Plays Sibelius 5th"
December 12, 1943	"Sibelius Birthday; On 78th Anniversary His Significance as a Composer Has Increased"
March 1, 1946	"Rodzinski Leads Sibelius' Fourth"

December 21, 1947   "Sibelius at 82" [reviews *The Music of Sibelius,* edited by Gerald Abraham]

November 24, 1948   "Borovsky Plays Work by Sibelius" [one of the op. 67 sonatinas, although which is not stated]

July 2, 1950   "Plight of Sibelius; No Royalties Have Been Paid to Finnish Composer for U.S. Performances"

December 3, 1950   "Classic Master; Sibelius Stands Alone as Composer Who Has Risen Above Passing Fads"

December 7, 1950   "Boston Symphony in Sibelius Works" [*Pohjola's Daughter,* Symphony no. 5]

December 8, 1950   "Szell on Podium for Philharmonic" [Symphony no. 7]

February 21, 1951   "Sibelius Honored at Concert Here" [Symphony no. 2, *Pohjola's Daughter,* Violin Concerto]

December 9, 1951   "Two Sibelius Scores; Excerpts from the 'Lemminkäinen Suite' Show Composer's Early Independence"

December 12, 1951   "Old Sibelius Suite Heard at Concert" [*Lemminkäinen Suite*]

February 6, 1952   "Beecham at Best in Concert Here"* [Symphony no. 6]

June 15, 1952   "Second Festival of Sibelius Held"

    "Paris Exposition in Sum" [laments paucity of Sibelius works represented]

June 29, 1952   "Sturdy Finland; Country's Art and Culture Exemplified by Symphonic Music of Sibelius"

December 5, 1954   "Sibelius Tributes; 90th Birthday Honors Planned for 1955"

March 16, 1955   "Music: Zimbalist and Ormandy; Works of Sibelius and Beethoven Presented" [Symphony no. 5]

September 29, 1957   "Downes on Sibelius; Excerpts From Writings on Finnish Genius by Late Critic of The Times"

Books by Olin Downes That Include Articles on Sibelius

Symphonic Broadcasts. Binghamton, N.Y.: Dial Press, 1931, 170–72; 269–75. Discussions of *En saga* and the Fourth Symphony, which originated as radio talks.

Symphonic Masterpieces. New York: Dial Press, 1935, 270–74. Revised version of the *En saga* and Fourth Symphony material from *Symphonic Broadcasts,* published here with a photograph of a granitic-looking Sibelius.

Articles by Olin Downes in Books by Other Authors or Editors

"Jean Sibelius." In *The Analytical Concert Guide,* edited by Louis Leopold Biancolli, 546–47. Garden City, N.Y.: Doubleday, 1951. Discussion of Symphony no. 4 reprinted from the *Boston Post,* October 19, 1913.

"Jean Sibelius: *En Saga.*" In *The Music Lover's Handbook,* edited by Elie Siegmeister, 221–22 et passim. New York: William Morrow, 1943. *En saga* material reprinted from *Symphonic Masterpieces,* 270–71.

"Jean Sibelius." In *Great Modern Composers,* edited by Oscar Thompson, 303–26. New York: Dodd, Mead, 1943. Virtually the same article that appears in the *International Cyclopedia of Music and Musicians,* below.

"Jean Sibelius." In *The International Cyclopedia of Music and Musicians,* edited by Oscar Thompson. New York: Dodd, Mead, 1938– , s.v. "Sibelius." A lengthy biographical article that includes a work list compiled from those of Cecil Gray and Karl Ekman; appears in the *International Cyclopedia's* current edition, 1985.

Other Articles by Olin Downes

"Downes on Sibelius/Ovation to Sibelius." Typescript, Yale Music Library, leaves A-G of Carl Stoeckel's *Some Recollections of the Visit of Jean Sibelius to America in 1914.* This essay was published as "Creative Genius in Music Honored at Norfolk," *Musical America,* June 13, 1914, 3–4.

"Impressions of Sibelius." Program notes commissioned by and written for the New York Philharmonic-Symphony Society, 1945–46 season.

"Jean Sibelius." Typescript, Yale Music Library. This essay was published as "Jean Sibelius," *New Music Review and Church Music Review* 13 (July, August, September 1914): 358–61; 403–7; 442–46.

"Olin Downesin kirjeitä Sibeliukselle" [Olin Downes's Letters to Sibelius], *Uusi Musiikkilehti* 2, Special Issue on the Occasion of the 90th Birthday (1955): 20–23. Includes three letters from Downes to Sibelius translated into Finnish. Two of these may be found in Appendix A, nos. 52 and 64. The location of the third, dated November 9, 1950, is not known.

"Olin Downesin lausuntoja Sibeliuksesta" [Olin Downes's Praises of Sibelius]. *Musiikkitieto* 9–10, Special Issue on the Occasion of the 80th Birthday (1945): 151–55. Articles by Downes from *Symphonic Broadcasts, The New Music Review,* and *The International Cyclopedia* translated into Finnish by Paul Sjöblom.

"Sibeliukselle ave atque laudatio." *Suomen Kuvalehti* 49 (1945) 1251. A reprint of Downes's introduction to *Sibelius,* published in Helsinki the same year. An English translation is found in GU MSS 688, SF "Sibelius, Jean."

"Sibelius Today and Tomorrow." *Saturday Review,* December 10, 1955, 30–31, 34, 36. Excerpt from *Sibelius the Symphonist.*

Books about Sibelius by Olin Downes

Sibelius. Edited and translated by Paul Sjöblom with the assistance of Jussi Jalas. Helsinki: Otava, 1945. A selection of Downes's articles on Sibelius translated into Finnish and published with a newly written introduction entitled "Ave atque laudatio."

Sibelius the Symphonist. New York: Philharmonic-Symphony Society of New York, 1956. Dedicated to the Radio Members of the Philharmonic-Symphony Society of New York, this book-length essay was corrected in proof on Downes's deathbed and published after he died. Excerpts from it appeared in the *Saturday Review.*

Typescripts in GU MSS 688, SF "Sibelius, Jean"

"Sibelius Facing his Tenth Decennium."

Introduction to *Sibelius* (elsewhere with the title "Ave atque laudatio"). This is not Downes's original, but a translation from the Finnish version by Paul Sjöblom.

Transcriptions of Radio Talks and Lectures in GU MSS 688

"Finland's Hero." Olin Downes Lectures, microfilm. Various lecture notes in typed and handwritten copy, with and without titles, abbreviated and complete, exist on three microfilm rolls along with the critic's other papers. One lecture bears the title above; additional notes may or may not be parts of the same lecture.

"Sibelius Birthday Program." Radio broadcast on the occasion of the 85th birthday, 1950, SF "Sibelius, Jean."

⌾ BIBLIOGRAPHY

Manuscript and Archival Sources

Allen A. Brown Collection. Boston Public Library. Boston, Mass.

Olin Downes Collection. MSS 688, Hargrett Rare Book and Manuscript Library. University of Georgia, Athens, Ga.

Olin Downes Collection. Robert Manning Strozier Library. Florida State University, Tallahassee, Fla.

Koussevitzky Collection. Correspondence "Sibelius, Jean." Library of Congress, Performing Arts Library, Washington, D.C.

Horatio Parker Papers. MSS 32, Yale Music Library. Yale University, New Haven, Conn.

Sibeliuksen Perheen Arkisto (The Sibelius Family Archives). Valtionarkisto (The National Archives of Finland), Helsinki, Finland.

Jean Sibelius Clipping File. New York Public Library for the Performing Arts, Lincoln Center, New York, N.Y.

Sibelius-Koussevitzky Correspondence. MS 634, Hargrett Rare Book and Manuscript Library. University of Georgia, Athens, Ga. (Copies of original correspondence in the Helsinki University Library.)

Stoeckel Family Papers. Misc. MS 247, Yale Music Library. Yale University, New Haven, Conn.

Books, Articles, and Dissertations

A reminder: The *Times* refers to the *Times* of London; the *Sunday Times* is its Sunday edition. These titles are not to be confused with the *New York Times.* Unless they were unusually important in the writing of this book, the many articles consulted in the various clipping files such as the Olin Downes Collection and the Jean Sibelius Clipping File at the New York Public Library are not listed separately here.

Aavatsmark, Fannie. "A Visit to Sibelius." *Musical America,* December 10, 1935, 7.

Abraham, Gerald, ed. *The Music of Sibelius.* New York: W. W. Norton, 1947.

Adorno, Theodor W. *Gesammelte Schriften.* Vol. 17, *Musikalische Schriften 4.* Edited by Rolf Tiedemann. Frankfurt: Suhrkamp, 1982.

———. "Glosse über Sibelius." Originally published as review of Bengt de Törne's *Sibelius: A Close-Up,* in *Zeitschrift für Sozialforschung* 7 (1938): 460-63.

———. *Introduction to the Sociology of Music.* Translated by E. B. Ashton. New York: Seabury Press, 1976.

———. *Minima Moralia. Reflections from Damaged Life.* Translated by E. F. N. Jephcott. London: NLB, 1974.

———. *Philosophy of Modern Music.* Translated by Anne G. Mitchell and Wesley V. Blomster. New York: Seabury Press, 1973.

———. "A Social Critique of Radio Music." *Kenyon Review* 7 (1945): 208-17.

———. "TWA Memorandum. Music in Radio." Princeton Radio Research Project, June 26, 1938, Series I, Box 26, Folder 1, Paul Lazarsfeld Papers, Rare Book and Manuscript Library, Columbia University.

Allgemeine Musik-Zeitung. September 20, 1901; December 13, 1901; November 18, 1902; November 21, 1902; June 20, 1905.

Andersson, Otto. *Jean Sibelius Amerikassa.* Helsinki: Otava, 1960.

Anthony, W. C. "American Appreciation of Sibelius." *Musical Times,* March 1936, 257.

Armsby, Leonora Wood. *Musicians Talk.* New York: Dial Press, 1935.

Austin, William. *Music in the 20th Century.* New York: W. W. Norton, 1966.

Axelsson, George. "Jan Sibelius Frowns on Plans for Benefit." *New York Times,* April 6, 1945.

Badal, James J. "The Strange Case of Dr. Karl Muck, Who Was Torpedoed by *The Star-Spangled Banner* During World War I." *High Fidelity,* October 1970, 55–60.

Bantock, Granville. "Sibelius, The Man and Artist." The *Times,* February 26, 1921.

Bantock, Myrrha. *Granville Bantock: A Personal Portrait.* London: J. M. Dent, 1972.

"Barbirolli Pays Honor to Sibelius." *New York Times,* December 9, 1940.

Barnouw, Erik. *A History of Broadcasting in the United States.* Vol. 1, *A Tower in Babel.* New York: Oxford University Press, 1966.

Bax, Arnold. *Farewell, My Youth.* London: 1943. Reprint. Westport, Conn.: Greenwood Press, 1970.

Bayley, Edwin R. *Joe McCarthy and the Press.* Madison: University of Wisconsin Press, 1981.

"Behind the Scenes. Jan Sibelius Wins Nation-wide Poll Among Listeners. . . ." *New York Times,* November 24, 1935.

Berger, Meyer. *The Story of The New York Times 1851–1951.* New York: Simon & Schuster, 1951.

Berk, Ellyn P. "An Analysis and Comparison of the Aesthetics and Philosophy of Selected Music Critics in New York: 1940–1975." Ph.D. diss., New York University, 1978.

"The Birmingham Festival." *Monthly Musical Record,* November 1, 1912, 285-86.

"Birmingham Festival/Sir H. Wood's Innovations." *Sunday Times,* October 6, 1912.

Blum, Fred. "Sibelius and America; A Centennial Survey." Typescript, Sibelius Museum, Turku, Finland.

Bonavia, Ferruccio. "New Symphony by Bax." *New York Times,* December 29, 1935.

———. "Popularity of Sibelius." *New York Times,* April 10, 1932.

Broadcasting. Broadcast Advertising, 1940 Yearbook Number. Washington, D.C.: Broadcasting Publications, 1940.

Broadcasting. Music—Literature—Drama—Art. Vol. 2. New York: National Broadcasting Co., 1935.

"Brooklyn Applauds Crooks and Downes." *Musical America,* November 10, 1934, 33.

Bruneau, Alfred. "La Musique à L'Exposition." *Figaro,* July 31, 1900.

Busoni, Ferruccio. "Offener Brief an die Allgemeine Musik-Zeitung." *Allgemeine Musik-Zeitung,* November 18, 1902, 817.

Cardus, Neville, "Diminished Sibelius." *Manchester Guardian,* April 25, 1962.

Cashman, Sean Dennis. *America in the Twenties and Thirties. The Olympian Age of Franklin Delano Roosevelt.* New York: New York University Press, 1989.

Chamberlin, Joseph Edgar. *The Boston Transcript. A History of its First Hundred Years.* Boston: Houghton Mifflin, 1930.

Chase, Gilbert. *America's Music from the Pilgrims to the Present.* Rev. 2d ed. New York: McGraw-Hill, 1966; rev. 3d ed. Urbana: University of Illinois Press, 1987.

Chase, Gilbert, ed. *Music in Radio Broadcasting.* New York: McGraw-Hill, 1946.

Coad, Philip. "Bruckner and Sibelius." Ph.D. diss., Queens' College, Cambridge, England, 1985.

Coghlan, Brian. *Hofmannsthal's Festival Dramas.* Cambridge, England: Cambridge University Press, 1964.

"Concert and Opera Asides: Two Movements of Sibelius Suite to Have First Performance in New York." *New York Times,* September 17, 1939.

"Concert Tribute to Jean Sibelius." *New York Times,* May 19, 1941.

"Concert Will Aid Sibelius Fund." *New York Times,* December 4, 1957.

Cone, Edward T. "The Authority of Music Criticism." *Journal of the American Musicological Society* 34 (1981): 1–18.

Copland, Aaron. *The New Music 1900–1960.* Rev. and enl. ed. New York: W. W. Norton, 1968.

Current Biography 1943, s.v. "Downes, Olin."

Dahlhaus, Carl. *Foundations of Music History.* Translated by J. B. Robinson. Cambridge, England: Cambridge University Press, 1983.

Dahlström, Fabian. *The Works of Jean Sibelius.* Helsinki: Sibelius Seura, 1987.

Daniel, Oliver. *Stokowski, A Counterpoint of View.* New York: Dodd, Mead, 1982.

Dickson, Harry Ellis. *"Gentlemen, More Dolce Please!" (Second Movement); An Irreverent Memoir of Thirty-Five Years in the Boston Symphony Orchestra.* Boston: Beacon Press, 1974.

Dictionary of American Biography, s.v. "Olin, Stephen." Supplement 5, s.v. "Downes, (Edwin) Olin."

Downes, Edward. "The Taste Makers: Critics and Criticism." In *One Hundred Years of Music in America,* edited by Paul Henry Lang, 230-44. New York: Schirmer, 1961.

Downes, Louise. *The New Democracy.* Boston: Sherman, French, 1910.

———. *The Sistine Madonna.* N.p.: German-American Publishing Co., [ca. 1901].

Downes, Olin. "Mahler Again." *New York Times,* November 21, 1948.

———. "Placing the Critics." *Modern Music* 2 (1925): 33–35.

———. "Time for Change in Music." *Boston Post,* June 22, 1913.

———. "Work by Poulenc Concert Feature." *New York Times,* November 12, 1948.

Dreams of a Summer Night. Scandinavian Painting at the Turn of the Century. Hayward Gallery, London, July 10 to October 5, 1986. Catalogue edited and produced for the Arts Council of Great Britain by Leena Ahtola-Moorhouse, Carl Tomas Edam, and Birgitta Schreiber. Uddevalla, Sweden: Bohusläningens Boktryckeri AB, 1986.

Dubbert, Joe L. *A Man's Place: Masculinity in Transition.* Englewood Cliffs, N.J.: Prentice-Hall, 1979.

Dunham, Richard Lee. "Music Appreciation in the Public Schools of the United States, 1897–1930." Ph.D. diss., University of Michigan, 1961.

Dykema, Peter W. "Music as Presented by the Radio." New York: Radio Institute of the Audible Arts, [ca. 1938].

Education on the Air. First Yearbook of the Institute for Education by Radio. Edited by Josephine H. MacLatchy. Columbus: Ohio State University, 1930.

Ekman, Karl. *Jean Sibelius: His Life and Personality.* Translated by Edward Birse. London: Alan Wilmer, 1936.

Emery, Edwin, and Michael Emery. *The Press and America: An Interpretive History of the Mass Media.* 5th ed. Englewood Cliffs, N.J.: Prentice-Hall, 1984.

Ennulat, Egbert. *Arnold Schoenberg Correspondence.* Metuchen, N.J.: Scarecrow Press, 1991.

"E. O. Quigley in Sing Sing Prison." *New York Times,* January 29, 1895.

The Essential Frankfurt School Reader. Edited by Andrew Arato and Eike Gebhardt. Oxford: Basil Blackwell, 1978.

"Extensive Operator in Bonds a Self-Confessed Forger." *New York Times,* January 19, 1895.

Farwell, Arthur. "Keeping in Touch with the World's Musical Growth Through the Piano: Jean Sibelius." *Musical America,* May 20, 1911, 22.

———. "Sibelius: A Musical Redeemer." *Musical America,* March 15, 1913, 14.

Faulkner, Harold Underwood. *The Quest for Social Justice 1898–1914.* Vol. 11 of *A History of American Life.* Edited by Arthur M. Schlesinger and Dixon Ryan Fox. New York: Macmillan, 1931.

"Festival to Mark Sibelius Birthday." *New York Times,* December 4, 1940.

"Finland's Voice." *New York Times,* January 2, 1939.

"Finland's Voice in the Symphonies of Jean Sibelius." *Current Opinion* 57 (1914): 108.

"Finland Salutes U. S. in Broadcast." *New York Times,* January 2, 1939.

"Finlandia." *New York Times,* June 16, 1944.

"Finnisches Konzert." *Signale für die Musikalische Welt* 78 (1920): 1219-20.

"Finnish Composer Coming." *New York Times,* January 25, 1921.

Fisher, Charles. *The Columnists.* New York: Howell, Soskin, 1944.

Fisher, Cyrus. "Radio Reviews. A New Year on the Air." *Forum and Century* 89 (January 1933): 62.

Fried, Richard M. *Nightmare in Red. The McCarthy Era in Perspective.* New York: Oxford University Press, 1990.

Gelatt, Roland. *The Fabulous Phonograph 1877–1977.* 2d rev. ed. New York: Macmillan, 1977.

———. "Not Beethoven's Successor." Review of *Jean Sibelius* by Harold E. Johnson. *New York Times Book Review,* July 26, 1959.

Gilman, Lawrence. "Music of the Month: From Stravinsky to Sibelius." *North American Review,* January 1922, 117-21.

———. "Sibelius in America." *New York Herald Tribune,* December 6, 1936.

Glanville-Hicks, P. "Olin Downes (1886–1955)." Epitaph delivered at the Memorial Service, broadcast over radio station WNYC, August 25, 1955. Printed in *Bulletin of American Composers Alliance* 5 (1955): 2.

Göhler, Georg. "Orchesterkompositionen von Jean Sibelius." *Kunstwart* 21 (1908): 261-69.

The Gramophone Shop Encyclopedia of Recorded Music. Compiled by R. D. Darrell. New York: The Gramophone Shop, 1936.

Graw, Jacob Bentley, ed. *Life of Mrs. S. J. C. Downs; or, Ten Years at the Head of the Woman's Christian Temperance Union of New Jersey.* Camden, N.J.: Gazette Printing and Publishing House, 1892. *History of Women,* no. 4252. New Haven, Conn.: Research Publications, 1975. Microfilm.

Gray, Cecil. *Sibelius.* London: Oxford University Press, 1931. Reprint. Westport, Conn.: Hyperion Press, 1979.

———. *Sibelius: The Symphonies.* London: 1935. Reprint. Freeport, N.Y.: Books for Libraries Press, 1970.

Greenfield, Thomas Allen. *Radio. A Reference Guide.* Westport, Conn.: Greenwood Press, 1989.

Greenberg, Clement. *The Collected Essays and Criticism.* Edited by John O'Brian. Vol. 2, *Arrogant Purpose, 1945–1949.* Chicago: University of Chicago Press, 1986.

Gross, John Bradford. "Philip Hale: Gentleman Critic." GU MSS 688, Subject File "Hale, Philip re."

Haggin, B. H. *Music in the Nation.* New York: William Sloane Associates, 1949.

———. "Sibelius: The Myth and the Reality." *Brooklyn Daily Eagle,* November 25, 1934.

———. *35 Years of Music.* New York: Horizon Press, 1974. (Originally published as *Music Observed.*)

"Hail Radioing of Score." *New York Times,* December 31, 1937.

[Hale, Philip]. *Great Concert Music: Philip Hale's Boston Symphony Programme Notes.* Edited by John H. Burk. New York: Garden City Publishing, 1939.

Hale, Philip. "New Symphony by Sibelius." *Boston Herald,* October 25, 1913.

Hamilton, David. "Sibelius the Symphonist." *Stagebill, Lincoln Center,* February 1980, 23, 26, 35.

Hanson, Howard. Review of *Jean Sibelius* by Harold E. Johnson. *Saturday Review,* July 25, 1959, 17.

Henderson, William J. "Klemperer Honors Sibelius." *New York Sun,* December 6, 1935.

———. "Music and Musicians." *New York Sun,* January 29, 1927.

Hepokoski, James. *Sibelius: Symphony No. 5.* Cambridge, England: Cambridge University Press, 1993.

H. F. P. "A New and Strange Sibelius Symphony." *Musical America,* March 8, 1913, 26.

Hill, Frank Ernest. *Tune In for Education: Eleven Years of Education by Radio.* New York: National Committee on Education by Radio, 1942.

Hill, W. G. "Some Aspects of Form in the Symphonies of Sibelius." *Music Review* 10 (1949): 165-82.

Hitchcock, H. Wiley. *Music in the United States: A Historical Introduction.* 3d ed. Englewood Cliffs, N.J.: Prentice-Hall, 1988.

"Hitler Awards Medal to Composer." *New York Times,* December 9, 1935.

Hodgson, Godfrey. *America in Our Time.* Garden City, N.Y.: Doubleday, 1976.

Holub, Robert C. *Reception Theory: A Critical Introduction.* London: Methuen, 1984.

"Homage to a Master." *Musical America,* December 10, 1935, 5–6.

Hood, Leon Crist. "The Programming of Classical Music Broadcasts Over the Major Radio Networks." Ed.D. diss., New York University, 1955.

Horowitz, Joseph. *Understanding Toscanini.* New York: Alfred A. Knopf, 1987.

"How Downes Came Up." *Times Talk,* January 1954, 4–5.

Howe, M. A. DeWolfe. *The Boston Symphony Orchestra 1881–1931.* Rev. and extended in collaboration with John N. Burk. Boston: Houghton Mifflin, 1931.

Howell, Tim. *Jean Sibelius, Progressive Techniques in the Symphonies and Tone Poems.* New York: Garland, 1989.

Hughes, Rupert. *Contemporary American Composers.* Boston: L. C. Page, 1900.

Humiston, William Henry. "New Sibelius Symphony a Puzzle." *Musical America,* August 9, 1913, 17.

Humphrey, Laning. "Olin Downes, Radio Interpreter." *Christian Science Monitor,* May 16, 1931, 18.

"Indictments Against Quigley." *New York Times,* January 25, 1895.

Instructor's Manual, NBC Music Appreciation Hour Ninth Season, 1936–1937. Conducted by Walter Damrosch, prepared by Lawrence Abbott. New York: National Broadcasting Company, 1936, Series D.

James, Henry. *The Bostonians.* Boston: 1886. Reprint. Edited by R. D. Gooder. Oxford: Oxford University Press, 1984.

Jay, Martin, *Adorno.* Cambridge, Mass.: Harvard University Press, 1984.

———. *The Dialectical Imagination. A History of the Frankfurt School and the Institute of Social Research 1923–1950.* Boston: Little, Brown, 1973.

Johnson, Harold E. *Jean Sibelius.* New York: Alfred A. Knopf, 1959.

———. *Jean Sibelius: The Recorded Music.* Helsinki: R. E. Westerlund, [1957].

Karsh, Yousuf. *In Search of Greatness.* New York: Alfred A. Knopf, 1962.

———. *Portraits of Greatness.* [London and New York: T. Nelson, 1960.]

Keene, James A. *A History of Music Education in the United States.* Hanover, N.H.: University Press of New England, 1982.

Keller, Hans. "The New in Review: Symphony and Sonata Today—II." *Music Review* 22 (1961): 172.

Kernochan, Marshall. "Notable Music. Concerts of the Week." *Outlook and Independent,* January 20, 1932, 85.

Kilpeläinen, Kari. *The Jean Sibelius Musical Manuscripts at the Helsinki University Library/Die Musikhandschriften von Jean Sibelius in der Universitätsbibliothek Helsinki.* Wiesbaden: Breitkopf & Härtel, 1991.

King, Richard. "Modernism and Mass Culture: The Origins of the Debate." In *The Thirties. Politics and Culture in a Time of Broken Dreams,* edited by Heinz Ickstadt, Rob Kroes, and Brian Lee, 120–142. Amsterdam: Free University Press, 1987.

Kinscella, Hazel Gertrude. *Music on the Air.* Garden City, N.Y.: Garden City Publishing, 1934.

Kirby, W. F. *Kalevala, The Land of Heroes.* London: The Athlone Press, 1985.

Koestler, Arthur. "The Intelligentsia." In *Writers & Politics: A Partisan Review Reader.* Edited by Edith Kurzweil and William Phillips, 79–92. Boston: Routledge & Kegan Paul, 1983.

Krehbiel, Henry E. "Work of Boston Orchestra on Its First Visit." *New York Herald Tribune,* November 7, 1920.

Kupferberg, Herbert. *Those Fabulous Philadelphians. The Life and Times of a Great Orchestra.* New York: Charles Scribner's, 1969.

Lambert, Constant. *Music Ho! A Study of Music in Decline.* 3d ed. London: Faber & Faber, 1966.

Layton, Robert. *Sibelius.* 4th ed. Master Musicians Series. New York: Schirmer, 1993.

Legge, Walter. "Conversations with Sibelius." *Musical Times,* March 1935, 218-20.

Leibowitz, René. *Sibelius, le plus mauvais compositeur du monde.* Liège: Aux Editions Dynamo, 1955.

Leichtentritt, Hugo. *Music, History, and Ideas.* Cambridge, Mass.: Harvard University Press, 1938.

———. *Serge Koussevitzky, The Boston Symphony Orchestra and the New American Music.* Cambridge, Mass.: Harvard University Press, 1946.

Leonard, Richard. Letter to the Music Editor of the *New York Times,* February 12, 1933.

Levas, Santeri. *Sibelius: A Personal Portrait.* Translated by Percy M. Young. Lewisburg, Pa.: Bucknell University Press, 1973.

Levy, Alan Howard. *Musical Nationalism: American Composers' Search for Identity.* Contributions in American Studies, no. 66. Westport, Conn.: Greenwood Press, 1983.

The Life and Letters of Stephen Olin. 2 vols. New York: Harper & Bros., 1853.

Lochner, Louis P. *Fritz Kreisler.* New York: Macmillan, 1950.

Lorenz, Robert. "Afterthoughts on the Sibelius Festival." *Musical Times,* January 1939, 13-14.

"Lost Choral Score Facsimile Radioed." *New York Times,* December 29, 1937.

Lowens, Irving. "L'affaire Muck, A Study in War Hysteria (1917-18)." *Musicology* 1 (1945-47): 265-74.

Lyle, Watson. "Jean Sibelius." *Living Age,* May 7, 1921, 360-61.

———. "The 'Nationalism' of Sibelius." *Musical Quarterly* 13 (1927): 617-29.

Lynes, Russell. *The Lively Audience. A Social History of the Visual and Peforming Arts in America, 1890–1950.* New York: Harper & Row, 1985.

Lyons, Louis M. *Newspaper Story. One Hundred Years of The Boston Globe.* Cambridge, Mass.: The Belknap Press of Harvard University Press, 1971.

Macdonald, Dwight. *Against the American Grain.* New York: 1962. Reprint. New York: Da Capo Press, 1983.

Manchester Guardian. "The Hallé Concerts," March 3, 1905; "M. Jean Sibelius," March 18, 1905; "The Liverpool Orchestral Society. Jean Sibelius," March 20, 1905; "Sibelius in Liverpool," December 4, 1905.

Mason, Daniel Gregory. *Tune In, America. A Study of Our Coming Musical Independence.* New York: Alfred A. Knopf, 1931.

Mueller, John H. *The American Symphony Orchestra. A Social History of Musical Taste.* London: John Calder, 1958.

Mueller, John H., and Kate Hevner. "A Survey of Trends in Musical Taste." *New York Times,* February 27, 1938.

Mueller, Kate Hevner. *Twenty-Seven Major American Symphony Orchestras: A History and Analysis of Their Repertoires, Seasons 1842-43 through 1969-70.* Bloomington: Indiana University Press, 1973.

Mueser, Barbara. "The Criticism of New Music in New York: 1919–1929." Ph.D. diss., City University of New York, 1975.

"Music for 'Tempest' Played in Cincinnati." *New York Times,* December 4, 1954.

Narodny, Ivan. "Music of Sibelius in America." *Musical America,* February 14, 1914, 13.

———. "Sibelius and Finnish Folk Songs." *Musical America,* June 15, 1912, 9.

National Cyclopedia of American Biography, s.v. "Downes, [Edwin] Olin"; "Olin, Stephen."

"Nature Boy at 90." *Time,* December 12, 1955.

Neilson, William Allan. *Charles W. Eliot: The Man and His Beliefs.* 2 vols. New York: Harper & Bros., 1926.

———. ed. *Lectures on Dr. Eliot's Five-Foot Shelf of Books.* New York: Collier's Lecture Service Bureau, 1913.

Neue Zeitschrift für Musik, s.v. January 18, 1905, 73.

"New Friends Mark Sibelius Birthday." *New York Times,* December 9, 1940.

New Grove Dictionary of American Music, s.v. "Criticism"; "Downes, Olin"; "Parker, Horatio."

New Grove Dictionary of Music and Musicians, s.v. "Criticism"; "Newman, Ernest"; "Niemann, Walter"; "Nietzsche, Friedrich"; "Nikisch, Arthur"; "Rolland, Romain."

Newlin, Dika. "Secret Tonality in Schoenberg's Piano Concerto." *Perspectives of New Music* 13 (1974-75): 137-39.

Newman, Ernest. *Essays from the World of Music. Essays from "The Sunday Times."* Selected by Felix Aprahamian. London: 1956. Reprint. New York: Da Capo Press, 1978. (See also articles under *Manchester Guardian.*)

———. *More Essays from the World of Music. Essays from the London "Sunday Times."* Selected by Felix Aprahamian. New York: Coward-McCann, 1958.

Newmarch, Rosa. *Jean Sibelius: A Finnish Composer.* Leipzig: Breitkopf & Härtel, [1906].

"New Trends in Radio Indicate Bright Future." *New York Times,* October 6, 1929.

"New York Critics Analyze the Words 'Classic' and 'Romantic.'" *CBC Times,* May 9–15, 1954, Clipping in the Canadian Broadcasting Corporation Reference Library, Toronto, Canada.

Niemann, Walter, *Jean Sibelius.* Leipzig: Breitkopf & Härtel, 1917.

———. "Jean Sibelius und die Finnische Musik." *Signale für die Musikalische Welt* 62 (1904): 185-91.

———. "Jean Sibelius und die Finnische Musik." [A different article from the one above.] *Die Musik* 13 (1913): 195–206.

———. *Die Musik Skandinaviens.* Leipzig: Breitkopf & Härtel, 1906.

"Olin Downes Dies; Times Music Critic." *New York Times,* August 26, 1955.

Olin Downes on Music. A Selection from His Writings during the Half-Century 1906 to 1955. Edited by Irene Downes. New York: Alfred A. Knopf, 1957.

Olsen, R. S. "The Reaction Against Sibelius." *Musical Opinion,* June 1962, 525, 527.

"Opera on the Air." *New York Times,* January 24, 1927.

Otis, Philo Adams. *The Chicago Symphony Orchestra. Its Organization Growth and Development 1891–1924.* Chicago: Clayton F. Summy, 1924.

Pakenham, Compton. "Recorded Music: Beethoven." *New York Times,* July 27, 1930.

Parker, Horatio. *Mona.* M1500.P288M7 Case. Library of Congress, Washington, D.C.

Paul, Adolf. "From a Friend of Sibelius." *New York Times,* December 29, 1935.

———. "Zwei Fennonenhäuptlinge: Sibelius/Gallén." *Deutsch-Nordisches Jahrbuch für Kulturaustausch und Volkskunde 1914.* Jena: Eugen Diederichs, 1914, 114-21.

"The People Now Shake Hands." *New York Times,* December 24, 1933.

Peyser, Herbert F. "An American Reveals Sibelius." *New York Times,* February 25, 1934.

———. "Janssen's Sibelius in Berlin." *New York Times,* March 19, 1933.

———. "Sibelius Revealed to Vienna." *New York Times,* December 22, 1935.

Pike, Lionel. *Beethoven, Sibelius and 'the Profound Logic'. Studies in Symphonic Analysis.* London: Athlone Press and University of London, 1978.

"Plans Completed for Sibelius Fete." *New York Times,* November 17, 1955.

Plaut, Alice S. Review of *Olin Downes on Music. MLA Notes* 14 (1956-57): 361.

Pleck, Elizabeth H., and Joseph H. Pleck, eds. *The American Man.* Englewood Cliffs, N.J.: Prentice-Hall, 1980.

"Plight of Sibelius Confuses Capital." *New York Times,* July 10, 1950.

Pratt, Harry Rogers. "Hardy Finland Speaks Through Sibelius." *New York Times,* December 8, 1935.

Price, Lucien. *We Northmen.* Boston: Little, Brown, 1936.

The Progressive Music Series. Vols. 3 and 4. Boston: Silver, Burdett, 1916.

Pudor, Heinrich. "Biographisches. Jean Sibelius (Mit Portrait)." *Musikalisches Wochenblatt* 31 (1900): 554-57.

———. "Zur Geschichte der Musik in Finnland." *Sammelbände der Internationalen Musikgesellschaft* 2 (1900–1901): 147-57.

"Quigley Stole $144,000." *New York Times,* January 19, 1895.

"Quigley's Forged Bonds." *New York Times,* January 22, 1895.

"Quigley's Operation in Bridgeport." *New York Times,* January 21, 1895.

"Quigley's Prison Term." *New York Times,* January 26, 1895.

"Quigley's Sentence Postponed." *New York Times,* January 24, 1895.

Raabe, Peter. "Zwei Legenden für Orchester von Jean Sibelius." *Allgemeine Musik-Zeitung,* May 31/June 7, 1901, 379-84.

Red Channels: The Report of Communist Influence in Radio and Television. New York: American Business Consultants, 1950.

"Reputation of Quigley." *New York Times,* January 20, 1895.

Réti-Forbes, Jean. "The Influence of Olin Downes, Music Critic, on American Concert Repertoire." Typescript, MSS 912, Jean Réti-Forbes Papers, Box R-Réti, Hargrett Library, University of Georgia.

──────. "The Olin Downes Papers." *Georgia Review* 21 (1967): 165–71.

Rich, Alan. "Whatever Happened to Jan Sibelius?" *New York,* June 9, 1975, 80.

Ringbom, Nils-Eric. *Jean Sibelius: A Master and His Work.* Translated by G. I. C. de Courcy. Norman: University of Oklahoma Press, 1954.

Robinson, Edward. "The Music Room: Jean Sibelius." *American Mercury* 25 (1932): 245–49.

Robinson, Paul. *Stokowski.* N.p.: Vanguard Press, 1977.

Rose, Gillian. *The Melancholy Science. An Introduction to the Thought of Theodor W. Adorno.* New York: Columbia University Press, 1978.

Rosenfeld, Paul. "The Beethoven of the North." *New Republic,* April 21, 1941, 526–28.

──────. *Discoveries of a Music Critic.* [New York]: 1936. Reprint. New York: Vienna House, 1972.

──────. *Musical Chronicle (1917–1923).* New York: Harcourt, Brace, 1923.

──────. *Musical Portraits: Interpretations of Twenty Modern Composers.* London: Kegan Paul, 1922.

Russell, Charles Edward. *The American Orchestra and Theodore Thomas.* Garden City, N.Y.: Doubleday, Page, 1927.

Rychnovsky, Ernst. Review of Symphony no. 4 by Jean Sibelius in *Die Musik* 11 (1912): 172.

Sabin, Robert. "American Music Criticism Before Its Golden Age." *Musical America,* February 10, 1937, 20.

Sablosky, Irving. *American Music.* Chicago: University of Chicago Press, 1969. Reprint. 1985.

Salmenhaara, Erkki. *Jean Sibelius.* Helsinki: Kustannusosakeyhtiö Tammi, 1984.

Sargeant, Winthrop. *Geniuses, Goddesses and People.* New York: E. P. Dutton, 1949.

Scherber, Ferdinand. Concert review in *Signale für die Musikalische Welt* 70 (1912): 469–70.

Schoenberg, Arnold. "New Music, Outmoded Music, Style and Idea." In *Style and Idea. Selected Writings of Arnold Schoenberg,* 113–23. Edited by Leonard Stein with translations by Leo Black. London: Faber & Faber, 1975. Rev. ed., 1984.

Schonberg, Harold C. *The Great Conductors.* New York: Simon & Schuster, 1967.

──────. *The Lives of the Great Composers.* Rev. ed. New York: W. W. Norton, 1981.

————. Review of *Olin Downes on Music. Musical Courier,* March 15, 1957, 30.

Schubart, Mark A. "Philharmonic Severs Red Tape of War to Assist Jan Sibelius." *New York Times,* April 7, 1945.

Schumann, Robert. *Gesammelte Schriften über Musik und Musiker.* 5th ed. Edited by Martin Kreisig. Leipzig: Breitkopf & Härtel, 1914.

Selected Letters of Virgil Thomson. Edited by Tim Page and Vanessa Weeks Page. New York: Summit Books, 1988.

Serious Music on the Columbia Broadcasting System. A Survey of Series, Soloists and Special Performances from 1927 through 1938. New York: Columbia Broadcasting System, [n.d.].

"Sibelius Appeals to U. S. to Understand Finn Case." *New York Times,* July 13, 1941.

"Sibelius at 90." *New York Times,* December 8, 1955.

"Sibelius, Bruckner, Mahler." *New York Times,* December 28, 1930.

"Sibelius, Composer, Dies at 91 of Stroke at Home in Finland." *New York Times,* September 21, 1957.

"Sibelius, Composer, Leads in Radio Vote." *New York Times,* December 2, 1935.

"Sibelius Is Host to U. S. Orchestra." *New York Times,* June 19, 1955.

"Sibelius Is Safe at Finnish Forest Home." *New York Times,* December 3, 1939.

"Sibelius Marks 77th Birthday." *New York Times,* December 9, 1942.

"Sibelius Once More." *New York Times,* January 4, 1931.

"Sibelius Program at Carnegie Hall." *New York Times,* January 12, 1941.

"Sibelius Score Lost on Atlantic Voyage." *New York Times,* December 28, 1937.

"The Sibelius Symphonies." *New York Times,* February 12, 1933.

"Sibelius's Ancestry." *New York Times,* February 7, 1932.

"Sibelius to Get U. S. Royalties." *New York Times,* December 3, 1954.

"Sibelius to Open Salutes to Fair." *New York Times,* December 27, 1938.

"Sibelius Visits the Musical Courier." *Musical Courier,* June 10, 1914, 6.

Simpson, Robert. *Sibelius and Nielsen: A Centenary Essay.* London: BBC Publications, 1965.

Sjöblom, Paul. "An Interview with Sibelius." *Musical America,* December 1940, 11, 34.

————. "New Sibelius Series Inaugurated." *New York Times,* July 1, 1951.

————. "No Statue for Sibelius." *New York Times,* December 22, 1940.

————. "Philadelphians Score in Helsinki." *New York Times,* July 3, 1955.

Slosson, Preston William. *The Great Crusade and After 1914–1928.* Vol. 12 of *A History of American Life.* Edited by Arthur M. Schlesinger and Dixon Ryan Fox. New York: Macmillan, 1930.

Smith, Carlton. "Sibelius Likes Music by Sibelius." *New York Times,* July 24, 1937.

Smith, John Boulton. *The Golden Age of Finnish Art, Art Nouveau and the National Spirit.* Helsinki: Ministry for Foreign Affairs, 1975.

Stavrou, C. N. *Whitman and Nietzsche: A Comparative Study of Their Thought.* Chapel Hill: University of North Carolina Press, 1964.

Stoeckel, Carl. "Some Recollections of the Visit of Sibelius to America in 1914." *Scandinavian Studies* 43 (1971): 53–88.

Stokowski, Leopold. *Music For All Of Us.* New York: Simon & Schuster, 1943.

Straus, Noel. "Sibelius Honored at Concert Here." *New York Times,* November 22, 1945.

———. "Sibelius Score. The Story of His 'Masonic Ritual Music' Told for the First Time." *New York Times,* October 3, 1948.

Stravinsky, Vera, and Robert Craft. *Stravinsky in Pictures and Documents.* New York: Simon & Schuster, 1978.

Stutsman, Grace May. "Koussevitzky Observes Sibelius Anniversary in Boston Concert." *Musical America,* December 25, 1935.

Subotnik, Rose Rosengard. "Musicology and Criticism." In *Musicology in the 1980s: Methods, Goals, Opportunities.* Edited by D. Kern Holoman and Claude V. Palisca, 145–60. New York: Da Capo Press, 1982.

Susman, Warren I. *Culture as History: The Transformation of American Society in the Twentieth Century.* New York: Pantheon Books, 1984.

———. "The Thirties." In *The Development of an American Culture.* Edited by Stanley Coben and Lorman Ratner, 179–218. Englewood Cliffs, N.J.: Prentice-Hall, 1970.

Susskind, Charles. *Janáček and Brod.* New Haven, Conn.: Yale University Press, 1985.

Swan, John C., ed. and comp. *Music in Boston: Readings from the First Three Centuries.* Boston: Trustees of the Public Library of the City of Boston, 1977.

"'Symphony in Wood' of Finns Has Debut." *New York Times,* May 5, 1939.

Tarasti, Eero. *Myth and Music. A Semiotic Approach to the Aesthetics of Myth in Music, Especially That of Wagner, Sibelius and Stravinsky.* The Hague: Mouton Publishers, 1979.

Taubman, Howard. "Music: Sibelius at 90." *New York Times,* December 5, 1955.

———. "Records: Anniversary. Companies Observe Birthday of Sibelius with New Disks—Recent Release." *New York Times,* December 8, 1940.

———. "Sibelius at 90: A Finnish Epic." *New York Times Magazine,* December 4, 1944.

Tawaststjerna, Erik. *Jean Sibelius.* 5 vols. Helsinki: Otava, 1965–1988. Vol. 1–3 translated and abridged in two English volumes by Robert Layton. London: Faber & Faber, 1976, 1986. Vol. 1–3 in Swedish. Helsinki: Söderström, 1992, 1991, 1993.

———. "Sibelius's Eighth Symphony—An Insoluble Mystery." *Finnish Music Quarterly* (1985): 61–70; 92–101.

———. "Über Adornos Sibeliuskritik," *Studien zur Wertungsforschung* 12 (1979): 112–24.

Terrace, Vincent. *Radio's Golden Years. The Encyclopedia of Radio Programs.* San Diego: A. S. Barnes, 1981.

Thompson, Oscar. "An American School of Criticism. The Legacy Left by W. J. Henderson, Richard Aldrich, and their Colleagues of the Old Guard." *Musical Quarterly* 23 (1937): 428–39.

Thomson, Virgil. *Music Right and Left.* New York: Henry Holt, 1951.

———. "Olin Downes: A Free Critical Spirit." *New York Herald Tribune,* January 27, 1957.

———. "Radio Examined." *New York Herald Tribune,* February 8, 1942.

———. *A Virgil Thomson Reader.* Boston: Houghton Mifflin, 1981.

The *Times,* February 15, 1909; October 2, 1912; October 3, 1912; September 11, 1913; February 12, 1921.

"Topics of the Times: Cigars for Sibelius." *New York Times,* December 8, 1948.

Törne, Bengt de. *Sibelius: A Close-Up.* Boston: Houghton Mifflin, 1938.

"Toscanini on the Air." *Fortune* 17 (January 1938): 62–68.

Tovey, Donald Francis. *Essays in Musical Analysis.* Vol. 2, *Symphonies (II): Variations and Orchestral Polyphony.* London: Oxford University Press, 1935.

"U. S. Taking Part in 'Sibelius Year.'" *New York Times,* January 1, 1965.

Voipio, Anni. "Sibelius—As His Wife Sees Him." *New York Times,* January 28, 1940.

Watkins, Glenn. *Soundings: Music in the Twentieth Century.* New York: Schirmer, 1988.

Weldy, Lloyd. "Music Criticism of Olin Downes and Howard Taubman in the *New York Times,* Sunday Edition: 1924–1929 and 1955–1960." D.M.A. diss., University of Southern California, 1965.

Whitman, Walt. *Leaves of Grass.* Comprehensive Reader's Edition. Edited by Harold W. Blodgett and Sculley Bradley. N.p.: New York University Press, 1965.

W. H. P. "Broadcast Cycle of Sibelius' Works Finds the Radio Public Responsive." *Musical America,* December 25, 1937, 25.

Wilkins, Robert Huchette. "The Role of Serious Music in the Development of American Radio, 1920–1938." M.A. thesis, University of North Dakota, 1969.

"Will Sentence Quigley Today." *New York Times,* January 23, 1895.

Wilson, William A. *Folklore and Nationalism in Modern Finland.* Bloomington: Indiana University Press, 1976.

Wister, Frances Anne. *Twenty-five Years of the Philadelphia Orchestra 1900–1925.* Philadelphia: Published under the Auspices of the Women's Committees for the Philadelphia Orchestra, 1925.

Wood, Henry J. *My Life of Music.* London: 1938. Reprint. Freeport, N.Y.: Books for Libraries Press, 1971.

Wooldridge, David. *Conductors' World.* New York: Praeger Publishers, 1970.

"Would Ban 'Finlandia' Now." *New York Times,* October 20, 1942.

Ybarra, T. R. "Music Maker." *Collier's,* April 17, 1937, 26, 46–48.

Åbo. *See* Turku, Finland
Addis, Enoch, 19
Addisville, Pa., 19
Adorno, Theodor W. (1903–69), 3, 128,
    131–32, 147, 148, 173, 174, 175
    in America, 132, 136
    American musicology and, 137
    "Glosse über Sibelius," 130, 132, 137
    on Hindemith, 142
    Introduction to the Sociology of Music, 139
    on Mahler, 131, 136
    Philosophy of Modern Music, 129, 139
    on radio, 128, 129
    on Sibelius, 129–30, 139
    on Stravinsky, 130, 139, 142
Aho, Juhani (1861–1921), 10
Ainola (JS's home) (*see also* Järvenpää),
    45, 72, 81, 86, 88, 145, 166, 176, 198,
    201, 218
Aldrich, Richard (1863–1937), 75
Alexander University (Helsinki), 9
Allgemeiner Deutscher Musikverein, 44
Altschuler, Modest (1873–1963), 58
American Business Consultants, 142
American Committee for Spanish Free-
    dom, 143
American Committee for Yugoslav Re-
    lief, 143
American consumer culture, 2, 97, 98,
    106, ch. 5 passim

American Labor party, 143
American School of the Air, 107
American-Soviet Music Society, 142
Amsterdam, 19
    Conzertgebouw Orchestra, 204
Anbruch, 131
Anderson, Marian (1897–1993), 199, 203
Antheil, George (1900–1959), 177
Apthorp, William Foster (1848–1913), 24
Armitage, Merle (1893–1975), 101
Artjärvi, Finland, 8
Atlanta, 19, 177
Axman, Gladys (fl. 1930s), 163

Babbitt, Milton (b. 1916), 147
Bach, Johann Sebastian (1685–1750), 24,
    25, 115, 204
    Concerto in D minor, 166–67
Bachet, Claude Gaspar, Sieur de Mezir-
    iac, *Commentaires sur les épistres
    d'Ovide,* 24
Baermann, Carl (1839–1913), 30, 157
Ballets russes, 158
Bantock, Sir Granville (1868–1946), 110,
    111, 112, 123, 162
Barber, Samuel (1910–81), 177
Barbirolli, Sir John (1899–1970), 118, 125,
    172
Barrère, Georges (1876–1944), 94
Bartók, Béla (1881–1945), 60, 135, 146

Basel, Switzerland, 30
Battell, Ellen. *See* Stoeckel, Ellen Battell
Battell, Robbins (1819–95), 40
Bax, Sir Arnold (1883–1953), 58
Bayreuth, Germany, 92, 191
BBC Symphony Orchestra, 99, 167
Bedelia, 30
Beecham, Sir Thomas (1879–1961), 132,
    213, 214, 229, 230, 231, 239
Beethoven, Ludwig van (1770–1827) (*see
    also* Sibelius, Jean), 88, 117, 169, 202,
    239
  Adorno on, 128, 136
  Damrosch on, 108
  Symphony no. 9, 115, 204, 210
Berezowsky, Nicolai (1900–1953), 237
Berg, Alban (1885–1935), 132
  Wozzeck, 125, 131
Bergman, Erik (b. 1911), 217
Berkshire Music Center (Lenox, Mass.),
    109, 197
Berkshire Music Festival, 202, 237
Berlin, 11, 14, 23, 82, 83, 103, 196
  New York Times office in, 187
Berlin Philharmonic Orchestra, 44
Berlioz, Hector (1803–69), 24
Bernstein, Leonard (1918–90), 142–43
Beveridge, Albert (1862–1927), *The
    Young Man and the World*, 157
Birmingham Festival, 112
Birmingham University, 112
Blitzstein, Marc (1905–64), 143
Bloch, Ernest (1880–1959), 87, 91, 109
Blomstedt, Jussi. *See* Jalas, Jussi
Bok, Mary Louise Curtis (1876–1970),
    193
Bonavia, Ferruccio (1877–1950), 112
Bordentown College, 19
Bori, Lucrezia (1887–1960), 119
Borovsky, Felix (1872–1956), 239
Boston (*see also* Downes, Edwin Olin;

Harvard University; Koussevitzky,
    Serge), 20, 21–32, 39, 41, 82, 218
  Sibelius cult in, 59
Boston Advertiser, 34
"Boston Classicists" (*see also* Chadwick,
    George W.; Paine, John Knowles;
    Parker, Horatio), 23, 25, 39
Boston Globe, 34, 197
Boston Herald, 25, 156
Boston Home Journal, 25
Boston Post, 15, 25, 26, 29, 54, 124, Appen-
    dix B passim
Boston Public Library, 32
  Allen A. Brown Collection, 158, 172,
    243
Boston Symphony Orchestra, 21, 32, 75,
    81, 84, 86, 87, 99, 103, 108, 115, 164,
    180, 181, 182, 190, 202, 204, 215, 237,
    238, 239, et passim
Boston Transcript, 24, 161
Boston University, 157
Bostonians, The (James), 23
Boulanger, Nadia (1887–1979), 124, 173
Boulez, Pierre (b. 1925), 147
Brahms, Johannes (1833–97), 24, 54, 111,
    113, 126
  Variations on a Theme of Haydn, 166,
    167
Brailowsky, Alexander (1896–1976), 228
Breitkopf & Härtel, 49, 58, 82, 223, 224
Brennan, William, 75, 180, 181, 182
Brevard Music Center (Brevard, N.C.),
    145
Brico, Antonia (1902–89), 81, 118, 201–2,
    226, 231, 238
British & Continental Music Agencies
    (London), 223
Brooklyn Institute of Arts and Sciences,
    108
Brown, Allen A. (1835–1916). *See* Boston
    Public Library

Bruckner, Anton (1824–96) (*see also* Sibelius, Jean) 45, 101
Burbank, Luther (1849–1926), 188
Burkhardt, Jakob (1818–97), *Civilization of the Renaissance,* 29
Busoni, Ferruccio (1866–1924), 9, 10, 83
  Berlin concert series, 44
  as Sibelius advocate, 58, 160

Canadian Broadcasting Company, 105
Carberry, Clifton Benjamin (1876–1940), 163
Carmen, Kevie, 102, 168
Carnegie Hall. *See* Downes, Edwin Olin, New York and
Carpelan, Baron Axel (1858–1919), 159
Carpelan family, 8
Carpenter, John Alden (1876–1951), 23
Caruso, Enrico (1873–1921), 103
Casella, Alfredo (1883–1947), 94
CBS. *See* Columbia Broadcasting System
Chabrier, Emmanuel (1841–94), 24, 26
Chadwick, George W. (1854–1931), 23, 25, 157, 186
  meets Sibelius, 40
  mentioned in Sibelius's diary, 59
  Viking's Last Voyage, The, 28
Charpentier, Marc-Antoine (1645/50–1704), 24, 26
Cherkassky, Paul, 190
Chicago, 103
Chopin, Frédéric François (1810–49), 103
Cincinnati, 84, 85
Civil Rights Congress, 143
Clark, Frances Elliot (1860–1958), 106, 170
Cleveland Symphony Orchestra, 119
Collins, Judy (b. 1939), 201
Columbia Broadcasting System (CBS), 103, 104, 106, 107, 175, 234

Columbia Graphophone Company, 98, 99, 119, 192–94
Columbia University, 131, 137
  Paul Lazarsfeld Papers, 174
Communist Party, 142, 143
Converse, Frederick Shepherd (1871–1940), 23
Copenhagen, 233
  Symphony no. 4 played in, 53
Copland, Aaron (1900–1990), 83, 127, 142
  The First of May, 142
  The New Music, 137
  on Sibelius, 137
Corson, Sarah Jane (1822–91) (OD's grandmother), 19–20, 120, 155, 213
Counterattack: The Newsletter of Fact on Communism, 142
Cowell, Henry (1897–1965), 84
Curtis Institute of Music, 193

Dagens Nyheter (Stockholm), 55
Damrosch, Walter (1862–1950) (*see also* Sibelius, Jean), 58, 94, 204
  music appreciation and, 107–8
  radio and, 103, 170
  Sibelius and, 40, 119
  Swan of Tuonela and, 108
  Symphony no. 4 and, 50, 54
  Tapiola and, 71, 89
Davenport, Marion. *See* Downes, Marion Amanda
Davies, Peter Maxwell (b. 1934), 177
Davison, Archibald (1883–1961), 124
De Contemptu Mundi, 28
Debussy, Claude (1862–1918), 26, 27, 82, 85, 113, 163, 168
  compared with Sibelius, 61–62
  Downes on, 24, 27, 77, 109, 175
  meets Sibelius, 112
  works: *La Mer,* 24, 27; *Pelléas et*

Debussy, Claude (cont.)
Mélisande, 24, 109; *Prelude to the After-noon of a Faun,* 85
Dempsey, Jack (1895–1983), 158
Dickson, Harry Ellis (b. 1908), 83
Dixie (Emmett), 25
Dixon, Richard Watson (1833–1900), "Autumn Song," 39
Downes, Edward Olin (b. 1911) (OD's son), x, 37, 81, 155, 167, 176, 191, 192, 195
Downes, Edwin Olin (1886–1955)
on Abraham's Sibelius symposium, 239
airplane crash of, 97, 167
ancestors of, 19–21
on Bach, 25, 156
"Be Your Own Critic," 108
in Berlin, 103, 187, 195, 200
Boston and, 15, 21, 76, 190, ch. 2 passim
Boston Post and, 26, 29, 75, 92, 124, 163, Appendix B passim
boxing and, 158
Carnegie Hall and, 94, 108
at Chatauqua, 108
childhood of, 17–18
made Commander of the Order of the White Rose, 114
correspondence of, 3, 105, 164, Appendix A, et passim
death of, 3, 145
democratic view of art, 2, 97, 108, 127, 130, 135
education of, 29, 30
Emerson and, 27–28
"Enjoyment of Music, The," 108
father and (*see also* Quigley, Edwin), 17, 27, 31, 37, 89
films and, 102; *Carnegie Hall,* 95
fishing and, 183–84, 185, 187, 190, 191
"Five-Foot Record Shelf" and, 102, 168
folk songs and, 204, 205
on Gershwin, 236
Harvard and, 29, 77, 108, 168
Hindemith and, 109, 142
as interviewer, 188
Janáček and, 97
jazz and, 205
Koussevitzky and, 29, 81, 83, 86–87, 109, 191, 196
Kreisler hoax and, 95–96
as lecturer, 95, 108–9
"the Mahler controversy," 132–35
marriages of, 120–21, 213
on Menuhin, 95
in Milan, 196
mother and (*see also* Downes, Louise Corson), 21, 27, 120, 121, 208, 213, 214
music appreciation and, 108–9, 126
on music criticism, 133–34
name, 20, 155
Nancy Downes Smith (OD's daughter) and, 167
New York and, 75–76, et passim
New York Times and, 1, 75, 163, Appendix B, et passim
Nietzsche and, 30–31
obituary, 29, 108, 170
Paderewski and, 103–4
papers of. *See* Olin Downes Collection
in Paris, 76, 85, 97, 142, 164, 182, 187, 196, 231, 232, 239
passport denied, 143, 176
personality of, 92, 94
physical appearance of, 37, 94; photographs of, 18, 79, 96, 144
as pianist, 17–18, 29, 94, 95, 166–67
political views of, 121, 213–14, 224–25
radio and, 102–6, 196
recordings and, 102
Red Channels and, 142–43
Rolland and, 26–27, 156

in Russia, 187, 188, 195
Schoenberg and, 57–58, 87, 134; on
    Five Pieces for Orchestra, 57; on
    Pierrot lunaire, 135
Sibelius and, 1, 13, 14, 15, 59; American
    conducting tour proposed, 75,
    180–82; cod-liver oil music,
    117–18; correspondence with, 1, 2,
    15, 27, 75, 78, 80, 81, 86, 87, 88, 99,
    116, 117, 120–21, 142, 143, 144–45,
    164, Appendix A, et passim; in di-
    ary of, 59, 80; first meeting with,
    39, 40, 41, 42; as hero, 26–27, 31,
    34, 60, 61, 105, 109, 120, 127, 241;
    and Joan of Arc, 67, 215; per-
    suades Sibelius to conduct, 205;
    on recordings of, 99, 192–93; re-
    views of, 57, 61–63, 77, 118, 119–
    20, 142, Appendix B; royalties
    for, 139, 141, 175, 219, 239; as un-
    washed Viking, 37, 109; visits to,
    66, 75, 78, 80, 81, 86, 94, 183, 185,
    190, 195–96, 236; Whitman and,
    34
on Sibelius's works: *Arioso,* 216; *Cap-
    tive Queen, The,* 238; Concerto for
    Violin, 193, 236, 237, 238, 239; *En
    saga,* 55, 105, 117, 169, 193, 198, 235,
    238, 239, 240; *Ferryman's Bride,*
    196; *Finlandia,* 117, 237, 238; *Im-
    promptu,* 196; *Kullervo* Symphony,
    219–25; *Lemminkäinen Suite,* 211,
    222, 224, 238, 239; *Lemmin-
    käinen's Homeward Journey,* 210;
    Night Ride and Sunrise, 236;
    Oceanides, The, 236, 238; *Oma
    maa (Our Land),* 196; *Origin of
    Fire,* 238; *Pohjola's Daughter,* 236,
    238, 239; Sonatinas, op. 67, 239;
    Swan of Tuonela, 207, 208, 210,
    212, 238; *Swanwhite,* 237; Sym-
    phony no. 1, 32–34, 193, 198, 235,

236, 237, 238; Symphony no. 2,
    32, 34, 125, 193, 211, 230, 231, 235,
    236, 237, 238, 239; Symphony no.
    3, 48–49, 54, 236, 237; Symphony
    no. 4, 54, 55, 56, 62, 105, 161, 210,
    212, 230, 233, 235, 236, 237, 238,
    239, 240; Symphony no. 5, 62, 63,
    231, 236, 237, 238, 239; Symphony
    no. 6, 80, 81, 187, 193, 195, 215,
    230, 237, 238, 239; Symphony no.
    7, 193, 198, 212–13, 214, 215, 216,
    230, 238, 239; Symphony no. 8,
    86–89, 115, 193, 194, 196, 198, 202,
    204; Symphony no. 9, 88, 202;
    Tapiola, 72, 236, 237; *Voces inti-
    mae,* 236, 237, 238
Stravinsky and, 77, 101, 135, 175, 232;
    compares Sibelius with, 81, 118,
    142; reviews of, 75, 76–77, 163,
    164
on Wagner, 57, 94, 120, 208
Whitman and, 34, 213
World's Fair and, 114–15, 117, 203–4
Writings *Sibelius,* 158; *Sibelius the Sym-
    phonist,* 145, 152, 157, 158, 159, 161,
    221, 222; *Symphonic Broadcasts,* 21,
    105, 155; *Symphonic Masterpieces,*
    198, 221, 222; *Treasury of American
    Song,* 205; Appendix B
Downes, Irene Lenore (OD's second
    wife), 145
Downes, Louise Corson (1857–1940)
    (OD's mother), 17–22, 121, 155
    death of, 21, 120
    photograph of, 22
    on Sibelius, 88, 202
    Whitman and, 20–21, 25, 30
Downes, Marion Amanda Davenport
    (OD's first wife), 21, 201
Downs, Charles S. (OD's grandfather), 19
Downs, Sarah Jane Corson. *See* Corson,
    Sarah Jane

Dukas, Paul (1865–1935), 26
Dwight, John Sullivan (1813–93), 25

Eastman School of Music, 59
Ekman, Karl, Jr. (1895–1961), 13, 44,
    145, 240
  Sibelius biography reviewed by
    Downes, 237, 238
Elgar, Edward (1857–1934), 85, 129
Eliot, Charles W. (1834–1926), 168
Elson, Louis Charles (1848–1920)
  on Symphony no. 2, 34
  on Symphony no. 4, 54
Emerson, Ralph Waldo (1803–82), 27–28,
    105, 134
Emmett, Dan (1815–1904), 25
Erskine, John (1879–1951), 94, 166–67
Everyman's Fair. See World's Fair
expressionism, 66

Farwell, Arthur (1872–1952), 23, 127
  on Sibelius, 56
fascism, 127–28
Fauré, Gabriel (1845–1924), 24, 26
Fiedler, Max (1859–1939), 37
Films for Democracy, 143
Finland, ix, 8, 10, 58, 116–17, 119, 121,
    123, 126, 146, 205, 206, 239, et
    passim
  folk songs of, 13, 34, 46
  government of, 10, 77, 98, 99, 100,
    146, 192, 194, 224, 238
  Karelia, 9, 10, 11, 13, 118
  language of, 8–9
Finlandia Male Chorus, 116
Finnish Male Choir, 55
"Finnish Renaissance," 11, 154
Fischer, Carl (1849–1923), 59
Fisher, Charles, 92, 94
  Columnists, The, 92
Fisher, Cyrus, 106
Flagstad, Kirsten (1895–1962), 115, 204

Florida State University, 171, 187, 225
Foote, Arthur (1853–1937), 23
"For Finland, Inc.," 119
Foss, Lukas (b. 1922), 177
Franck, César (1822–90), 26, 168
Frank, Alan (b. 1910), 113, 114
Frankenstein, Baron, 191
Frankfurt Institute for Social Research,
    128, 131
Frankfurt University, 131, 139
Fromm, Erich (1900–1980), 131

Gallen-Kallela, Akseli (1865–1931), 10–
    11, 154
  Aino, 10
  Symposium, The (The Problem), 11,
    154
Garbo, Greta (1905–90), 85
Gericke, Wilhelm (1845–1925), 32
Germany, 23, 24
Gershwin, George (1898–1937), 94, 167,
    236
  Dawn of a New Day, 116
Giannini, Dusolina (b. 1902), 236
Gieseking, Walter (1895–1956), 94, 108
Gilbert, Henry (1868–1928), 109
Gilman, Lawrence (1878–1939), 76, 109–
    10, 113–14, 171
Ginn, Father, 116
Gluck, Alma (1884–1938), 40, 193
Glyndebourne, England, 229
Godmilow, Jill, 201
Godowsky, Leopold (1870–1938), 218
Goerll, Mrs., 216–17
Goethe, Johann Wolfgang von (1749–
    1832), 21, 126
Goldmark, Karl (1830–1915), 10
Goossens, Sir Eugene (1893–1962), 119
Gounod, Charles (1818–93), 116
Granfelt, Hanna Lilian (1884–1952), 197
Gray, Cecil (1895–1951), 36, 110, 132,
    240

Sibelius biography, 8, 112–13; reviewed by Downes, 113, 237
Greenberg, Clement (b. 1909), 128, 173
Grimm, Jacob Ludwig (1785–1863), 9
Grozier, Edwin Atkins (1859–1924), 29, 163

Hadley, Henry (1871–1937), 80–81, 185–86
 Lucifer, 186
 meets Sibelius, 40
Haggin, Bernard H. (1900–1987), 125
Hale, Philip (1854–1934), 24–25, 156
 on Sibelius, 37; Symphony no. 1, 25, 156; Symphony no. 2, 37; Symphony no. 4, 54
 on Whitman, 25, 156
Hämeenlinna, Finland, 7, 9
Handel, George Frideric (1685–1759), 102
Handel and Haydn Society (Boston), 21
Hansen, Wilhelm, 58, 77
Hanson, Howard (1896–1981), 119, 146, 177
Hargrett Rare Book and Manuscript Library (University of Georgia), 151, 165, 179
Harty, Sir Hamilton (1879–1941), 112
Harvard, John (1607–38), 23
Harvard Classics, 168
Harvard Glee Club, 124
Harvard University (*see also* Downes, Edwin Olin), 23, 24, 25–26, 27, 108, 157, 191
Haydn, Franz Joseph (1732–1809) (*see also* Handel and Haydn Society), 166
 compared to Sibelius, 45, 63
 Creation, The, 68
Heidelberg Festival, 44
Heilman, William Clifford (1877–1946), 30, 157

Helsingfors. *See* Helsinki
Helsingin Sanomat, 11
Helsinki, 15, 53, 116, 179, Appendix A, et passim
 Esplanade, 188, 217, 225
 Finlandia Hall, 154
 Helsinki University (formerly Alexander University), 9
 Helsinki University Chorus, 82
 Helsinki University Library, 165, 177, 201, 225, 243
 Hotel Kämp, 11, 185, 188, 190, 200, 226, 227, 233
 Philharmonic Orchestra, 116, 194
 Polytech Chorus, 140, 218–21
 Tuomari Kirkko, 145
Helsinki Music Institute. *See* Sibelius Academy
Henderson, William J. (1855–1937), 110
Hill, Edward Burlingame (1872–1960), 124
 Modern French Music, 26
Hindemith, Paul (1895–1963), 84
 Adorno on, 142
 Austin on, 146
 Downes on, 109
His Master's Voice (H.M.V.), 100, 193
Hitler, Adolf (1889–1945), 126, 127, 131, 173
Hofmann, Josef (1876–1957), 94, 119, 167
Hofmannsthal, Hugo von (1874–1929), 64, 66
 Jedermann (Everyman), 64–65, 162
Hollywood, Calif., 3, 102, 124, 136
Horkheimer, Max (1895–1973), 128, 131
Horne, Lena (b. 1917), 143
Hotel Kämp. *See* Helsinki

Ilves, Eero (1887–1953) (JS's son-in-law), 189, 190, 199, 205
Ilves, Katarina (JS's daughter), 190

immigration, 28–29
impressionists, 24
Indianapolis, 119
Indy, Vincent d' (1851–1931), 26
    Downes on, 24, 236
    meets Sibelius, 112
Institute of Radio Education, 107
intelligentsia, 60, 127, 149, 152
    American, 125, 127, 137, 146
    defined by Arthur Koestler, 136, 175
Iso lintu (Finnish folksong), 158
Iturbi, José (1895–1980), 119, 238
Ives, Burl (b. 1909), 143
Ives, Charles (1874–1954), 23, 27, 157, 159
    democratic view of art, 127
    on Philip Hale, 25

Jalas, Jussi (1908–85) (JS's son-in-law), 144, 221, 222, 223, 233
Jalas, Margareta (JS's daughter), 223, 233
James, Henry (1843–1916), *The Bostonians,* 23
Janáček, Leoš (1854–1928), 167
Janssen, Werner (1899–1990), 119, 237
Järnefelt, Aino. *See* Sibelius, Aino
Järnefelt, Arvid (1861–1932), 10
Järnefelt, Eero Nikolai (1863–1937), 10
Järvenpää, Finland, 14, 15, 67, 190, 198, 238, Appendix A, et passim
Joan of Arc (1412–31) (*see also* Sibelius, Jean), 120, 215
Johann Wolfgang Goethe University, 131
Johannes de Garlandia (fl. mid-13th century), 54
Johnson, Theodate (b. 1907), 238
Joyce, James (1882–1941), 124

Kajanus, Robert (1856–1933), 10, 11, 55, 194, 222
    Aino Symphony, 9, 10
    Sibelius recordings and, 98, 100, 194

Kalevala (*see also* Sibelius, Jean), 9, 10, 13, 111, 154, 220
Kallio, Kyösti, 116, 171, 205
Kaltenborn, Hans von (1878–1965), 233, 234
Karelia. *See* Finland
Karsh, Yousuf (b. 1908), 217–18
Kelterborn, Dr. Louis (1891–1933), 30
Kindler, Hans (1892–1949), 119
Klemperer, Otto (1885–1973), 170
Klinsky-Pix (fl. 1930s), 200
Kniesel String Quartet, 236
Kolehmainen, Hannes (1889–1966), 29
Koussevitzky, Serge (1874–1951) (*see also* Downes, Edwin Olin; Paris; Sibelius, Jean), 108, 132, 191, 218
    background, 82–83, 164
    Boston and, 83–84
    competition with Stokowski, 85–86
    as conductor, 82–84
    correspondence of, 86, 87, 165, 243
    named Commander of the Order of the White Rose, 82
    Sibelius and, 81, 82, 91, 126, 196; cycle of seven symphonies, 81, 86–87, 196; performances of, 81, 86–87, 215, 216, 230, 237: *Swanwhite,* 81, 237; Symphony no. 1, 81, 237; Symphony no. 2, 118, 237; Symphony no. 6, 118, 191, 237; Symphony no. 7, 118, 202, 213, 216; *Tapiola,* 81, 237; recordings of, 99, 101, 167–68, 193; Symphony no. 8 and, 86–87, 115, 204
    Stravinsky and, 76, 81, 82–83, 126, 191, 196
    Tanglewood and, 82, 197
Koussevitzky, Natalia Uškov, 83
Krehbiel, Henry (1854–1923)
    hears Sibelius conduct, 40
    on Sibelius's symphonies, 48, 54
Kreisler, Fritz (1875–1962), 95–96

Krips, Alfred, 83
Krohn, Ilmari (1867–1960), 10
"Ku Klux Klan school of anthropology,"
    28–29
Kurck family, 8
Kuula, Toivo (1883–1918), 55

La Forge, Frank (1879–1953), 203
La Guardia, Fiorello (1882–1947), 116
Lambert, Constant (1905–51), 113, 132
    Music Ho!, 113, 171
Lang, Paul Henry (1901–91), 145, 175
    Music in Western Civilization, 137
Laulu-Miehet, 118
Leblanc, Georgette (1876–1941), 109
Leibowitz, René (1913–72), 173
    *Sibelius, le plus mauvais compositeur du
    monde*, 124, 145, 173
Leino, Eino (1878–1926), 10, 11
Leipzig, 23, 49, 82
Leningrad. *See* St. Petersburg
Leon, Mischa, 123
Lhévinne, Josef (1874–1944), 167
Library of Congress. *See* Washington,
    D.C.
Lienau, Robert (1866–1949), 58
Listener, The, 113
Liszt, Franz (1811–86), 30, 236
Liverpool, 111, 112, 171
Liverpool Orchestra, 111, 170
Loeffler, Charles Martin (1861–1935), 24,
    172
    Poème païen, 24
London, 14, 131, 194, 210, 214, 218, 223
    London Concert Goers' Club, 111
    Promenade Concerts, 132
    Queen's Hall, 112
    Symphony no. 4 played in, 53
Longfellow, Henry Wadsworth (1807–
    82), *Song of Hiawatha*, 9
Lönnrot, Elias (1802–84), 8–9, 154
Los Angeles, 177

Louis XIV (1638–1715), 24
Lowenthal, Leo (b. 1900), 131

Macdonald, Dwight (1906–82), 128,
    173
MacDowell, Edward (1860–1908), 157
    Piano Concerto, 95
MacDowell Chorus, 196
MacDowell Colony, 94
Macleod, Fiona. *See* Sharp, William
Mahler, Gustav (1860–1911), 2, 44, 45,
    60, 132, 148, 149
    recordings of, 101
    Sibelius and, 44, 47
    Symphony no. 2, 132, 133
    Symphony no. 5, 132
    Symphony no. 7, 132, 134
"Mahler controversy," 132–35, 148
Manchester Guardian (*see also* Newman,
    Ernest), 111, 170, 171
Mann, Thomas (1875–1955), 66
    Doctor Faustus, 136
Mannes, Leopold Damrosch (1899–
    1964), 218
Marcuse, Herbert (1898–1979), 131
Marshall, John Patton (1877–1941), 30,
    157
Martinelli, Giovanni (1885–1969), 116
Mason, Daniel Gregory (1873–1953), 23
Masterpieces of the Twentieth Century
    Festival (Paris), 142, 232
McCarthy, Joseph (1908–57), 142, 176
Menassen, Pa., 198
Mendelssohn, Felix (1809–47)
    admired by Sibelius, 52
    March of the Priests, 116
    Ruy Blas, 132
Menuhin, Yehudi (b. 1916), 95
Mercantile National Bank. *See* New York
    City
Merikanto, Oskar (1868–1924), 11
Miles, Irene. *See* Downes, Irene Lenore

minimalists, 177
Minneapolis, 101, 109, 119
Mitropoulos, Dmitri (1896–1960), 119
Monteux, Pierre (1875–1964), 59, 119
  conducts Symphony no. 3, 61
  conducts Symphony no. 5, 62
Montreal, 103
Morel, Paul (b. 1918), 238
Moscow, 187, 195
Moscow Art Theatre, 143
Moscow Conservatory, 82
Moussorgsky, Modeste (1839–81), 187, 235
Mozart, Wolfgang Amadeus (1756–91), 17, 45, 52, 97
  Concerto in D minor, 166
  Downes on, 227
  Magic Flute, 52, 53
  Prague Symphony, 160
  Sibelius on, 52
Muck, Karl (1859–1940), 15, 58, 85, 132, 201
  conducts Sibelius, 77, 236; Symphony no. 1, 32
  imprisoned, 59, 161
  mentioned in Sibelius's diary, 59
Munch, Edvard (1863–1944), 11
Munich, 23, 58
Munich Opera, 191
music appreciation (see also Downes, Edwin Olin), 106–9, 126, 170
Musical America, 42, 56
Musical Art Quartet, 237
Musicians Committee to Aid Spanish Democracy, 143
Musik, Die, 54
Mussolini, Benito (1883–1945), 127

Nation, 125
National Archives of Finland, 153, 160, 243
National Arts Foundation, 228

National Broadcasting Company (NBC), 103, 234
  NBC Music Appreciation Hour, 107
  NBC Symphony Orchestra, 107, 119, 219
National Committee on Education by Radio, 107
National Council of American-Soviet Friendship, 143
National Negro Congress, 142–43
National Sibelius Festival (U.S.), 118–19
National Symphony Orchestra, 146
Naumburg, George, 191
Naumburg, Walter W. (1867–1959), 190–91, 192
Nazis, 121, 126, 131
NBC. See National Broadcasting Company
neoclassicism, 45, 60, 142, 163
Neue Zeitschrift für Musik, 44–45
New England Conservatory, 23, 186
New Jersey Courier, 19
New Music Review and Church Music Review, 57
New Republic, 61, 127
New York City (see also Downes, Edwin Olin); 17, 82, 85, 86, 94, 177, et passim
  Carnegie Hall, 81, 94, 108, 118, 145, 172, 238
  Central Park concerts, 191
  Hotel Astor, 94
  Jewish population of, 126
  Madison Square Garden, 95, 158
  Mannes School of Music, 218
  Mercantile National Bank, 17
  Metropolitan Opera, 94, 103, 115, 192, 199, 203, 204, 236
  Musicians' Club, 203
  Radio City Music Hall, 116
  Sibelius's reaction to, 42–43

Stravinsky cult in, 76–77, 87
Tapiola premieres in, 71
Town Hall, 108, 191
Women's Symphony Orchestra, 201
New York Herald Tribune, 3, 76, 114, 121, 124, 125, 136, 145
New York Philharmonic, 103, 104, 105, 119, 125, 132, 186, 238, 239
New York Post, 125
New York Public Library, 228, 243
New York Symphony Society, 71
New York Times, 1, 2, 8, 17, 19, 26, 75, 78, 80, 82, 87, 92, 123, 125, 126, 133, 134–35, 156, 228, Appendix B, et passim
    announces Sibelius's acceptance of Eastman position, 59
    Paris office of, 182, 184, 231
New Yorker, The, 95
Newman, Ernest (1868–1959), 111–12
    Adorno and, 112, 129
    compared to Olin Downes, 108
    Kreisler hoax and, 95
    on Sibelius, 112; in England after World War I, 58; on *Tapiola,* 72
    on Wagner, 57
Newmarch, Rosa (1857–1940), 13, 160
    on Sibelius, 111
    on Symphony no. 3, 48
Nicholas II (1868–1918), 10
Niemann, Walter (1876–1953), 54, 61
Nietzsche, Friedrich (1844–1900), 30–31
    Thus Spake Zarathustra, 31
    Übermensch, 31
    Whitman and, 31, 158
Nikisch, Arthur (1855–1922), 44
Norfolk, Conn., 44, 56, 57, 60, 81, 183, 184, 193, 194, 240
    Chamber Music Festival, 39
    Music Festival, 15, 39, 40, 180, 183, 186

Norris, Homer (1860–1920), 30, 157
    Practical Harmony on a French Basis, 157
Nuori Suomi. See Young Finland

Ohio State University, 107
Olin, Stephen (1797–1851), 20, 155
Olin Downes Collection
    at Hargrett Rare Book and Manuscript Library (MSS 688), 3, 4, 152, 243, Appendix A, et passim
    at Robert Manning Strozier Library, 171, 225, 243
Olympic Games (1940), 116
Orange, N.J., 17
Ormandy, Eugene (1899–1985), 101, 118, 119, 232, 239

Paderewski, Ignace (1860–1941), 103–4
Paine, John Knowles (1839–1906), 23, 25
Päivälehti. See Helsingin Sanomat
Palestine Post, 134
Palestrina, Giovanni (1525/26–1594), 67
Palmgren, Selim (1878–1951), 55
Paloheimo, Arvi (1888–1940) (JS's son-in-law), 120, 121, 141, 187, 188, 189, 190, 194, 195, 198, 199, 200, 201, 202, 205, 206, 207–8, 209, 210, 214, 219, 220, 221, 227
Paloheimo, Eva (JS's daughter), 120, 188, 214, 228, 233
Paloheimo, Yrjö, 198
Paraske, Larin (c. 1834–after 1891), 13, 154
Paris, 14, 26, 157, 163, 175
    Concerts Koussevitzky, les, 83
    Sibelius and, 55
Parker, Horatio (1863–1919), 28, 41, 159
    as Boston Classicist, 23, 25, 39
    Hora novissima, 28, 204
    Mona, 39, 158–59

Parker, Horatio *(cont.)*
  music played at the World's Fair, 115,
    204
  papers of, 243
  Progressive Music Series, 39
  Sibelius and, 39, 40, 41, 42, 56, 59
Partisan Review, 127, 128, 175
Paul, Adolf (1863–1942), 11, 154
  A Book About a Man, 130–31, 174
Paul Lazarsfeld Papers. *See* Columbia
  University
Paulist Choristers, 116
Pekkala estate (Artjärvi, Finland), 8
Pennington Female Institute, 19
Pennington Seminary, 19
People's Fair. *See* World's Fair
Philadelphia, 84, 85
Philadelphia Orchestra, 77, 230
Pittsburgh Symphony Orchestra, 119
PM, 125
Poe, Edgar Allan (1809–49), 105
  Raven, The, 169
Politiken (Copenhagen), 158
Pollock, Friedrich, 131
Pons, Lily (1898–1976), 108
Poulenc, Francis (1899–1963), 133, 174
  Concert champêtre, 132
Powell, Maud (1867–1920), 40
Prague, 14
Prague Music Festival, 97
Pratt, Harry Rogers (1884–1956), 97–98,
    167
Price, Lucien (1883–1964), 197, 198
  on Downes, 29, 94, 166
  on Sibelius, 97, 167
  We Northmen, 198
Princeton Radio Research Project, 129,
    174
Procopé, Hjalmar (1868–1927), *Belshaz-*
    zar's Feast, 119
Procopé, Hjalmar J. (1889–1954), 116,
    211, 212, 214, 216, 224

Progressive Citizens of America, 143
Progressive Music Series. See Parker,
  Horatio
Prohibition, 20
Prokofiev, Serge (1891–1953), 135, 146
Pugnani, Gaetano (1731–98), 95
Purcell, Henry (1659–95), 115, 204
Puritans, 21, 23

Queen of Belgium Piano Competition.
  See Ysaÿe Piano Competition
Quigley, Edwin (OD's father) (*see also*
    Downes, Edwin Olin), 1, 17, 19, 27,
    147

Rabaud, Henri (1873–1949), 59
Rachmaninoff, Sergei (1873–1943), 85
  Isle of the Dead, 164
radio (*see also* Downes, Edwin Olin),
    102–6
  Adorno's critique of, 128–29
  classical music on, 168–69
  "I Love a Mystery," 105, 169
  music education and, 106–7, 170
  Wagner on, 124
Radio City Music Hall, 116
Rautawaara, Aulikki (1906–90), 216,
    217
Ravel, Maurice (1875–1937), 24, 26
RCA Victor. *See* Victor Talking Machine
  Company
reception history, 3, 5, 133–34, 151–52,
    158
recordings, 98–102
*Red Channels: The Report of Communist
  Influence in Radio and Television,*
    142–43, 176
Reger, Max (1873–1916), 142
Reiner, Fritz (1888–1963), 119
Repin, Ilya (1844–1930), 187–88
Réti, Rudolf (1885–1957), 152
Réti-Forbes, Jean (1911–1972), ix, 152

Rezeptionsgeschichte. See reception
history
Rich, Alan (b. 1924), 146, 176
Richter, Hans (1843–1916), 110
Riga, Latvia, 200
Rimsky-Korsakov, Nicolai (1844–1908),
168, 187
Robert Manning Strozier Library (Florida
State University), 171
Roberts, William. *See* Newman, William
Rodzinski, Artur (1892–1958), 119, 238
Rolland, Romain (1866–1944) (*see also*
Downes, Edwin Olin), 26
Roosevelt, Franklin Delano (1882–1945),
121, 214
Roosevelt, Theodore (1858–1919), 24
Rosenfeld, Paul (1890–1946), 127
on Sibelius, 61, 123, 127
Ross, Hugh (1898–1990), 196–97
Runeberg, Johan Ludwig (1804–77), 8, 9,
217
Rychnovsky, Ernst, 54

Saarinen, Eliel (1873–1950), 82
St. Petersburg, Russia, 179, 187, 188, 197
St. Petersburg Imperial Orchestra, 82–83
San Francisco Symphony, 119, 186
Sargeant, Winthrop (1903–86), 146, 151
Sargent, Sir Malcolm (1895–1967), 112
Sarnoff, David (1891–1971), 119, 210
Satan (*see also* Stravinsky), 20, 65, 66, 86,
189
Satie, Erik (1866–1925), 124
Schall, Roger (b. 1904), 200, 201
Schenkerian analysis, 218
Schindler, Kurt (1882–1935), 196
Schnéevoigt, Georg (1872–1947), 220,
222, 238
Schoenberg, Arnold (1874–1951) (*see also*
Downes, Edwin Olin; Sibelius, Jean),
ix, 2, 54, 59, 60, 70, 84, 113, 124, 130,
132, 135, 136, 147, 149, 173

on the composer as critic, 148
defends Mahler, 134–35
works: *Five Pieces for Orchestra,* 57,
161; *Glückliche Hand, Die,* 57;
Kammersymphonie, 55; *Pierrot lu-
naire,* 135, 154; Quartet no. 2,
55–56; *Verklärte Nacht,* 57
Schola cantorum (New York), 116,
196–97
Schonberg, Harold C. (b. 1915)
on Downes, 94
on Sibelius, 146
on Stokowski, 84
Schumann, Robert (1810–56), 51
Scott, Sir Walter (1771–1832), "The Sun
upon the Lake Is Low," 39
Scriabin, Alexander (1872–1915), 60, 82
Second Viennese School (*see also* Berg, Al-
ban; Schoenberg, Arnold; Webern,
Anton), 131, 135, 148
Seeger, Pete (b. 1919), 143
Sharp, William (1855–1905), "A Cavalry
Catch," 39
Shostakovitch, Dmitri (1906–75), 135
Sibelius, Aino (JS's wife), 9, 13–14, 194,
Appendix A
Sibelius, Christian (1869–1922) (JS's
brother), 67–68
Sibelius, Christian Gustaf (1821–68) (JS's
father), 7, 153
Sibelius, Eva (JS's daughter). *See* Palo-
heimo, Eva
Sibelius, Jean
alcohol and, 78
ancestry of, 7–8
baldness of, 2, 58, 60, 162
Beethoven and, 67, 74, 109, 126–27,
146
Berlin and, 44, 49, 55, 58
birthdays of, 77, 118–19, 127, 139, 145,
172, 175, 176, 206, 211, 215, 216,
224, 237, 238, 239, 240, 241

Sibelius, Jean *(cont.)*
  Bruckner and, 69
  burns his music manuscripts, 89
  cigars and, 228, 229
  compositional techniques: church
      modes and, 65, 67; circular
      themes, 34, 35, 48; key use and
      symbolism, 13, 53, 65–66, 68–69;
      orchestration, 40–41, 70, 73; osti-
      nato, 13, 35, 72; pedal points, 32;
      "profound logic" and, 46, 47, 71;
      silence, 72; structure, 41, 45, 48,
      69; themes, 70; theory of "coalesc-
      ing fragments" in, 36–37, 110;
      working out ideas in his head, 194
  conducts, 15, 40, 41, 44, 53, 110, 112,
      116, 205, 207
  correspondence of, 1, 3, 9, 56, 59, 78,
      86, 99–100, 141–42, 143–44, 161,
      176, Appendix A, et passim
  creative crisis, 44, 49–59
  critics and *(see also individual names)*,
      2–3; American, 48, 54, 56–57, 59,
      171; British, 53, 59, 88, 171; Finn-
      ish, 48, 53; German, 32, 53–54,
      59
  death of, 145
  on the democracy of art, 130–31
  diary of, 9, 49, 53, 55, 59, 72, 80, 88,
      153, 160, 162, 164
  on Downes, 1, 80, 164
  Eastman School of Music and, 59,
      161–62
  education, 9
  fax and, 82
  folksong and, 13, 34, 46
  funeral of, 51, 160
  Goethe medal awarded, 126, 173
  government stipend, 14, 77, 154
  "Hellenic rondo" and, 71
  image: bohemian, 2, 11, 60; celebrity,
      84; conservative, 60, 61, 101–2;

  "fat and juicy," 55; godlike, 80, 81;
      heroic, 26–27, 58, 84, 147; impres-
      sionistic, 41; popular, 58; national-
      ist, 58, 59, 61; Romantic, 2, 61,
      123, 127; self, 2, 146
  indecision of, 55, 59, 78, 111, 162
  Joan of Arc and, 67, 120
  Kalevala and, 42, 49, 60
  language of, 9
  on modern music, 64, 67, 71
  Mozart and, 52–53
  on musical analysis, 63
  nature and, 72, 86, 194
  Norfolk and, 39–44, 56, 69
  opera and, 60
  as poet, 72
  recordings and, 98–101, 119, 168,
      192–94
  religion and, 69, 70
  retirement of, 14, 15, 74
  Schoenberg and, 55
  "silence of Järvenpää," 14, 15
  as Sillén in *A Book About a Man,* 130–
      31, 174
  sketchbook, 56–57
  symphonies (general), 14, 59–60, 66,
      74, 148, 183; as professions of
      faith, 53, 64, 67
  throat tumor, 49
  travel, 14; to England, 58, 110–12; to
      Germany, 44; to U.S., 39–44
  tuba and, 41
  voted Americans' favorite living sym-
      phonist, 105, 169
  Wagner and, 60, 159
  World War I and, 15, 58, 112
  Yale and, 42, 43 (photograph)
  works *(see also* Downes, Edwin Olin):
      Aallottaret, 40–41, 73; *Andante
      Festivo,* 116; *Arioso,* 216, 217; "Au-
      tumn Song," 39; *Belshazzar's
      Feast,* 119; *Building of the Boat,*

The, 60, 159; *Canzonetta,* 105, 169; "Cavalry Catch, A," 39; Concerto for Violin, 76, 101, 177, 190, 193; *En saga,* 105, 106, 112, 118, 169, 177; *Everyman,* 64–66, 68, 115, 171; *Ferryman's Bride, The,* 196; *Finlandia,* 14, 42, 58, 60–61, 66, 110, 111, 112, 113, 114, 115, 118, 119, 120, 126, 147, 170, 173; *Four Legends,* 159, 177, 220, 222, 238; *Impromptu,* 196; *In memoriam,* 160; *Jedermann,* 64–66, 68, 115, 171; *Karelia Suite,* 177; *King Christian II Suite,* 42, 110; *Kullervo* Symphony, 11–14, 74, 140, 154, 177, 219–25; *Lemminkäinen and the Maidens of Saari,* 222, 223; *Lemminkäinen in Tuonela,* 222, 223; *Lemminkäinen Suite,* 159, 177, 220, 222, 238; *Lemminkäinen's Return,* 119, 210, 222; *Oceanides,* 40–41, 73; *Oma maa* (*Our Land*), 196, 197; *Onward, Ye Peoples,* 196; Overture in E major, 169; *Pohjola's Daughter,* 27, 42, 119, 177, 194; *Rondo der Wellen,* 40–41; *Rondo of the Waves,* 40–41; *Song of the Athenians,* 110; Songs, op. 61, 55; *Spring Song,* 42; String Quartet in A minor, 10; String Quartet in B-flat major, 10; Suite in A major, 10; "Sun upon the Lake Is Low, The," 39; *Swan of Tuonela,* 42, 60, 108, 119, 120, 159, 207, 208, 210, 212, 222; *Swanwhite,* 81; Symphony no. 1, 15, 25, 32–34, 48, 81, 98, 99, 110, 111, 112, 118, 180, 194; Symphony no. 2, 32, 34–37, 41, 44, 45, 46, 48, 69, 98, 99, 110, 112, 118, 170, 180, 186, 193, 194, 201, 211, 230–31; Symphony no. 3, 45–49,

61, 69, 112, 160; Symphony no. 4, 2, 44, 49–56, 58, 69, 86, 91, 105, 112, 160–61, 169, 180, 183, 210; Symphony no. 5, 2, 57, 58, 62–64, 69, 77, 85, 86, 112, 114, 231; Symphony no. 6, 57, 64, 66–69, 85, 86, 99, 114, 118, 187, 193, 195, 230; Symphony no. 7, 15, 57, 64, 66, 69–71, 73, 85, 86, 99, 114, 118, 167–68, 193; Symphony no. 8, 15, 74, 86–89, 115, 118, 166, 194, 195; *Tapiola,* 15, 49, 57, 69, 71–74, 81, 89; *Three Songs for American Schools,* 39; *Tulen synty* (*Origin of Fire*), 82; *Valse triste,* 14, 42, 58, 66, 105, 112, 113, 114, 147; *Vårsång,* 42; *Voces intimae,* 51, 101; *War Song of Tyrtaeus,* 110
Sibelius, Katarina (JS's daughter), 190
Sibelius, Kirsti (JS's daughter), 190
Sibelius, Margareta (JS's daughter), 223, 233
Sibelius, Maria Charlotta Borg (JS's mother), 7, 8
Sibelius Academy (Helsinki), 9, 160, 223
Sibelius cult. *See* Boston
Sibelius Festival (Finland), 82, 168, 195, 225, 226, 231–32, 233, 239
Sibelius Museum. *See* Turku
Sibelius Society, 198
Siegmeister, Elie (b. 1909), 205, 240
Siloti, Alexander (1863–1945), 236
Sing-Sing prison, 19
Sjöblom, Paul, 164, 166, 198, 216, 217, 220, 225
Sjöblom, Yrjö, 143, 153, 198, 204
Smith, Carleton (b. 1910), 228, 229–30
Smith, Carleton Sprague (b. 1905), 228
Snellman, Johan Vilhelm (1806–81), 8, 9
Sokoloff, Nikolai (1859–1922), 119
Sousa, John Philip (1854–1932), 103

Spaeth, Sigmund (1885–1965), 119

Spalding, Albert (1888–1953), 103, 237

Spivacke, Harold (1904–77), 95

Stein, Gertrude (1874–1946), 124

Stock, Frederick (1872–1942), 237

Stoeckel, Carl (1858–1924), 14, 39–42, 56, 59, 159, 161, 180, 183, 186, 243

Stoeckel, Ellen Battell (1851–1939), 14, 39–42, 59, 159

Stokowski, Leopold (1882–1977) (see also Downes, Edwin Olin), 84–86, 165, 172

    competition with Koussevitzky, 85–86

    conducts Stravinsky, 75, 76

    correspondence of, 168

    Everyman and, 102

    Fantasia and, 102

    Sibelius and, 85, 91, 132; performances of: Concerto for Violin, 193; Symphony no. 1, 237; Symphony no. 4, 52, 237; Symphony no. 5, 77, 85, 86; Symphony no. 6, 85, 86; Symphony no. 7, 85, 86; recordings of, 100–101

Stransky, Josef (1872–1936), 58

Strauss, Richard (1864–1949), 44, 45, 85, 135, 197

    compared with Sibelius, 61–62

    declines Yale invitation, 159

    Downes on, 31, 77, 109, 175, 236

    Heldenleben, Ein, 31

    recordings of, 168

Stravinsky, Igor (1882–1971) (see also Downes, Edwin Olin; Sibelius, Jean), 2, 60, 76, 84, 109, 147, 148, 232

    admired by Thomson, 124

    as devil, 80, 81

    Koussevitzky and, 82, 83

    receives Sibelius Prize, 169

    recordings of, 101, 168

    works: *Chant du Rossignol, Le,* 76; *Concertino for String Quartet,* 76; *Fire-*
bird (Oiseau de feu), 75, 76; *Histoire du soldat, L',* 76, 80; *Octuor Ragtime,* 76; *Oedipus Rex,* 154; *Petrouchka,* 76; Piano Concerto, 77, 164; *Pulcinella,* 76; *Sacre du printemps, Le,* 76, 83, 163, 236; *Song of the Haulers on the River Volga,* 76; *Symphonies of Wind Instruments,* 76, 163

Stravinsky cult. See New York City

Strindberg, August (1849–1912), 11

Sweden, 8, 144, 233

    Symphony no. 4 played in, 53

Szell, George (1897–1970), 239

Taft, William Howard (1857–1930), 40

Tanglewood (Lenox, Mass.) (see also Berkshire Music Center), 197

Tavastehus. See Hämeenlinna, Finland

Tawaststjerna, Erik (1916–93), 4, 7, 137, 152–53

Taylor, Deems (1885–1966), 119

Tchaikovsky, Peter Ilyich (1840–1893), 26, 111, 127

Telefunken, 216

Thompson, Dorothy (1894–1961), 94, 166

Thomson, Virgil (1896–1990), 1, 2–3, 95, 124, 125, 126, 145, 147

    Adorno and, 136

    on Downes, 92, 166

    Harvard and, 26, 29, 124

    homosexuality and, 125

    as music critic, 121, 124–26, 148

    on Sibelius, 123; likens music to Hollywood class-A picture, 124; as "not adult," 125; on Symphony no. 1, 125; on Symphony no. 2, 124, 125

    Variations on a Sunday School Tune, 127

Tibbett, Lawrence (1896–1960), 119

Time, 85, 145

Tollet, Marcus, 214
Törne, Bengt de (1891–1967), *Sibelius: A
    Close-up,* 132, 238
Toscanini, Arturo (1867–1957), 4–5, 130,
    132, 198, 207
    at Bayreuth, 191
    conducts all-Sibelius program, 119,
        172, 209, 210, 238
    conducts *En saga,* 106, 193
    conducts Symphony no. 2, 211
    conducts Symphony no. 4, 91, 210,
        230
    described by Downes, 208–9, 210
    on radio, 129, 219
Tovey, Sir Donald Francis (1875–1940),
    63, 110, 170
Turku (Åbo), Finland, 179, 187
    Sibelius Museum, 4

University of Georgia (Athens), 3, 155,
    179, 187
Urchs, Ernest (1864–1928), 94, 166–67

Vanderbilt, Gloria (b. 1924), 85
Varèse, Edgard (1883–1965), 84
    friendship with Downes, 216–17
    interest in Sibelius's music, 177,
        216–17
Vaughan Williams, Ralph (1872–1958),
    142, 177, 196, 232
Verdi, Giuseppi (1813–1901), 103
    Otello, 115, 203
Victor Book of Concertos, The, 106
Victor Book of the Opera, The, 106
Victor Book of the Symphony, The, 106
Victor Red Seal records, 98
Victor Talking Machine Company, 98, 99,
    193
    music education and, 106, 107
Vienna, 13, 29, 46, 57, 60, 95, 194, 196
Villa-Lobos, Heiter (1887–1959), 142,
    232

Virolle, Professor, 189
Vu, 200

Wagner, Richard (1813–1883) (*see also*
    Downes, Edwin Olin; Sibelius, Jean),
    42, 57, 103, 111, 115, 124, 135, 191,
    204, 208
    works: *Liebestod,* 31; *Lohengrin,* 159;
        Parsifal, 94, 120, 191, 208; *Ring of
        the Nibelungen,* 92, 154, 191; *Tann-
        häuser,* 191; *Tristan und Isolde,* 31,
        83, 159, 191
Wall Street, 17, 102
Walter, Bruno (1876–1962), 133, 134
Walter W. Naumburg Foundation, 191
Warsaw, 103
Washington, George (1732–99), 19
Washington, D.C.
    Constitution Hall, 199
    Library of Congress, 30, 95, 151,
        243
    National Symphony Orchestra, 146
Webern, Anton (1883–1945), 147
Wegelius, Martin (1846–1906), 9
    History of Western Music, 44, 159
Weil, Irving (1878–1933), 123
Westerlunds Musikhandel (Helsinki),
    217
Whitman, Walt (1819–92), 20, 25, 28, 34,
    213
    Leaves of Grass, 130
    Nietzsche and, 31
    So Long!, 31
    Song of Myself, 30
    Song of Occupations, 32
Widor, Charles-Marie (1844–1937), 26,
    157
Wiesengrund, Oskar, 131
Willkie, Wendell (1892–1944), 125
Wilson, Woodrow (1856–1924), 121,
    214
Winter War, 117, 198, 206

Women's Christian Temperance Union, 19–20, 155

Wood, Sir Henry (1896–1944), 110, 112, 132, 170

World Congress for Peace, 143

World-Telegram, 125

World War I (*see also* Sibelius, Jean), 15, 82, 85, 127, 183

World War II, 137, 139, 147, 213–14, 217

World's Fair, 114–16, 118, 171, 196, 205, 207, 213

    musical programs of, 114–15, 203–4, 238

Yale University, 23, 39, 40

    awards Sibelius honorary degree, 42

    Collegium musicum of, 109

    Hale and, 24

    Music Library, 240, 243

    Parker and, 159

Ybarra, Thomas Russell (b. 1880), 199–200

Young Finland (*Nuori Suomi*), 11

Ysaÿe Piano Competition, 231, 232

Zimbalist, Efrem (1889–1985), 91, 94, 193, 239